MW01620553

Reinhold Heller

GABRIELE MÜNTER

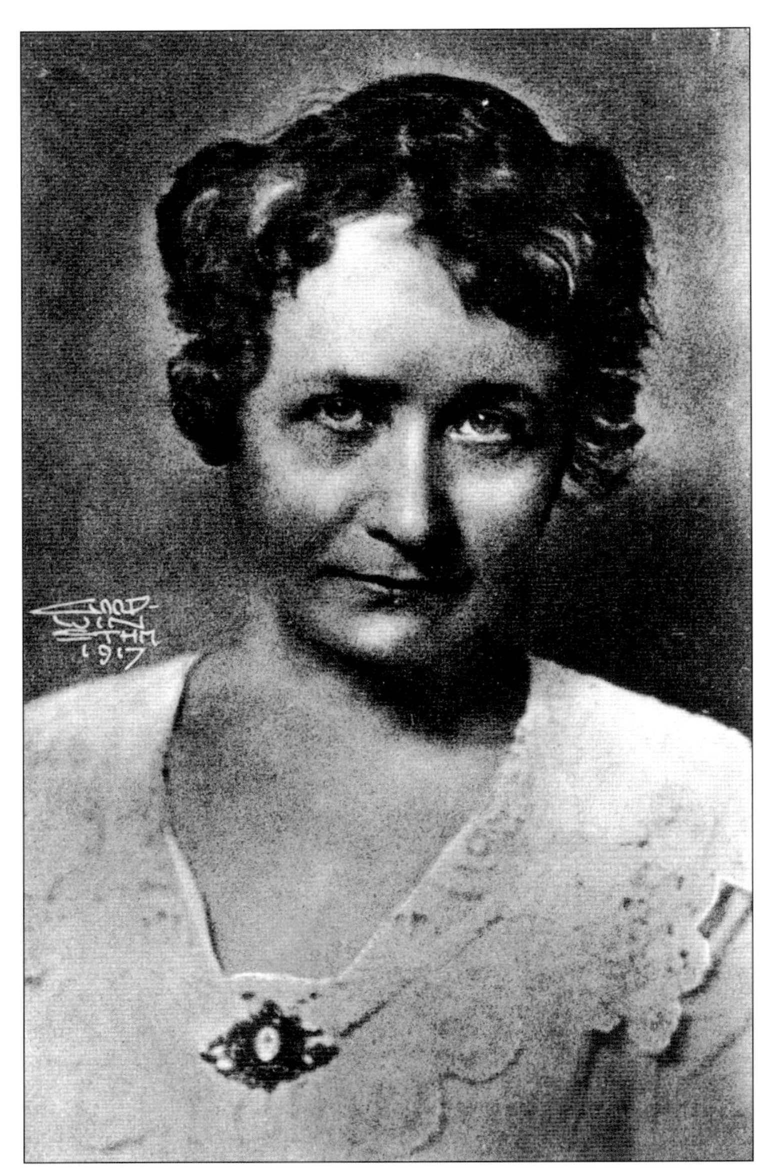

Reinhold Heller

GABRIELE MÜNTER

The Years of Expressionism

1903–1920

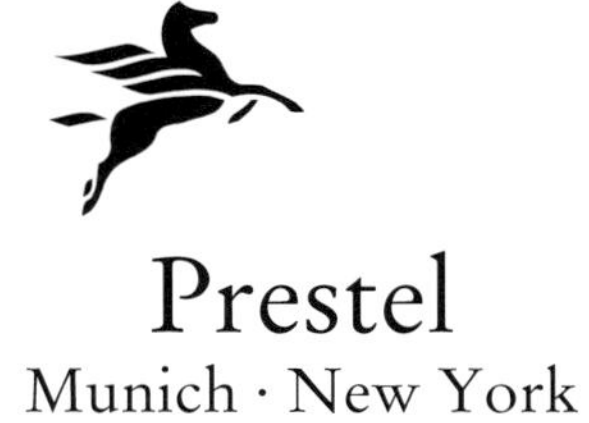

Prestel
Munich · New York

First published on the occasion of the exhibition
*"Gabriele Münter:
The Years of Expressionism, 1903–1920,"* held at the following venues:
Milwaukee Art Museum, Milwaukee, Wisconsin, 5 December 1997–1 March 1998;
Columbus Museum of Art, Columbus, Ohio, 18 April–21 June 1998;
Virginia Museum of Fine Arts, Richmond, Virginia, 13 July–20 September 1998;
Marion Koogler McNay Art Museum, San Antonio, Texas,
3 November 1998–3 January 1999

Front cover: *Boating*, 1910 (detail; Cat. No. 47)
Back cover: *Still Life, Red*, 1909 (Cat. No. 31)
Frontispiece: Gabriele Münter, Stockholm, 1917,
postcard published by "Der Sturm"

Photographic Acknowledgments: p. 184

The Cataloguing-in-Publication data is available from the Library of Congress.

Prestel-Verlag
Mandlstrasse 26 · 80802 Munich · Germany
Tel. (+49 89) 38 17 09 0; Fax (+49 89) 38 17 09 35
e-mail: prestel@compuserve.com
and 16 West 22nd Street, New York, NY 10010, USA
Tel. (212) 627-8199; Fax (212) 627-9866

Prestel books are available worldwide.
Please contact your nearest bookseller or write to either
of the above addresses for information concerning
your local distributor.

Copyedited by Michele Schons
Designed by Maja Thorn
Type: Stempel Garamond, Linotype AG
Typesetting and Lithography: LVD, Berlin
Printed by Aumüller Druck KG, Regensburg
Bound by Buchbinderei Almesberger GmbH, Salzburg

Printed in Germany

Printed on acid-free paper

ISBN 3-7913-1866-7

Foreword

The Milwaukee Art Museum has a long tradition of collecting and exhibiting German art. Though a number of nineteenth-century German academic works were among the holdings of the Layton Art Collection, which was founded in 1888 and eventually became part of the Milwaukee Art Museum, the collection was significantly expanded in the 1950s and the early 1960s with works by preeminent German Expressionist artists, many of which were kindly given to the museum by Mrs. Harry Lynde Bradley. In 1962, René von Schleinitz began to donate works from his singular collection of nineteenth-century German genre paintings. In 1977–78, Mrs. Bradley bequeathed her entire collection to the museum, which contained works by Gabriele Münter, Franz Marc, Marianne von Werefkin, their Russian compatriots Vassily Kandinsky and Alexei Jawlensky, as well as Lyonel Feininger, Paul Klee and Kurt Schwitters. Thus, by 1980, the museum was able to represent a wide spectrum of early twentieth-century German art, ranging from the *Brücke* group to the Blue Rider and the Blue Four. In more recent years, the museum has acquired contemporary German art by such seminal artists as Georg Baselitz, Joseph Beuys, Anselm Kiefer and, through the René von Schleinitz Memorial Fund, a major selection of prints and drawings by Caspar David Friedrich, Max Liebermann, Adolf Menzel, Philipp Otto Runge and Karl Friedrich Schinkel, to name but a few. These nineteenth- and twentieth-century works—together with the 1991 bequest of the Flagg Collection of medieval and Renaissance sculpture and metalwork from Augsburg and other German centers and the promised gift of the Ritz Collection of German Expressionist paintings, drawings and prints—make it one of the most comprehensive collections of German art in an American museum today.

Consequently, the Milwaukee Art Museum has held numerous exhibitions of German art over the years, including "The Robert Gore Rifkind Collection of German Expressionist Art" in 1979 and "Art in Germany: From Expressionism to Resistance, 1909–1936," an exhibition of the Marvin and Janet Fishman Collection, which traveled in Germany and America from 1990 through 1992. The present exhibition, "Gabriele Münter: The Years of Expressionism, 1903–1920," is particularly relevant owing to the fact that the museum holds the largest American collection of her works—eleven paintings in all. Though the museum is fortunate to be able to present these works with examples of her Blue Rider colleagues, its aim is to offer an American audience an in-depth view of the extraordinary achievement of this somewhat neglected artist.

This exhibition was proposed to the museum by Reinhold Heller, Professor of Art History at the University of Chicago, a distinguished scholar specializing in Symbolist and German Expressionist art and guest curator of the museum's exhibition of the Fishman Collection. I am grateful to Professor Heller for his confidence in the Milwaukee Art Museum and for his dedication to the project. This exhibition also came to the museum through the efforts of Sue Taylor, former Curator of Prints and Drawings and now Professor of Art History at Portland State University. I would also like to acknowledge Michael Maegraith, Executive Publisher, Prestel-Verlag, for his interest and support, which have helped make this publication possible.

Finally, I wish to thank the many generous lenders to the exhibition, especially the Städtische Galerie im Lenbachhaus in Munich. Moreover, without the generous endorsement of Olsten Staffing Services, through their President, Anthony J. Petullo, The National Endowment for the Arts and Lufthansa, the exhibition would not have been possible. I am, likewise, grateful to the directors of the participating institutions, Irvin Lippman at the Columbus Museum of Art, Katherine Lee at the Virginia Museum of Fine Arts, and William Chiego at the Marion Koogler McNay Art Museum for their support in presenting Gabriele Münter's work to a wider American audience.

Russell Bowman
Director, Milwaukee Art Museum

Acknowledgments

I am deeply indebted to a collector and benefactor, who wished to remain anonymous, for making his collection of works by Gabriele Münter available for my study, for supporting and encouraging my initial research and for enthusiastically suggesting an exhibition of Münter's works to be held here in the United States. Sadly, he will not see this exhibition so marked by, and so inconceivable without, his remarkable generosity and inimitable spirit.

Among many scholars who have discussed Münter's work with me, Peg Weiss must be singled out. After many years of research on Kandinsky, she gained notable appreciation for and knowledge of Münter's person and work. She shared her wisdom readily with me, and was kind enough to introduce me to several collectors and to the dean of American Kandinsky scholars, Kenneth Lindsay, who related to us his personal memories of Gabriele Münter and made available his correspondence with her. Peg, her unique scholarship and her warm friendship, are greatly missed.

Numerous other scholars, among them some of my students, have discussed aspects of Münter's career and work with me. I am immensely indebted to them all, but especially to Vivian Endicott Barnett, Shulamith Behr, Alessandra Comini, Michelle Facos, Susanne Grimm, Adrienne Kochman, Rose-Carol Washton Long, Sarah Gregg Skerker, Martha Ward, Bessie Tina Yarborough and Anika Öhrner.

Dr. Annegret Hoberg, at the Städtische Galerie im Lenbachhaus in Munich, shared her vast knowledge of Münter's work with me and contributed significantly to the realization of this exhibition, which owes much to the example of the comprehensive Münter retrospective she organized in 1992. In their unfailing, friendly support she, the Director, Dr. Helmut Friedel, the former director, Dr. Armin Zweite, and numerous other members of staff at the Städtische Galerie opened the museum's extensive collection of Münter's works to me, which aided me immeasurably in my research. Furthermore, I am indebted beyond measure to Ilse Holsinger, who oversees operations at the Gabriele Münter- und Johannes Eichner-Stiftung, Munich; she made available an impressive array of archival material to me, helped decipher cryptic handwriting, offered freely her knowledge and gave continued encouragement.

The curatorial, conservation, publicity and other staff at the Milwaukee Art Museum have transformed the exhibition from an idea into a reality. Their untiring work cannot be sufficiently valued. Russell Bowman, the museum's Director, long recognized the value of its collection of works by Münter—the largest outside Germany—and has enthusiastically supported the exhibition, not least by making the services of his assistant, Marilyn Charles, available at critical junctures in its planning and organization. Warm thanks are due to her for her capable assistance. Also at the Milwaukee Art Museum, Margaret Andera, Curatorial Assistant, and Leigh Albritton, Registrar, were responsible for many aspects of the exhibition's realization, while John Irion oversaw its installation.

I have been repeatedly grateful for the skills and talent, extreme patience and conscientiousness demonstrated by the designer of this catalogue, Maja Thorn, and its editor, Michele Schons. Michael Maegraith of Prestel-Verlag long had faith in both the exhibition and the catalogue, and has helped immensely in seeing it to its completion.

Without the cooperation of many private collectors and the curatorial staff of museums in possession of Münter's paintings, neither the exhibition nor the catalogue could have been realized. Numerous collectors generously took me into their homes, allowed me to examine their collections and have made works from them available for the exhibition. For their endorsement, I wish to extend my heartfelt thanks.

Finally, I would like to thank my wife, Vivian Hall Heller, without whose help and patience there would be no acknowledgments.

REINHOLD HELLER
Chicago, Fall 1997

Biographic Chronology

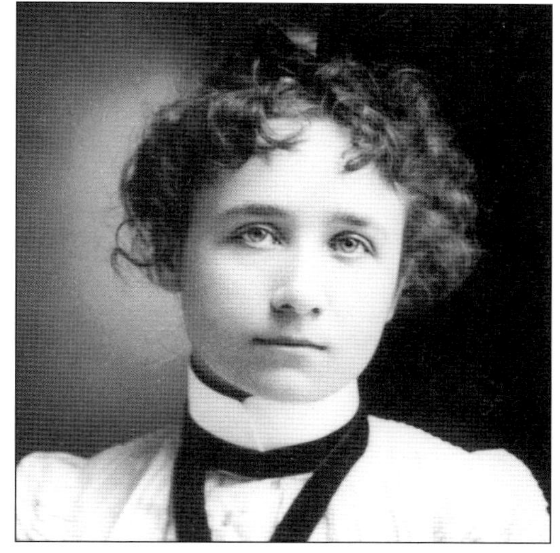

Gabriele Münter, St. Louis, 1900

1877 Gabriele Münter is born on 19 February in Berlin. Her father, Carl Friedrich Münter, descended from a Westphalian family of merchants and clergymen, was born on 19 December 1826 in the city of Herford. He emigrated to the United States, according to his daughter's recollections, to avoid arrest and scandal due to his liberal ideals and revolutionary advocacy of personal freedom in 1847. In the United States, he initially ran a general store, and obtained a degree in dentistry from the Dental College, Cincinnati, Ohio. In 1852, he was in Quincy, Illinois, apparently to serve as an agent for groups of emigrants from Herford. On 11 July 1852, according to church records, he married Mary Lucinde Richardson of Cincinnati at the German Evangelical church of St. Jacobi in Quincy, Illinois, settling in Jackson, Tennessee; in 1856, after the death of his first wife, he visited his family in Germany, then returned to Tennessee, where in 1857 he married Gabriele Münter's mother, Wilhelmine Scheuber. Born in 1836 in the Swabian village of Siglingen an der Jagst, the eldest of nine children in a carpenter's family, she had emigrated to the United States with her family in 1845. The outbreak of the American Civil War and the fact that they were expecting their first child led the Münters to return to Germany in December 1864 and to settle in Berlin at Unter den Linden 58, where Carl Münter established a practice as an "American dentist." Their first son, August, was born in April 1865; Carl Theodor ("Charly"), in October 1866 and Emmy, in June 1869.

1878 The Münter family moves to Herford, into a house newly constructed at Bielefelder Strasse 9.

1884 While Münter is in the second grade, the family moves briefly to the resort town of Bad Oeynhausen, then to the city of Koblenz, situated on the Rhine River. In the early summer, Wilhelmine Münter undertakes a trip to the United States to visit her parents at Coffeelanding, Tennessee.

1886 Carl Münter dies on 16 April in Koblenz at age fifty-nine.

1887 In January, Münter's eldest brother, August, dies at the young age of twenty-two.

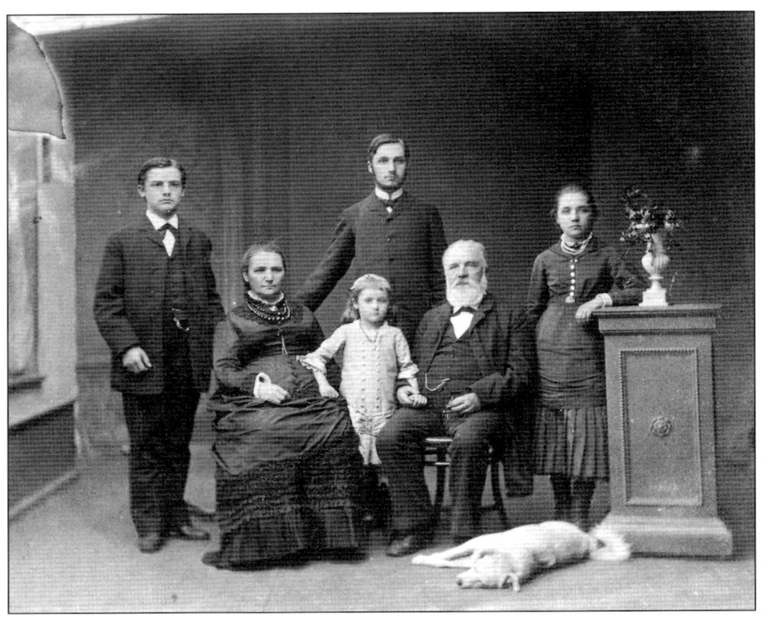

Minna and Carl Münter with their children (from left to right): Carl (Charly), Gabriele, August and Emmy, ca. 1882

1890–1892 While attending the Lyceum for Girls in Koblenz, Münter receives her first formal drawing lessons as part of her curriculum, in which she is required to make accurate schematic drawings of ornaments, heads, flowers and leaves in exercise books according to established models and with the help of a grid system.

1896 During the spring, Münter receives private art lessons from a member of the Herford art organization "Malkiste." Her interest in bicycles and cycling develops after she participates in a bicycle race in June.

1897 On 15 May, Münter arrives in Düsseldorf to begin private drawing lessons with the portrait and genre painter Ernst Bosch; she lives with the family of the Norwegian landscape painter Morten Müller. In July, she is given her first bicycle. For the fall semester, she enrolls in the private "Women's Atelier" of the Düsseldorf Academy professor Willy Spatz. When her mother becomes seriously ill, she returns to Koblenz early in November. On 15 November, Wilhelmine Münter dies at age sixty-one. Through the death of their mother, the Münter children receive a significant inheritence, which is administered by the surviving son, Carl.

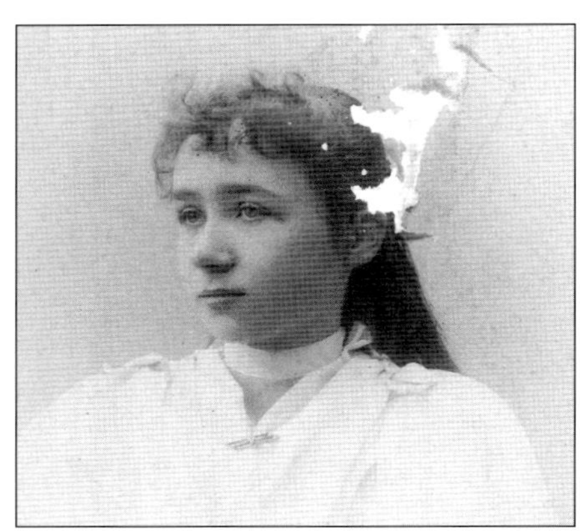

Gabriele Münter, 1893

1898 In July, Münter returns to Düsseldorf to her studies under Spatz. Her brother, Carl, marries the American singer Mary Quint. After Münter and her sister Emmy receive an invitation to visit their relatives in the United States, the two leave from Rotterdam on the S.S. Statendam on 29 September. They arrive in New York on Sunday, 9 October, then leave by train on 20 October for St. Louis, where they arrive the next day. They stay with the family of their mother's sister, Albertine Happel. While there, they visit the St. Louis Exposition and attend musical performances and plays at the Imperial Theater. An excursion takes them to Niagara Falls and Buffalo on 20 December; they return to St. Louis on 22 December, then leave for Columbia, Mississippi the day after Christmas.

1899 Gabriele and Emmy Münter arrive in Moorefield, Arkansas, on 6 February, where they stay with their aunt, Caroline Schreiber at the "Schreiber Mill," a rolling mill and cotton gin owned by her relatives. For her twenty-second birthday, she receives a new Kodak camera. On 12 April, an explosion at the mill puts it out of service for over a month. On 8 June, the two sisters leave for Marshall, Texas to visit their cousin Willy Scheuber; while they are there, their "uncle Mike" dies on 30 July. In August, they visit their uncle Joe Donohoo and attend the wedding of his son in Plainview, Texas. They participate in a "cowboy reunion" between 17 and 19 August, and from 30 August to 3 September they join a cattle drive at a nearby ranch.

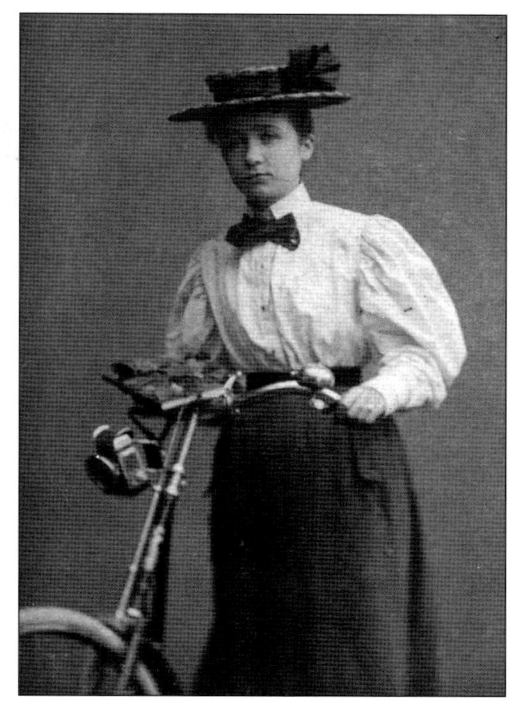

Gabriele Münter with her first bicycle, 1897

1900 In February, Gabriele and Emmy Münter go by way of Fort Worth and Abilene to Guion, to the farm of a widowed cousin. They return to Marshall on 18 May, to Moorefield on 12 July, and to St. Louis on 29 July, where they prepare to return to Germany. By train they leave for New York on 1 October, arrive in Hoboken the next day and sail from New York on 6 October on the S.S. Pennsylvania for Hamburg, where they arrive on the 19th. They return to Koblenz after visiting relatives in Bonn and Cologne. With a view to continuing her training as an artist, Münter begins studies in November with the sculptor Hermann Küppers in Bonn.

1901 On 15 January, Münter breaks off studies with Küppers and returns home the next month on the 24th. Following the advice of her friend Margarete Susman, she decides to go to Munich to study portrait drawing under Maximilian Dasio at the "Ladies' Academy" of the "Association of Women Artists," where she registers on 1 May. She lives in Munich's artist and bohemian district of Schwabing, at the Pension Bellevue, Theresienstrasse 30, where Susman also lives. She visits exhibitions at the Glaspalast and regularly attends performances of the avant-garde political cabaret "Eleven Executioners" as well as operas and the theater. From 25 July to 12 August, she joins Dasio's landscape draw-

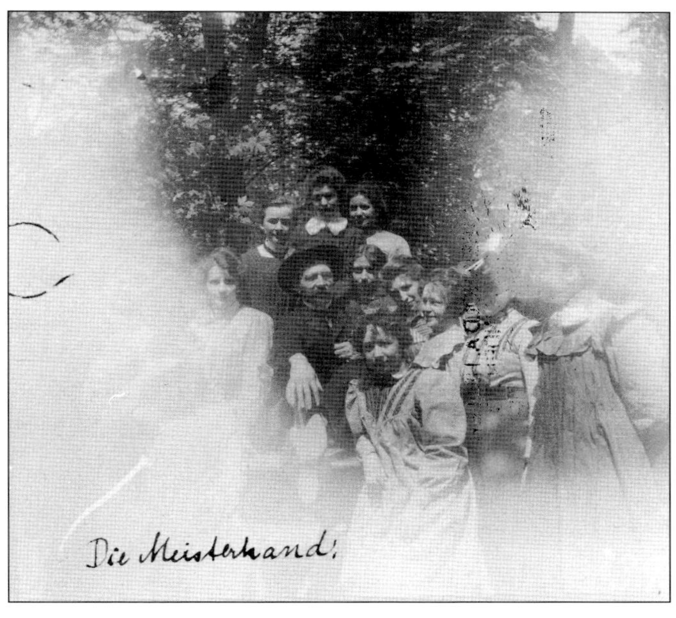

"The Master's Hand": The Ladies' Academy class taught by Maximilian Dasio (Gabriele Münter, foreground center), Munich, 3 June 1901

ing class at Fürstenfeldbruck. In late August, she travels to Darmstadt to see the newly inaugurated Mathildenhöhe artists' colony with its innovative *art nouveau* architecture, then returns in the late summer to Bonn, where she undertakes numerous bicycle tours in the countryside. She returns to Munich on 12 October, visits Lake Starnberg the next day, then enrolls in Angelo Jank's portrait drawing class. For the Christmas holidays, she returns to Bonn.

1902 In January, the Darmstadt artists' colony is featured in the second exhibition of the Phalanx Society in Munich. Chaired by Vassily Kandinsky, its members include the "Eleven Executioners" artists Wilhelm Hüsgen, Ernst Stern and Ernst Neumann, who with Kandinsky also form the faculty of the Phalanx School. After seeing the exhibition, Münter enrolls in Hüsgen's sculpture class at the Phalanx School and attends evening classes for drawing after the nude model, supervised by Kandinsky. "The masks of the Eleven Executioners appealed strongly to me. My fingers itched—I wanted to sculpt. Soon I began to attend the Phalanx School and registered for Hüsgen's sculpture class in the afternoons. Linked to it then was the evening class for drawing after the nude with Kandinsky. There then I had a new artistic experience, how—unlike other teachers—Kandinsky explained things in detail, clearly, and treated me as though I were a consciously striving person who can set herself problems and goals. That was something new for me and it impressed me."[1] On 22 February, she attends a lecture by the *Jugendstil* designer and theorist Hermann Obrist. On 26 June, she joins Kandinsky's landscape class in Kochel; she makes her first small *plein air* landscape paintings under his tutelage, and frequently accompanies him on bicycle tours. On 29 June, with Kandinsky's class, she visits Walchensee. After the group is joined by Kandinsky's wife, Anja, he remarks to Münter that he is "uncomfortable" when both are present and asks her to withdraw from his class, to which she agrees. On 22 August, she leaves for Munich, and then joins her family in Bonn, where she continues to paint small landscape studies during bicycle tours. On 7 October, she returns to Munich. She and Kandinsky are frequently together, visiting each other and going on bicycle tours. Münter signs up for Angelo Jank's figure drawing class at the Ladies' Academy. However, on 1 December, she returns to Kandinsky's class.

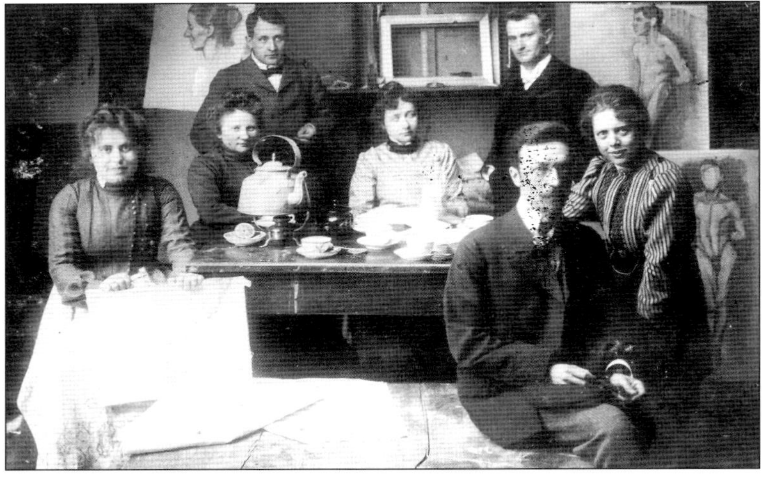

Vassily Kandinsky's evening life drawing class at the Phalanx School (Kandinsky in foreground, Münter seated at table, center), Munich, 1902

1903 On 3 May, Münter leaves Munich for Herford to visit relatives. She and Kandinsky, who has been in the eastern Bavarian town of Kallmünz with his Phalanx class, arrange a rendezvous in Ansbach on 10 June, then go by way of Nuremberg back to Munich, and from there to Kallmünz on 19 June. At the Wirtshaus zur Roten Amsel (Inn to the Red Blackbird), Kandinsky arranges for them to have adjoining rooms. She makes numerous sketches of the town and its outlying cliffs and paints using the palette knife according to Kandinsky's instructions. Münter and Kandinsky pledge faithfulness to each other and become secretly engaged to be married after he has obtained a divorce. Together, they visit Regensburg on 29 July and again on 18 August. Münter leaves for Munich and Bonn on 20 August, where she informs her brother and sister of her relationship with Kandinsky. In their correspondence, she and Kandinsky begin to plan a trip to Paris together to test their compatability. Münter remains in Bonn while Kandinsky goes to Russia, then returns to Munich on 8 October. She leaves for Würzburg to meet Kandinsky on 3 November; together, they visit Rothenburg ob der Tauber before returning to Munich on 9 November, when she moves into her first own studio at Schackstrasse 4. On 12 November, Kandinsky suggests they expand their planned trip to include North Africa and Spain, as well as a summer in Sweden. In December, she prints her first woodcuts.

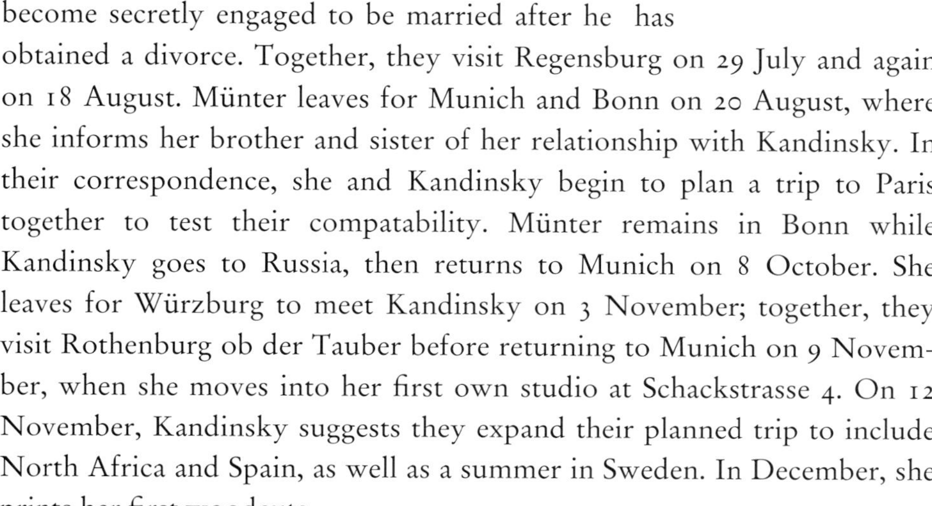

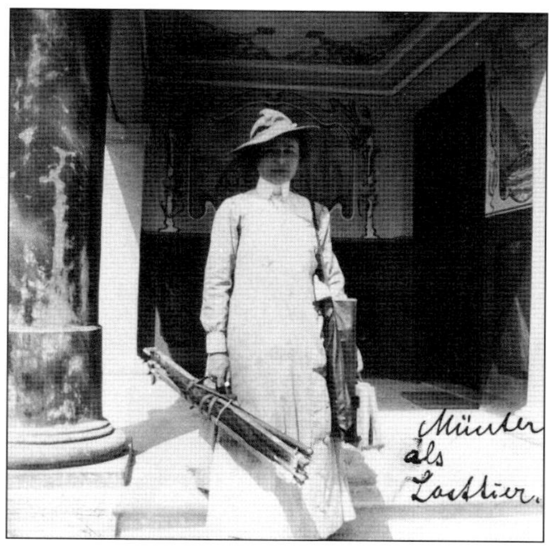

"Münter as Pack Animal," Kochel, summer, 1902

1904 In January, Münter sees a performance of Oscar Wilde's *Salome* and a dance performance by Isadora Duncan. On 31 March, Münter meets Kandinsky at a hotel before leaving for Bonn for the baptism of her niece, Elfriede (Friedel), on 1 April and, again, to fulfill Kandinsky's wish that she not be in Munich, where his wife is living. She rejoins Kandinsky on 11 May in Krefeld, and travels with him to Düsseldorf and Cologne before returning with him to Bonn on 18 May to present him to her family. Together, they depart by Rhine steamer for Rotterdam on 23 May to travel further in Holland to The Hague, Haarlem, Amsterdam, Zaandam and other towns; Münter returns to Germany alone on 22 June. She remains with her family for the next six months, with the exception of one meeting in October with Kandinsky in Frankfurt, following his formal

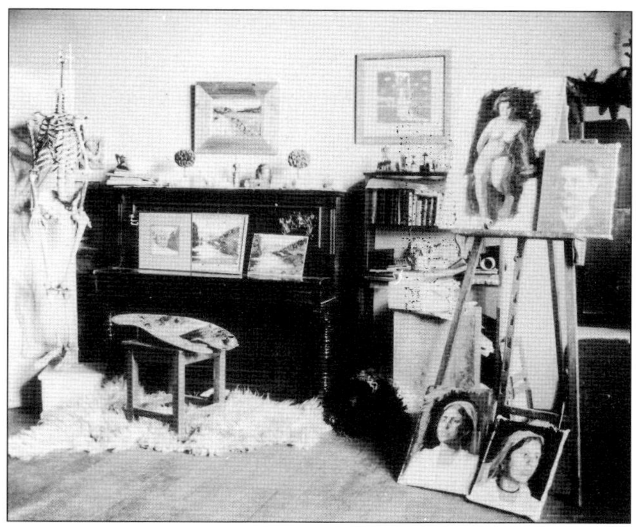

Gabriele Münter's studio, Schackstrasse 4, Munich, winter, 1903–04. Photograph by the artist

separation from his wife. On 2 December, he arrives in Bonn, having been in Russia to begin divorce proceedings, and in Paris. Together, they set out for Tunis on 6 December by way of Strasbourg, Basel, Lyon and Marseilles, and arrive there on 25 December. They rent separate rooms in a hotel on the outskirts of the city.

1905 In Tunis, they remain near their hotel, make sketches and paint together, and Münter completes tapestries and pearl stitchings after Kandinsky's *art nouveau* designs. On 8 February, they visit the ruins at Carthage, to which they return in March while making other trips to Sousse and Kairouan. On 5 April, they return to Europe, separating in Innsbruck after having visited Palermo, Naples, Rome, Florence, Bologna and Verona together. Münter returns to Munich to rent a room at the Pension Stella, Adalbertstrasse 48, where another Phalanx School student, Emmy Dresler, lives. On 24 May, Münter meets Kandinsky in Reichenbach in Saxony and, together, they undertake a bicycle tour from Lichtenstein to Dresden via Chemnitz, Freiberg and Meissen. After arriving in Dresden on 1 June, they move into separate rooms at Schnorrstrasse 4. They take a walking tour through Saxon Switzerland and separate on 15 August, when he leaves for Munich and she for Bonn.

In November, Kandinsky rejoins her, and they again leave Germany. By way of Cologne, they travel initially to Belgium, to Liège on 18 November, then to Brussels on 25 November. By way of Milan, Genoa and Sestri, they arrive in Rapallo around Christmas, and rent the "Casa Valle Bella" at 24 Via Montebello, where they remain until May 1906.

1906 In Rapallo, Münter sketches and paints scenes she encounters while cycling in the town. They are visited by Kandinsky's father and two students of the Phalanx School, Emmy Dresler and Carl Palme. On 1 May, Münter and Kandinsky leave for Paris via Genoa, Milan, Lucerne and Basel, and arrive on 22 May. They rent rooms at 12, Rue des Ursulines, then on 28 June move to Sèvres, 4, Petite Rue des Binelles, near the park at St. Cloud, where they paint numerous oil studies. Münter works on linocuts, making portraits of Kandinsky and French neighbors. Kandinsky's father visits again, as do other Russian relatives of Kandinsky, and Olga Meerson. They also befriend the painter Elisabeth Epstein. On 17 November, Münter takes a room at 58, Rue Madame in Paris and participates in Théophile Steinlen's figure drawing class at the Académie Grande Chaumière. She ceases to attend these lessons and returns to Sèvres on 18 December.

1907 Münter and Kandinsky continue their studies of Sèvres and the park at St. Cloud. They take a trip to Chartres from 4 to 5 January, where she renders drawings to be used for linocuts. She returns to Paris on 13 February to resume studies with Steinlen, but, on 19 March, gives in to Kandinsky's pleas that she come back to Sèvres. At the Paris Salon des Indépendants she exhibits six paintings in March and April. The periodical *Les Tendances Nouvelles* reproduces several of her woodcuts. On 1 June, they leave Sèvres, spend several days in Paris and continue on to Cologne on 11 June. Alone, she travels to Bonn to visit her brother, while Kandinsky goes to Munich. She recommences work on lino- and woodcuts, a selection of which she exhibits at the Paris Salon d'Automne from October through November, and arranges for some of her paintings to be exhibited at the Galerie Lenoble in Cologne. On 30 July, she meets Kandinsky in Stuttgart, whence they undertake a lengthy walking and bicycle tour in the Swiss Alps until 19 August, a trip marred for Münter by a severe toothache. While in Switzerland, they briefly meet Kandinsky's mother. By way of Frankfurt, Bonn, Hanover and Hildesheim, they then go to Berlin, where Münter's sister, Emmy Schroeter, and her family live; they arrive on 8 September. In the fall, they attend lectures by Rudolf Steiner and come into contact with his "Theosophical Society." Münter again briefly attends classes in figure drawing and painting, and works on a series of linocuts devoted to motifs of dolls and other toys.

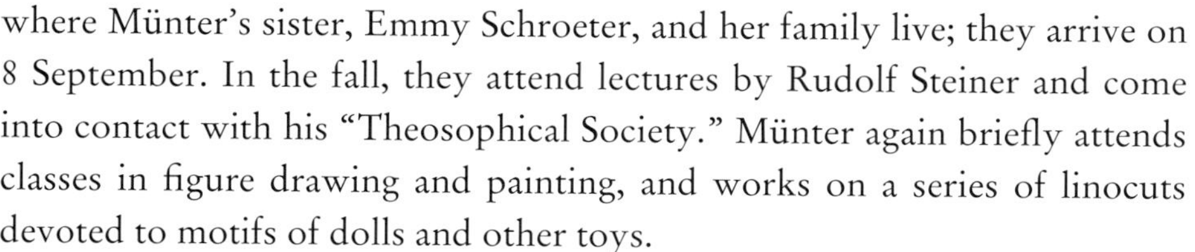

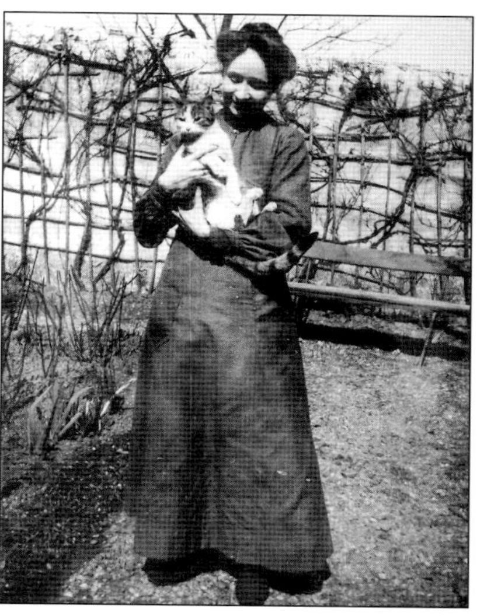

Gabriele Münter with "Waske," Sèvres, 1906–07. Photograph by Vassily Kandinsky

1908 In January, the Kunstsalon Lenoble in Cologne shows eighty paintings by Münter; a selection of these works is shown at the Kaiser Wilhelm Museum in Krefeld and the Silesian Museum of Fine Arts in Breslau. In Bonn, the art publisher and book dealer Friedrich Cohen exhibits twenty-four of her wood- and linocuts.

After returning to Munich from Berlin in late April, Münter and Kandinsky take a trip to southern Tyrol, where they undertake several walking tours through the mountain valleys, then sojourn for several weeks in Lana. They return to Munich by way of horse-drawn carriage, mail coaches and train on 10 June, and within a week begin touring in the Bavarian countryside near Munich in search of a place to spend time together. Between 17 and 20 June, they visit the areas around the lakes Starnberger See and Staffelsee. There, they are particularly attracted to the town of Murnau on Staffelsee. Returned to Munich, they report on Murnau to the Russian artists Marianne von Werefkin and Alexei

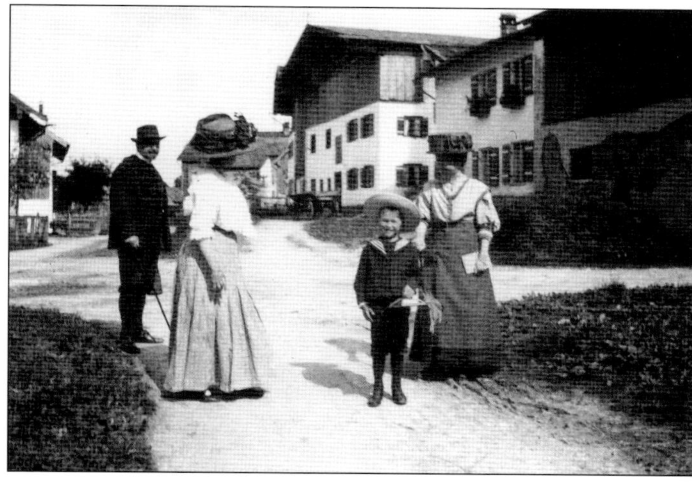

Alexei Jawlensky, Marianne Werefkin, Andreas Jawlensky and Gabriele Münter in Murnau, summer, 1908 or spring, 1909

Jawlensky, who then visit the town and rent rooms there for the remaining summer months. Münter and Kandinsky, in the meantime, engage in a tour of Chiemsee, Salzburg and the Austrian alpine lakes of Mondsee, Attersee and Wolfgangsee. Returned to Munich on 8 August, they are encouraged by Jawlensky and Werefkin to join them in Murnau, and arrive there that same week, taking rooms at the "Griesbräu" inn on the village's main street. Münter later recalled: "We saw Murnau during a brief trip we took and recommended it to Jawlensky and Werefkin—who in the fall also invited us there. We stayed at the Griesbräu and liked it very much.

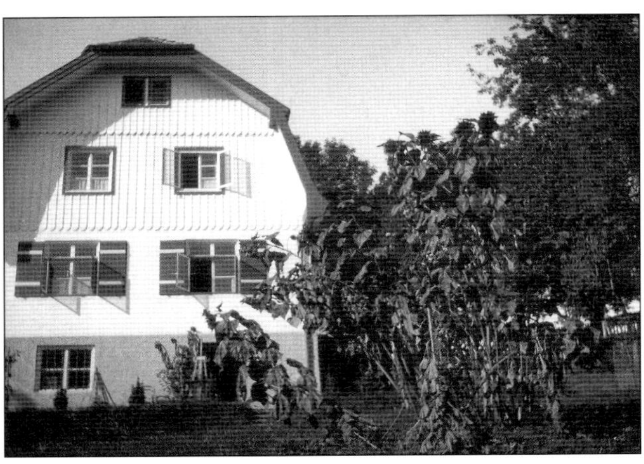

Gabriele Münter's house at Kottmüllerallee, Murnau. Photograph by the artist

"After a brief time of experimentation, I took a major leap there—from painting after nature, more or less impressionistically, to the feeling of a content to abstracting to the presentation of an extract.

"It was a wonderful, interesting, happy period of work with many discussions about art with the enchanting 'Giselists' [i.e. Werefkin and Jawlensky, who lived in Gisela Strasse in Munich]. I especially liked to show my works to Jawlensky—on the one hand because he liked to praise,... on the other hand because he explained several things to me as well—offered me the fruits of his experience and what he had learned—and spoke of 'Synthès.' He is a pleasant colleague. We all tried hard and each one of us matured [in our art]. I made a mass of studies. There were days when I made five studies (the cardboard measuring 33 x 41 [cm]) and many when there were three, and a few when I did not paint at all. We all worked hard."[2]

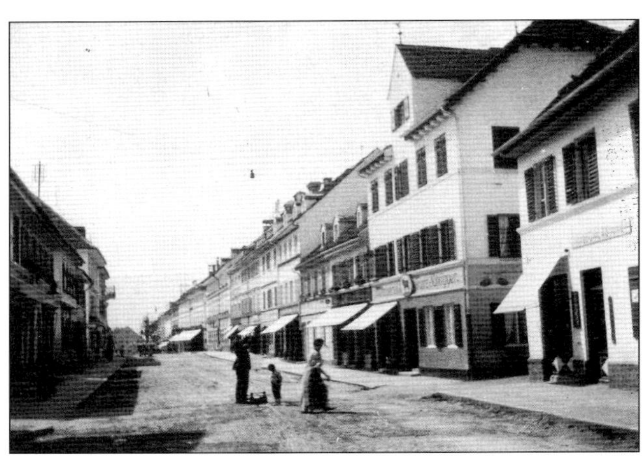

Main Street in Murnau, 1908 or 1909. Photograph by the artist

Early in September, Kandinsky goes to Munich for several days to move into a new apartment at Ainmillerstrasse 36 in Schwabing. At the end of September, Münter returns to Munich and rents a room in the Pension Stella. She uses studies made in Murnau as the basis for her paintings.

1909 At the end of January, the artists meeting in the home of Werefkin and Jawlensky form the avant-garde "Neue Künstlervereinigung München" (New Artists' Association Munich). Founding members include Werefkin and Jawlensky, Münter and Kandinsky, the painters Adolf Erbslöh and Alexander Kanoldt and the art patrons Heinrich Schnabel and Oskar Wittenstein. The association is officially registered on 22 March, and, according to Münter's recollections, "Kandinsky resolved to become its head since no one else could do it."[3] In addition to her room in the Pension Stella, Münter rents studio space nearby.

She and Kandinsky go by train and sled on 20 February via Garmisch and Mittenwald to visit the Russian composer Thomas von Hartmann and his wife Olga Archádina in the alpine town of Kochel, near Murnau, for two weeks. Together, they paint numerous studies of the snow-covered village, its cemetery and the surrounding landscape. On 9 March, they return to Munich. They spend much of late April and part of May in Murnau with Werefkin and Jawlensky. "In spring 1909, the Giselists rented us the rooms next to theirs in the 'Volks Bazar' with the Echter family. We stayed there with one break until June—then we moved... into the newly constructed villa with which Kandinsky had fallen in love at first sight. To this love he remained faithful."[4] On 21 August, Münter purchases this house on the outskirts of Murnau, in the Kottmüllerallee, at Kandinsky's urging and after obtaining the approval of her brother-in-law Georg Schroeter, who visits Murnau with his wife and their daughter Friedel. In September, they return to Munich, where, on the 16th, Kandinsky moves into the first-floor apartment of the garden house at Ainmillerstrasse 36. Soon thereafter, Münter leaves the Pension Stella and moves in with him, returning to Murnau and Starnberger See for a week. Kandinsky's father visits for nearly a month. At the Paris Salon d'Automne in October, she exhibits two recent paintings.

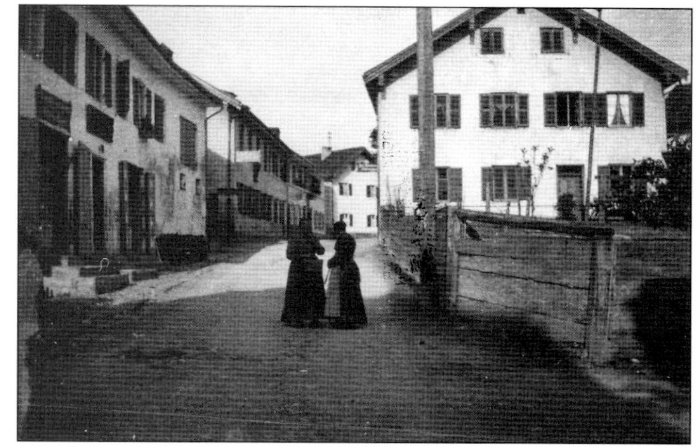

Grüngasse in Murnau, 1908 or 1909. Photograph by the artist

At the Galerie Thannhauser in Munich, from 1 to 15 December, the first exhibition of the New Artists' Association Munich is held. It includes ten paintings and eleven prints by Münter, and travels during 1910 to numerous other German cities, thereby giving the artists' group significant publicity and exposure outside Munich. Between December 1909 and February 1910, Münter and other New Artists' Association members exhibit works in the Salon Izdebsky in Odessa. Kandinsky spends the Christmas and New Year holidays with his wife, Anja, but reassures Münter on New Year's Eve: "At the end of this coming year, you might not remain as lonely, as abandoned as has become the case now. I too am lonely and sad and certainly worse off than you are, because I sit here in the midst of the ruins of my prior life. And everything that meets my eye causes me pain."[5]

1910 Münter and Kandinsky spend a week in Murnau in February, return there in April and July, and again briefly between 10 and 11 September. They spend much of the time there working in the garden and on the house and its furnishings.

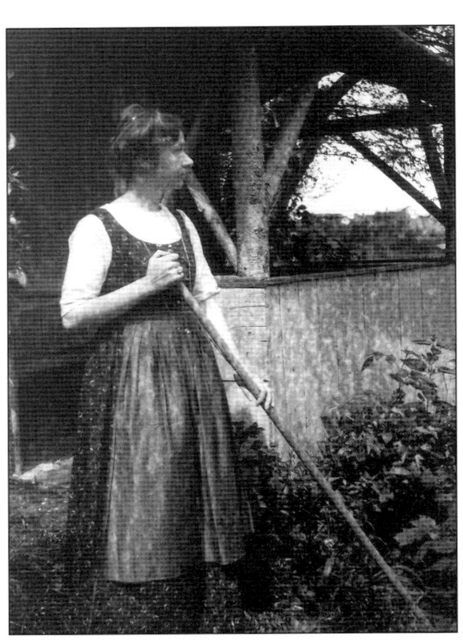

Gabriele Münter in her garden, Murnau, summer, 1910. Photograph by Vassily Kandinsky

The second exhibition of the New Artists' Association Munich takes place in the Thannhauser Gallery from 1 to 14 September, and includes a larger contingent of French artists, notably Georges Braque, André Derain, Kees van Dongen, Pablo Picasso and Georges Rouault. Münter exhibits seven large paintings. The exhibition travels to Karlsruhe, Mannheim, Hagen, Berlin and Dresden.

On 9 October, Kandinsky leaves for Russia by way of Weimar and Berlin—where he visits Münter's sister Emmy and her husband Georg Schroeter—to visit his parents, renew contacts with Russian artists and to continue the proceedings for his divorce. He returns to Munich on 22 December.

Münter, in the meantime, spends ten days in Murnau with Hedwig Fröhner in October, then remains in Munich, where she is frequently together with Kandinsky's wife, Anja, and the Fröhner sisters. Kandinsky arranges for the inclusion of works by himself, Münter and other New Artists' Association members in the Second International Salon Izdebsky and in the "Karo Bube" (Jack of Diamonds) exhibition in Moscow in December.

1911 On New Year's Day, at the home of Werefkin and Jawlensky, Münter and Kandinsky meet the painter Franz Marc, "our new, wonderful friend," who had applied to join the New Artists' Association, and who also introduced August Macke to it. On 11 January, Kandinsky resigns as head of the New Artists' Association; with Münter and Marc, he begins plans for an alternative exhibition society and an "almanac." On 2 February, she, Kandinsky, Marc and other New Artists' Association members attend a concert of works by Arnold Schönberg. In February, Fanny Dengler joins Münter and Kandinsky as housekeeper, a position she had formerly held with Kandinsky and his wife: "[It was] Kandinsky's old wish. Because of her mother's illness, she returned from America—where it seems she liked it."[6] Later, Münter dates her and Kandinsky's increasing alienation as beginning at this time.

From 20 to 28 January, Münter and Kandinsky are in Murnau. On 15 March, at an auction sponsored by the NKVM, Marc purchases Münter's painting *Village Street in Snow*.

In mid-May, Kandinsky goes alone to Murnau and visits Franz and Maria Marc in the nearby village of Sindelsdorf. During this time, Münter writes her brief, diary-form synopsis of her life with Kandinsky since 1905.

In late May, both return to Murnau until Münter leaves for Berlin to visit her sister's family on 26 June. There she makes the acquaintance of the collector Bernhard Koehler, an uncle of August Macke's, and visits the exhibition of the Berlin Secession. On 21 July, she arrives in Herford to visit relatives there, then leaves for Bonn to visit her brother Charly on 31 July. On 2 August, August Macke visits her, "a tall, handsome, young man, very likable. Stayed until midnight";[7] and she is together with him and his wife in Macke's Bonn studio repeatedly during the next few days. She makes a series of contacts with museum directors and gallery owners in Düsseldorf, Hagen, Essen and Cologne to encourage them to exhibit and purchase works by the artists of the New Artists' Association Munich. On 21 August, she returns to Munich and Murnau. She and Kandinsky meet with Franz and Maria Marc in Sindelsdorf from 12 to 15 October to discuss plans for their planned almanac.

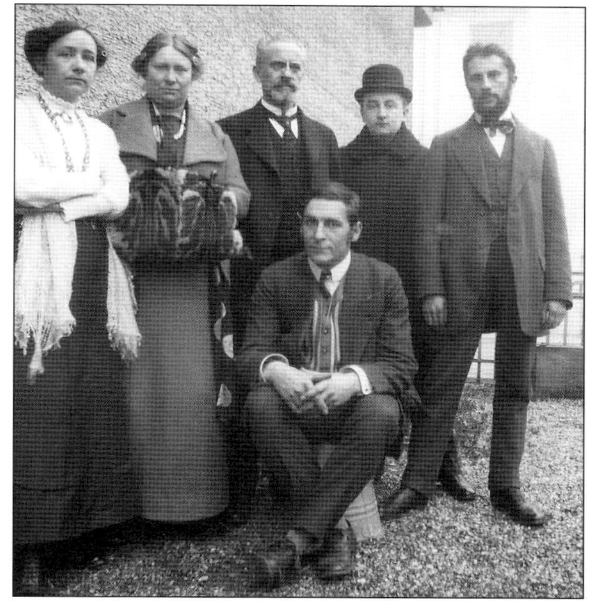

Gabriele Münter, Maria Marc, Bernhard Koehler, Thomas von Hartmann, Heinrich Campendonk and Franz Marc (seated) on the terrace of the apartment at Ainmillerstrasse 36, Munich, 1911

From November to January 1912, Münter participates in the fourth exhibition of Berlin's New Secession with four paintings along with other New Artists' Association members. Tensions and differences exist within the organization, however, and on 2 December, Kandinsky's painting *Composition V* is rejected by the exhibition jury on grounds that it is larger than permitted. As a result, Münter, Marc and Kandinsky resign from the New Artists' Association, as does Alfred Kubin, who is kept informed by telegraph, and they form a new group "The Blue Rider." They organize, extraordinarily rapidly, a counter-exhibition in response to the winter exhibition of the New Artists' Association, to be shown simultaneously from 18 December to 1 January 1912 at the Galerie Thannhauser. This "First Exhibition of the Editorship The Blue Rider" contains some forty-five works by the German-American painter Albert Bloch, the Russian painters David and Vladimir Burliuk, Heinrich Campendonk, Robert Delaunay, Elisabeth Epstein, Heinrich Kahler, Kandinsky, Macke, Marc, Münter, Jean Bloé Niestlé, Henri Rousseau and Arnold Schönberg.

1912 Slightly reduced in size, the exhibition of the "Blue Rider" opens in mid-January at the Gereon Club in Cologne. Expanded with works by Paul Klee, Jawlensky, Werefkin, Franz Flaum and Oskar Kokoschka, it forms part of the opening exhibition at Herwarth Walden's avant-garde "Der Sturm" Gallery in Berlin on 12 March. The Blue Rider exhibition travels further to Hagen and Frankfurt.

On 12 February, at the Munich gallery of Hans Goltz, the "Second

Exhibition of the Editorship The Blue Rider: Black and White" opens. Devoted solely to works on paper, it contains 315 prints, drawings and watercolors by 31 artists of diverse nationalities as well as a selection of Russian folk woodcuts.

The Blue Rider artists also exhibit with the Modern League in Zurich, and Münter again sends two paintings to the Paris Salon des Indépendants. As of May, she and Kandinsky spend most of the summer in Murnau, with periodic extended trips to Munich, notably for a hernia operation Kandinsky undergoes on 10 July.

On 5 October, by way of Berlin, Kandinsky leaves for Moscow and Odessa, where he remains until mid-December.

On 10 October, Hans Goltz includes four of Münter's works in a group exhibition at his Gallery New Art in Munich. Late in the month, Herwarth Walden goes to Munich to hang an exhibition of Italian Futurist paintings; he visits Münter with Hans Goltz, begins to make plans for an exhibition of her works at his Berlin gallery, and invites her to contribute prints to his periodical *Der Sturm.* She visits the Futurist exhibition at the Thannhauser Gallery and an Emil Nolde exhibition at Max Dietzel's gallery.

1913 Münter visits Murnau from 13 to 15 January. On 7 February, she attends the Picasso exhibition at the Thannhauser Gallery in Munich. Le Fauconnier visits Münter and Kandinsky on 11 February. Other frequent visitors during the year include Campendonk, Marsden Hartley, Jawlensky and Werefkin, Klee, Kubin, Franz and Maria Marc and the art historian Wilhelm Hausenstein.

Walden's "Der Sturm" Gallery in Berlin opens its eleventh exhibition, a retrospective of eighty-four paintings from 1904 to 1913 by Gabriele Münter, on 6 January. After seventeen paintings are selected by Walden, the exhibition travels to Munich, where, with sixty-seven paintings, it is the opening exhibition of Max Dietzel's "Neue Kunstsalon" from the end of March to 30 April. Walden further selects thirty of these paintings to show in Copenhagen on 8 April. In its reduced form, the Münter exhibition travels to Frankfurt, Dresden and Stuttgart.

After the opening of her exhibition in Munich, Münter and Kandinsky go to Murnau on 29 March and stay until 4 April. For the Easter holidays, Kandinsky's mother Lydia Kojevnikoff joins him and Münter at their Ainmillerstrasse apartment. On 28 April, Münter and Kandinsky leave for Murnau, where they remain until 5 May; they return again on 10 June, are joined on 25 June by Kandinsky's former wife Anja, and go back to Munich on 30 June. Kandinsky leaves for a stay of several months in Moscow, via Berlin on 5 July.

Münter begins a trip to visit her relatives on 17 July, first in Berlin, then on 2 August in Herford, on 17 August in Osnabrück, and on 21 August in

Bonn. During the trip, she paints several portraits of family members and gives painting lessons to her niece, Friedel. She returns to Munich on 30 August, where Kandinsky rejoins her on 6 September. Together with Franz and Maria Marc and Robert and Sonia Delaunay, they visit Berlin to see the First German Autumn Salon at Walden's "Der Sturm" Gallery around 20 September; Münter is represented in the exhibition with six paintings. Towards the end of the year, she helps Kandinsky hang his exhibition at the Galerie Thannhauser in Munich.

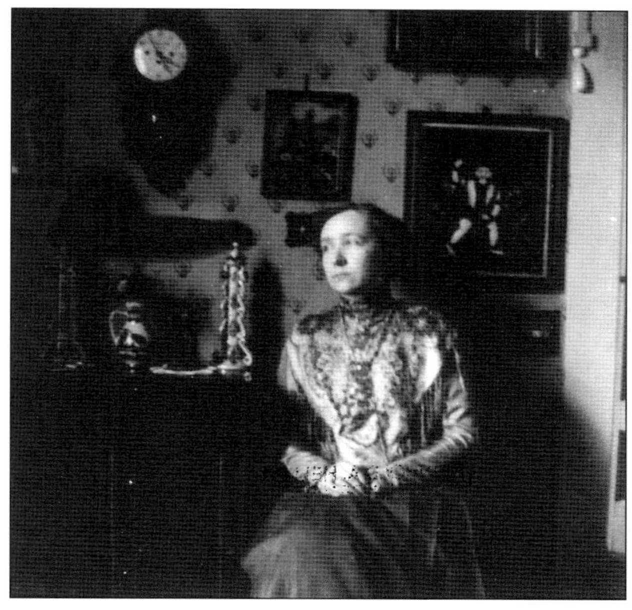

Gabriele Münter in the living room of her apartment in the Ainmillerstrasse 36, ca. 1913. Photograph by Vassily Kandinsky

1914 During the early months of the year, Münter and Kandinsky are frequently in the company of Munich writers and artists, as well as the Croatian utopian writer Dimitrije Mitrinovic. In February, they spend several days in Murnau.

Münter participates in the exhibition "Expressionist Painting" at the Galerie Arnold in Dresden and Breslau. At the "Jury-Free Exhibition" of the Leipzig Secession she shows three paintings from February to April. The first Blue Rider exhibition is meanwhile being shown in Scandinavia in Helsingfors, Trondheim and Göteborg.

Kandinsky vacations with his mother in Meran from 9 to 20 April. Münter and Kandinsky spend the summer in Murnau, beginning in June. On 1 July, they begin a three-day tour of the nearby villages of Oberammergau, Ettal and Garmisch-Partenkirchen. In Murnau they are visited by Arnold Schönberg and Herwarth and Nell Walden.

Following the mutual declarations of war between the German and Russian Empires on 1 August, Münter and Kandinsky return to Munich; late in the evening of 3 August, they flee together to Switzerland. On 6 August, they arrive at Mariahalden near Goldach, where they live in a villa owned by their Munich landlord. They are joined by Kandinsky's former wife Anja as well as four other Russian relatives who, together, make plans to return to Russia. They are frequently in the company of artists of the Swiss Modern League and on 4 September are visited by Paul and Lily Klee. On 16 November, Münter and Kandinsky leave for Zurich. On 25 November, Kandinsky begins the trip back to Russia, where he arrives on 13 December, leaving Münter behind with instructions to break up their Munich household.

1915 Until mid-January, Münter remains in Zurich, where she arranges an exhibition of eleven of her paintings at the Salon Wolfsberger from mid-

February through the end of March. Returned to Munich, she occasionally visits the Klees, the Blochs, Campendonk, Anatol Schiemann and Elisabeth Epstein. She helps Anja Kandinsky to prepare for her departure for Moscow, by way of Stockholm and St. Petersburg on 16 February; Anja arrives in Moscow on 1 March. To enable her to continue to correspond with Kandinsky, Münter arranges for mail to be forwarded via Sweden, which remains neutral during the war, by Knut Ljunggren, Nell Walden's brother-in-law. She urges Kandinsky to join her in Stockholm as soon as possible, but he repeatedly rejects her urging, pleading financial difficulties, fear of not being able to return to Russia and the need to remain with his mother, who has been ill. In his twelfth letter to her since leaving Zurich, on 11 March, he implores Münter to wait until July for the trip to Sweden, then continues:

"Now I have been living alone for three months and realize that this is the appropriate way of life for me. I miss you often. Often I want to go out with you, speak with you, take a short trip with you, etc. Linked to that are my sorrow and worry about you, about your feeling of loneliness, about your fear of the future. But clarity about myself continues to elude me.... It simply is not my talent—to be clear in myself concerning my personal life. I am too impulsive in this respect, too distracted and maybe too moody. Only in art do I really know, completely and unerringly, what I want. That is why I achieve something too. In my personal life, I do not know *what* I should, or want, to give to whom. I really want only one thing (*that* I know): that no one suffer because of me.... Such a person must live alone. Only at this point where my art and life meet must I have absolute freedom. Every restriction is true suffering for me. I sometimes terribly envy those people who go out together, come home together, spend the night together and wake up with the feeling, with the knowledge: 'he is here,' 'she is here.' I know that this envy is unproductive, because such a life can only make me happy for a brief moment, then I immediately long for freedom, to be alone. Above all to be alone. Perhaps it is only due to the fact that my ideal of love is greater than my ability to realize it. Perhaps sometime in my life I really loved 'her' and failed to meet her in this life again. Perhaps I am looking for her. If these words hurt you, don't forget that I suffer no less from them. I want to give my heart away and am incapable of doing it. Perhaps I lack the ability. Love (according to my ideal) must be infinite and fruitful in every way. I only love art *that* way. Perhaps two such loves are impossible in my heart. Or perhaps I am impotent in terms of human love. This love, of which I speak, you have also never experienced and never had. That is why I tell you (maybe half unconsciously) that you never loved me. And life together as husband and wife without this love is a compromise with a greater or lesser aftertaste of a lie, that is, of sin.... Today my heart aches and today I almost feel like crying. When I think of you, then my heart aches as if it would burst sometimes and I want to shed my blood for you. You must never forget and must constantly feel that I, who ruined your life, actually am prepared to shed my blood for you. Those are not exaggerated and not insignificant words, my dear, dear, good, kind Ella."[8]

Expecting nonetheless to be reunited with Kandinsky in July, at the beginning of May, she goes to Murnau for ten days to close the house, then returns to Munich on 18 May to clear out the apartment in Ainmillerstrasse. On 3 June, she arrives in Berlin to visit her sister, Emmy, and to arrange her own and Kandinsky's business affairs with Herwarth Walden and "Der Sturm" Gallery. Through Erich Gutkind, she is introduced to the Swedish mystic and psychologist Poul Bjerre.

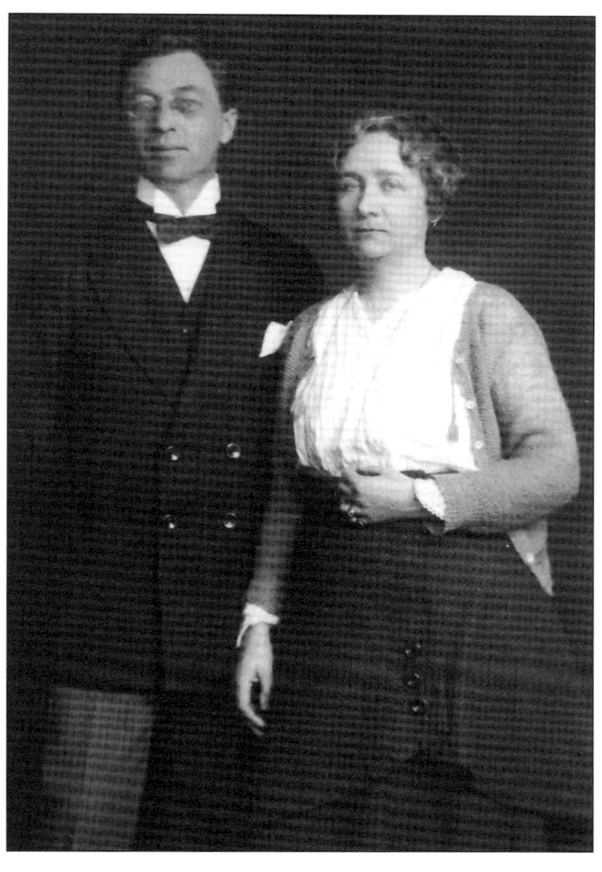

Gabriele Münter and Vassily Kandinsky, Stockholm, winter, 1916–17

On 3 July, Münter leaves for Copenhagen; she stays at the Pension Lindhardt, where she waits in vain for news from Kandinsky, then proceeds to Stockholm on 17 July and telegraphs him her address at a boardinghouse belonging to Clara Louise Palm, Stureplan 2, on 19 July. She seeks out the artists Isaac Grünewald and Sigrid Hjertén, who are associated with Herwarth Walden's "Sturm" Gallery, as well as the sculptor Andreas Wissler and his wife.

Münter becomes reacquainted with Carl Palme, who was a fellow student at the Phalanx School in Munich in 1902–03, and undertakes numerous excursions into the countryside around Stockholm with his wife and other women. On 21 September, Kandinsky repeats that he is financially unable to come to Sweden, and argues: "I do not believe you are right to force me to make a trip now and I would do so against my will. I will do it only because you wish it.... As to the marriage, I must warn you that it is absolutely impossible before the end of the war."[9]

In October, a collection of her works is shown at Carl Gummeson's art gallery in Stockholm. Meanwhile, in Berlin, the thirty-fifth "Sturm" exhibition, opening on 24 October, is devoted to fifty-three of her paintings and prints. After Münter arranges for an exhibition of his work at Gummeson's, Kandinsky finally agrees to go to Stockholm and arrives from Russia on 23 December. He resides at Clara Palm's boardinghouse, sharing double rooms with Münter.

1916 Kandinsky and Münter pose together for several formal photographs, taken at the department store A. B. Nordiska Kompaniet. They frequently visit Bjerre, Thyra Wallin, the Palmes, the Grünewalds and the Swedish artist and collector Prince Eugene. She helps Kandinsky hang his works at Gummeson's gallery, where his exhibition opens for fourteen days, beginning on 1 February. From 1 to 15 March, Gummeson again shows Münter's works; in conjunction with the exhibition, Kandinsky publishes his essay "On the Artist," dedicated to Gabriele Münter and edited by her, in Swedish translation, but excluding the passages specifically devoted to her work that describe her as a "...talent of pronounced national character—an indisputable sign of individuality, of personality, i.e. of an artistic, creative personality."[10] He leaves to return to Russia on 16 March, the day after Münter's exhibition closes, with the promise to return before the year's end. Selections from the Kandinsky and Münter exhibitions are sent to Blomquist's Art Gallery in Kristiania (now Oslo) during the summer under sponsorship of Walden's "Der Sturm."

Remaining alone in Stockholm, Münter again is largely in the company of women, especially Thyra Wallin. In numerous letters to Kandinsky, she continues to urge him to return to Stockholm. He initially resists, because "things would be the same as they were during the winter,"[11] but by the summer promises to come soon, after his fiftieth birthday on 4 December, to marry her. However, in September, he begins a relationship with Nina von Andreevskaya, whom he marries on 11 February 1917.

On 8 July, Münter begins a trip to Lapland with Gertrude Holz. She arrives, by train by way of Kiruna and Abisko, at Narvik on 14 July, and on 17 July begins traveling along the west coast of Norway via Svolvær and Trondheim to Kristiania, where she arrives on 23 July. Within a few days, she travels back to Sweden, going by way of Göteborg to the small village of Aplared, near Borås in southwestern Sweden, and the Arnäsholm estate as guest of Carl Leopold Sundbeck. Before leaving for Stockholm on 9 September, she paints some fifteen paintings, among them landscape motifs from the Norway trip and portraits of her host and his family. Three of her earlier paintings, in the meantime, are included in Berlin at "Der Sturm" Gallery's summer "Expressionists, Futurists, Cubists" exhibition.

In Stockholm, Münter lives briefly at the home of Thyra Kleen, a student of Max Klinger, then travels on to the suburb of Stocksund, where she lives as of 21 September. She paints portraits, in part on commission, showing many of them in an exhibition organized by the Red Cross in Stocksund. She remains there all winter, renting rooms in various boardinghouses.

1917 Münter is the invited guest, exhibiting thirty-one paintings from her Scandinavian period, at the joint exhibition of the "Association of Swedish Women Artists" and the "Association of Women Artists of Austria," at Liljevalchs Konsthall, Stockholm. In reduced format, the exhibition travels to Helsingborg in April. She is also represented with three paintings in March at "Der Sturm" exhibition devoted to artists associated with the gallery in Berlin.

She does not know of Kandinsky's marriage in February; without explanation, he fails to respond to her letters and ceases to write to her after May.

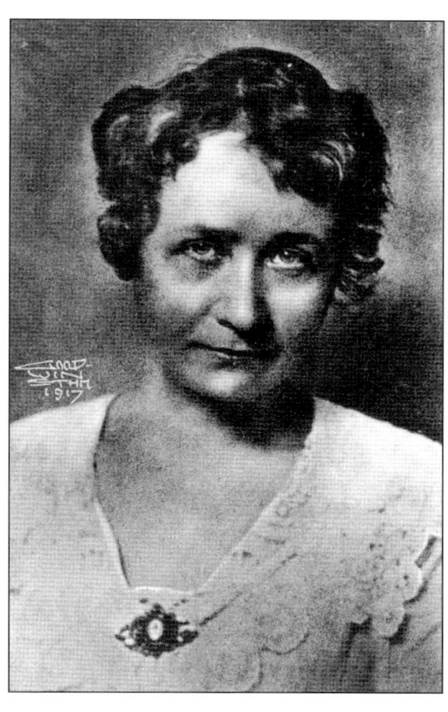

Gabriele Münter, Stockholm, 1917. Postcard published by "Der Sturm"

In spring, she paints a series of largely symbolic portraits of Gertrude Holz, her preferred model of the time. In a joint exhibition with Georg Pauli, she shows a total of ninety-five works, including thirty-two new paintings at Arturo Ciacelli's Nya Konstgalleriet, Stockholm. Following the exhibition on 16 June, she returns to Stocksund and then goes to Arlid, where she spends several days and visits Nell and Herwarth Walden at the nearby village of Landscrona. Thereafter, she spends two weeks with the artists Agnes Cleve and John Jon-And at their estate in Bohuslän. Later, she spends a week with Lilly Rydström-Wickelberg before going to Göteborg on 7 September, remaining there until 20 October as she waits to be issued a visa to go to Copenhagen. While in Göteborg, she arranges an exhibition of her reverse-glass paintings at a book dealer's, then returns to Stockholm for three weeks where she continues to wait for visa difficulties to be cleared up. Late in the fall, she leaves for Copenhagen. The first two weeks she spends with Nell Walden's sister, Anna Roslund, then lives in various pensions. With recommendations from Herwarth Walden, she arranges an exhibition of her work at "Den Frie Udstilling" (Independent Exhibition) in Copenhagen.

1918 Münter's exhibition at "Den Frie Udstilling" takes place from 7 to 13 March. With one hundred paintings, including earlier ones sent by Walden from Berlin, twenty reverse-glass paintings and prints, it is the largest exhibition devoted to her work up to this time. She is in contact with the Danish artists' circle associated with the radical cabaret "Edderkoppen." At this time, Münter begins to participate regularly in spiritualist meetings and séances.

In the spring, she is forced to change her accommodation several times as her financial situation becomes increasingly precarious. Encouraged by Olga Meerson, a fellow student at the Phalanx School, on 27 June she leaves for Saunte in northern Denmark, where she spends the summer. Meerson visits her several times, as does Anna Roslund once. For the winter, she returns to Copenhagen. In December, Walden includes her works, along with those of the Swedish artists Sigrid Hjertén and Gösta Adrian-Nilsson, in "Der Sturm" exhibition "International Expressionists and Cubists" in Berlin.

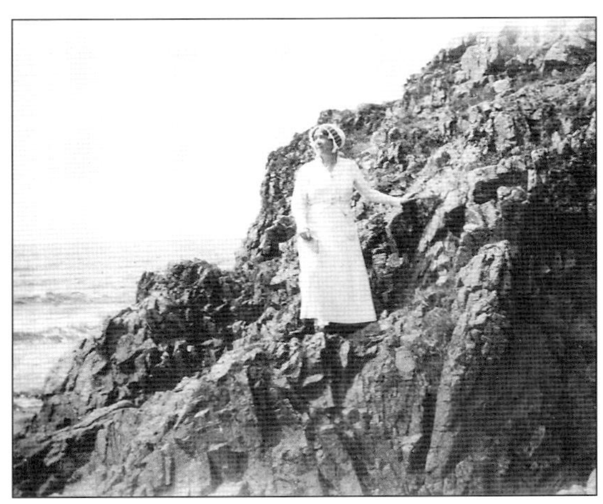

Gabriele Münter at Bornholm, 1919

1919 Münter's efforts to obtain commissions for portraits and other works fail. Early in summer, in another effort to earn money, she advertises for students to study under her at the Danish Baltic Sea island of Bornholm. On 22 June, she leaves for Bornholm to be joined by her sole student, Elfriede Nyemann, whom she instructs in landscape painting at the seaside town of Sandvig and whose portrait she paints.

Returned to Copenhagen, Münter's personal isolation and critical financial situation become increasingly desperate. Nonetheless, she is able to arrange another exhibition of ninety-three oils and eighteen reverse-glass paintings, including her newest landscapes, that opens on 5 October at "Københavns Ny Kunstsal" (Copenhagen's New Art Salon). In November, she again participates, with six paintings, in the annual "Den Frie Udstilling." In December, she is featured at "Der Sturm" Gallery in the exhibition "Gösta Adrian-Nilsson, Paul Klee, Gabriele Münter."

1920 In January, Münter begins to ship paintings back to Germany. She leaves Copenhagen for Berlin on 28 February, and on 12 May travels on to Munich and spends the summer in Murnau. She establishes contact with the Munich New Secession and in December has a collection of her works shown at the Galerie Thannhauser in Munich. Over Christmas and the New Year, she stays in Schloss Elmau for the first time.

1921–1928 Münter lives alternately in Munich, Murnau, Cologne and Berlin during this time, frequently moving between them. She exhibits with the Munich New Secession and is included among its artists at the "International Art Exhibition Düsseldorf" in 1922—the first international avant-garde exhibition in postwar Germany. As of 1926, she exhibits with the "Association of Women Artists in Berlin" as well as other women's art societies, and in 1927 is included in the important "Women's Art Exhibition," organized by Johannes Hinrichsen at Berlin's "Künstlerhaus." She has major retrospectives in 1925–26 in the Rhineland cities of Cologne, Essen, Krefeld, Duisburg and Braunschweig. Beginning in 1925, uncertain of her art and seeking new inspiration, she attends informal classes supervised by the Berlin artist Arthur Segal.

She continues to attempt to correspond with Kandinsky, but receives no response to her letters; she is contacted, however, by Captain Ludwig Baehr, who acts as Kandinsky's agent in an effort to obtain payment from Herwarth Walden for paintings he had sold, and learns through Baehr of Kandinsky's marriage, as well as of the birth and death of his son. After Kandinsky returns to Germany in 1921 to teach at the Bauhaus in Weimar, he attempts through Baehr to have some of his works and other property stored by Münter returned to him, but persistently refuses her condition that he contact her personally. What communication there is, is through lawyers as Kandinsky demands his property and Münter demands that he admit that they were husband and wife in a "marriage of conscience" and that he broke all promises and vows to her. Finally, however, in response to a very lengthy, bitter and accusatory letter she had sent on 13 July 1922, he sends a registered letter on 22 July to "Frau Gabriele Münter-Kandinsky": "I do not want to deny my guilt. But it does not consist in the failure of our marriage to work out, that our life together was a constant torture for both of us. We both are guilty of that, insofar as a person can be guilty for possessing a particular type of character or another. At any rate, a marriage can only last when both parties consider it possible and desire it. My guilt consists of having broken my promise to marry you legally. And for that I am more than sorry.... Because I—deliberately or not deliberately—have broken my word, therefore, it is my sincere intention at least to meet your wishes in material concerns as much as I am able.... Hate on my part is out of the question. You brought much pain into my life, but are yourself unhappy enough that I could not have any hard feelings towards you. I wish you would also not hate me."[11]

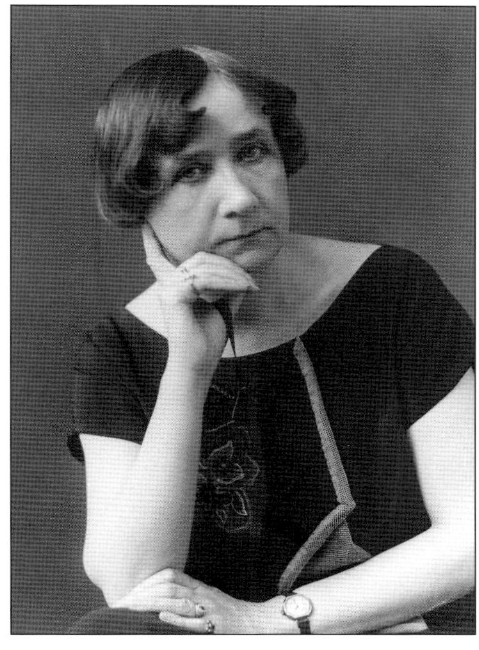

Gabriele Münter, Berlin, 1920

They do not reach agreement about the division of property until 1926.

In March 1925, she begins a lengthy manuscript in five notebooks and numerous loose papers. Entitled "Confession and Accusation," it is a composite of diary entries, drafts of letters, notes, reminiscences and personal reflections concerning her relationship with Kandinsky, as well as excerpted quotations from folk songs, poems and books by various authors; she continues writing in the notebooks irregularly until the fall of 1928. She summarized her relationship with Kandinsky as follows:

"I allowed myself to be lied to and cheated out of my life. Now I have nothing and never had anything. [I was recently asked:] Did you gain nothing from him as an artist? I said, yes, certainly, though, I remember how in the beginning I accused him that, while others always learned so much from his correction, he never said anything to me! He replied, yes, that 'as a student' I was hopeless—he could teach me nothing, unlike the others. And now I think that even what I gained from him as an artist was only half—only a small quarter—nothing complete, no totality. He could give me nothing—I did not understand how to demand and how to take. We did not live with each other—I did not understand or see it clearly—but I probably could sense it. He was always turned inwards to himself—never offered an open friendship and companionship—only promises. Beautiful words, beautiful gestures, lies. He lied to himself and cheated himself, because I'm sure he certainly believed that he could neither want nor do something evil. He overrated himself immensely, otherwise he would not have promised so much."[12]

At a New Year's Eve party in 1927, Münter meets the free-lance art historian, philosopher and journalist Johannes Eichner. In 1928, their relationship develops as they go to exhibitions together and he visits her in Munich. "Now joy has come to me. (Am I ready for it?)," she recorded among the last entries in "Accusation and Confession."[13]

1929–1936 Münter and Eichner develop their life together, initially in Paris and southern France in 1929–30, then largely in Murnau. Eichner begins to write about her art, and in 1933 organizes the exhibition "Gabriele Münter: 1908–1933" of fifty paintings that travels to Bremen, Bochum, Jena, Eisenach, Altenburg and Stuttgart during the next two years. The exhibition is repeatedly attacked by partisans of the reactionary National Socialist aesthetic, and Eichner urges Münter to adopt a more compliant approach in her work while seeking support from Nazi Party members. Following his advice to be more commercial and to adapt to current tastes, she begins a series of paintings concentrated on the construction of the Olympiastrasse, a major Nazi highway project associated with the winter Olympic Games, which take place in Garmisch in 1936. One of the paintings is included in the traveling exhibition "Adolf Hitler's Streets in Art." Münter's financial situation worsens significantly during this time, and she agrees to transfer ownership of the Murnau house to Eichner, who undertakes extensive renovation and "winterization" of the summer villa.

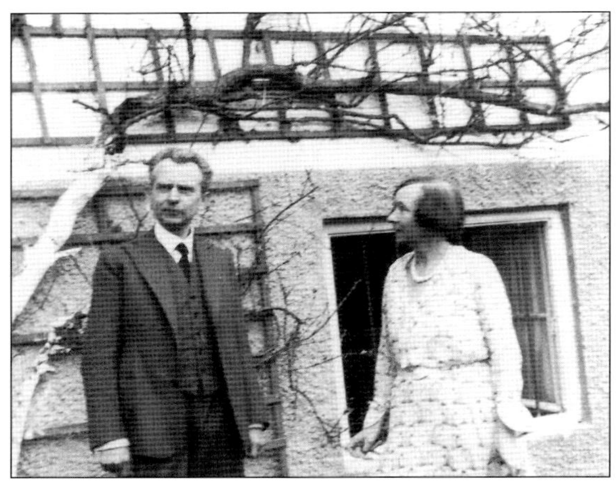

Gabriele Münter and Johannes Eichner, 1933

1937–1945 In 1937, an exhibition of fifty-six paintings is shown at the Heimatmuseum in Herford in honor of Münter's sixtieth birthday. An exhibition of thirty-five paintings, mostly recent, organized by Erwin Pixis for the Munich Art Association in March receives negative criticism in the Nazi press and is vehemently attacked by the Bavarian Nazi Minister of State, Adolf Wagner, when he visits it. Münter accompanies the exhibition to the Galerie Valentien in Stuttgart, and there establishes contact with followers of the pioneer of abstract painting, Adolf Hölzel. Works submitted by Eichner for her to the "Great German Art Exhibition" in Munich are rejected. On 11 August, she and Eichner visit this official exhibition intended to show "healthy" German art in juxtaposition to the infamous simultaneous "Degenerate Art Exhibition," which they also visit. Thereafter, she exhibits only sporadically in Murnau and other small Bavarian towns until after World War II. She occasionally receives portrait commissions, and is able to sell or barter flower still lifes during the remaining years of the Nazi regime, but lives largely in isolation with Eichner in Murnau. She remains, however, officially recognized as a professional artist through membership in the "National Cartel of Fine Artists." In the basement of her house, in a secret room, she hides her collection of Blue Rider works, initially to prevent them from being confiscated by the Nazis, then by the American occupation troops that arrive in Murnau on 29 April 1945.

1946–1962 Münter reestablishes contact with several of her American cousins, some of whom visit her and send her packages of food and clothing in the late 1940s and early 1950s.

With the revival of modernist art in Germany, Münter, too, begins to be rediscovered; she is sought out in Murnau by critics, art historians and museum directors who recognize and honor her as one of the few surviving members of the Blue Rider and the classic age of German modernism. Ludwig Grote begins to organize a large exhibition devoted to the Blue Rider, jointly sponsored by the Bavarian State Painting Collection and the Allied military government's Central Collection Point for Art in Munich; Münter is appointed to the exhibition's honorary advisory committee. The exhibition opens on 3 September 1949. She is also included in several exhibitions surveying contemporary art in Germany, beginning in 1948, as well as in the German section of the Venice Biennale in 1950, which she visits, noting in her diaries: "Hardly anybody stops before my pictures."

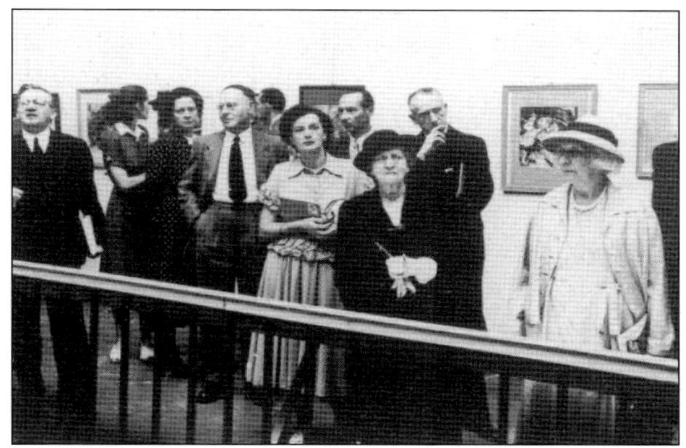

Gabriele Münter at the opening of the Blue Rider exhibition, Haus der Kunst, Munich, 1949

Eichner organizes the first postwar exhibition devoted to her, "Gabriele Münter: Works of Five Decades," which tours for four years to twenty-two German cities, beginning in Braunschweig in 1950. He also begins a monograph on Münter's work; published in 1957 and entitled *Kandinsky and Gabriele Münter: Concerning the Origins of Modern Art*, it is the first book-length study of her art and makes extensive use of her vast collection of letters and other documents, as well as her own recollections.

Throughout the 1950s, Gabriele Münter exhibitions are held uninterruptedly, with at least one a year, in German museums and art galleries. A collection of her portrait drawings is published in honor of her seventy-fifth birthday by Georg Friedrich Hartlaub in 1952, while Hans Konrad Roethel issues a volume devoted to her paintings in 1957. As director of the

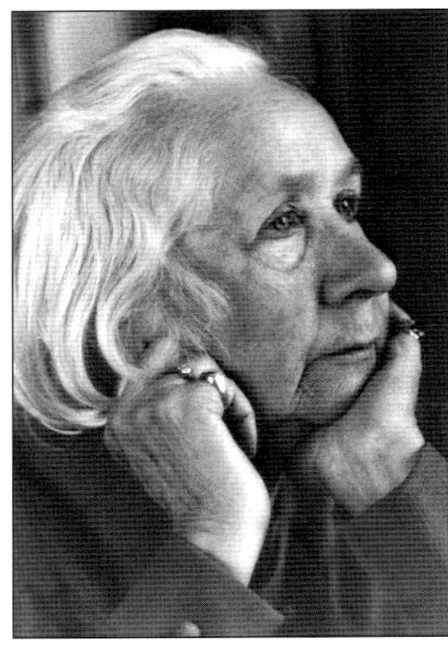

Gabriele Münter at the age of seventy-five, Murnau, 1952

Municipal Gallery of the City of Munich (Städtische Galerie im Lenbachhaus München), Roethel also negotiates with her concerning her collection of Blue Rider works and documents, a large part of which—including more than ninety paintings by Kandinsky and twenty-five by herself—she donates to the city in 1957.

On 11 February 1958, Johannes Eichner dies unexpectedly. Münter now continues to live alone in Murnau. She is visited repeatedly by art historians, especially by Kandinsky scholars, including Will Grohmann, Klaus Brisch and the American, Kenneth C. Lindsay, as well as by the American collector, Norbert Adler, who purchases several works from her. The first exhibitions devoted to her work in the United States, arranged through Roethel, are held in 1960–61 at the Dalzell Hatfield Galleries in Los Angeles and the Leonhard Hutton Galleries in New York.

On 19 May 1962, Gabriele Münter dies in her Murnau house.

Through her will, the Gabriele Münter and Johannes Eichner Foundation is created in order to "generate and deepen understanding for the artistic efforts of modern art as well as to encourage the production of this type of art." The Foundation also receives her entire estate, including all works not donated to the Municipal Gallery, her papers and letters and her Murnau house.

The American Journey, 1898–1900

An Album of Drawings and Photographs by Gabriele Münter

St. Louis, Missouri
Moorefield, Arkansas
Marshall, Texas
Plainview, Texas

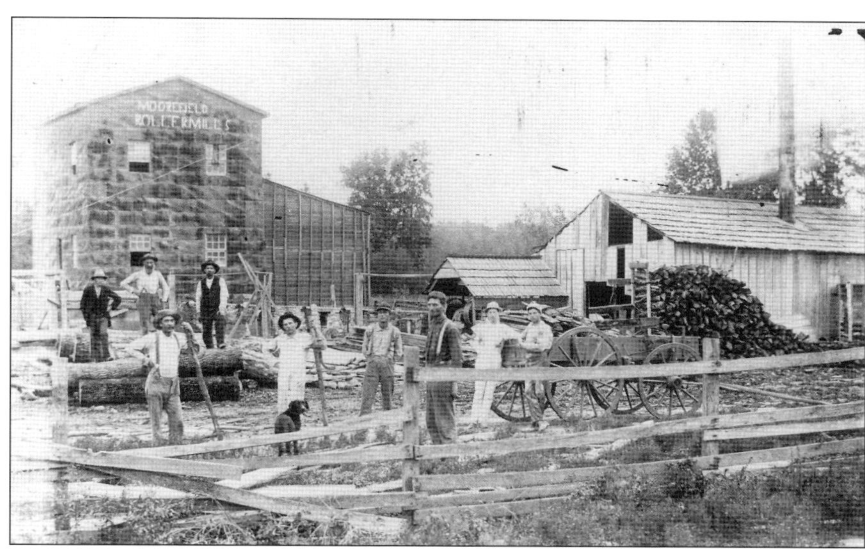

The mill in Moorefield, 1899. Photograph by Gabriele Münter. Gabriele Münter- und Johannes Eichner-Stiftung, Munich

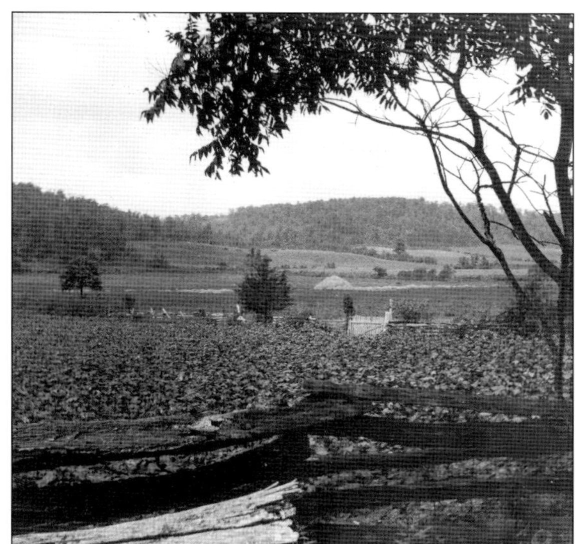

View of the countryside near Marshall, 1899. Photograph by Gabriele Münter. Gabriele Münter- und Johannes Eichner-Stiftung, Munich

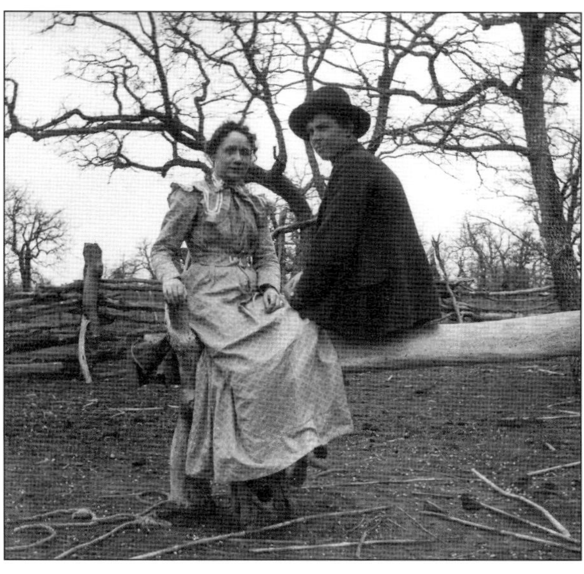

Gabriele Münter with an American relative, Marshall, March, 1900. Photographer unknown. Gabriele Münter- und Johannes Eichner-Stiftung, Munich

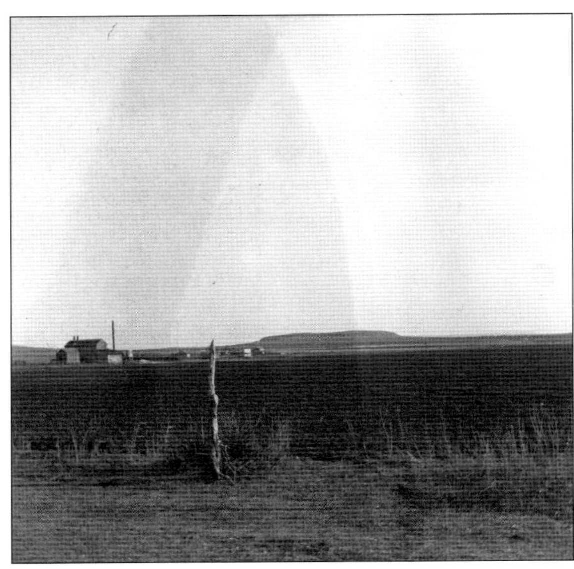

House on the prairie near Marshall, 1899. Photograph by Gabriele Münter. Gabriele Münter- und Johannes Eichner-Stiftung, Munich

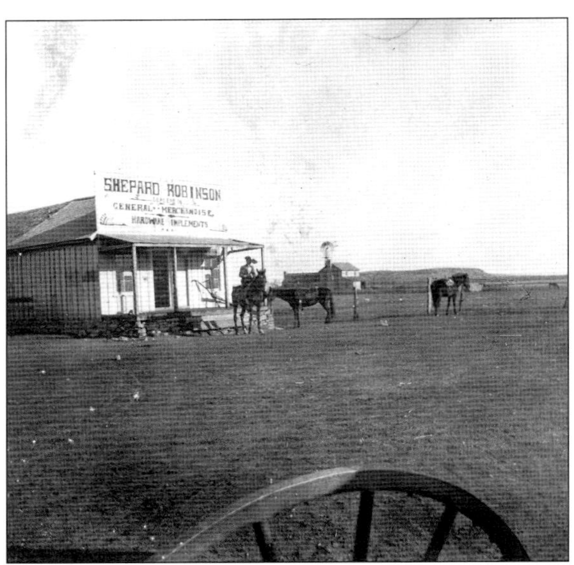

Shepard Robinson General Store, Marshall, 1900. Photograph by Gabriele Münter. Gabriele Münter- und Johannes Eichner-Stiftung, Munich

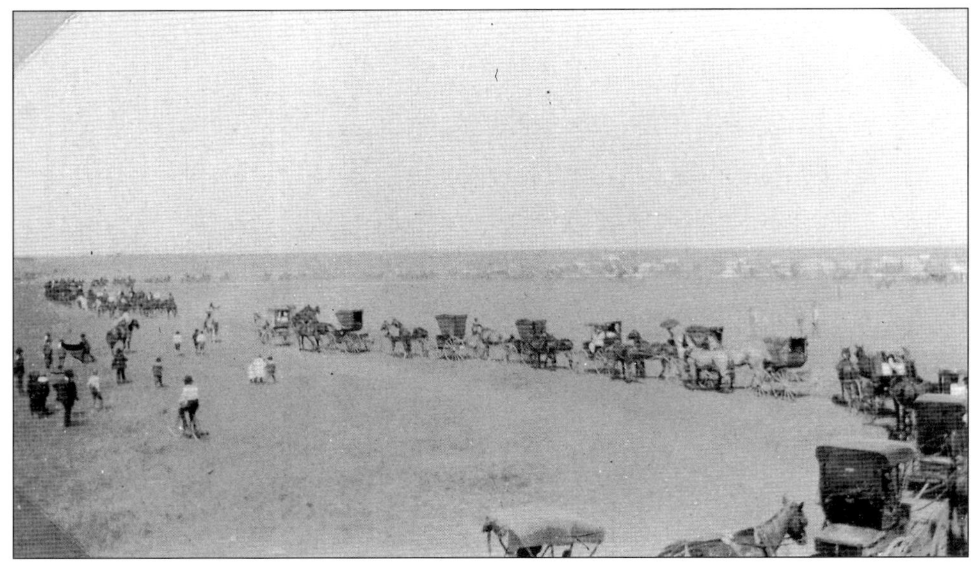

Plainview Cowboy Reunion, 17 August 1899. Photograph by Gabriele Münter. Gabriele Münter- und Johannes Eichner-Stiftung, Munich

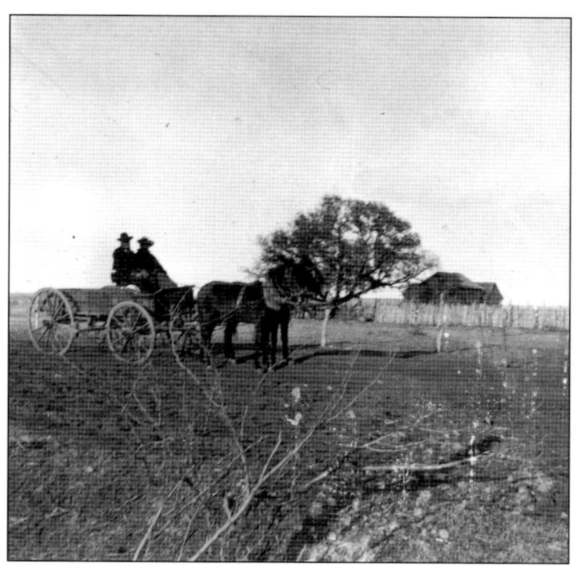

Left: "Life Oak Tree," Marshall, 28 February 1900. Photograph by Gabriele Münter. Gabriele Münter- und Johannes Eichner-Stiftung, Munich

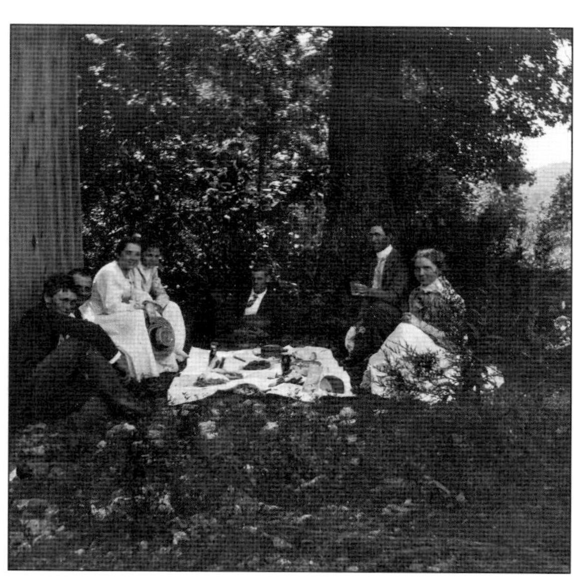

Picnic, Marshall, 19 June 1899. Photograph by Gabriele Münter. Gabriele Münter- und Johannes Eichner-Stiftung, Munich

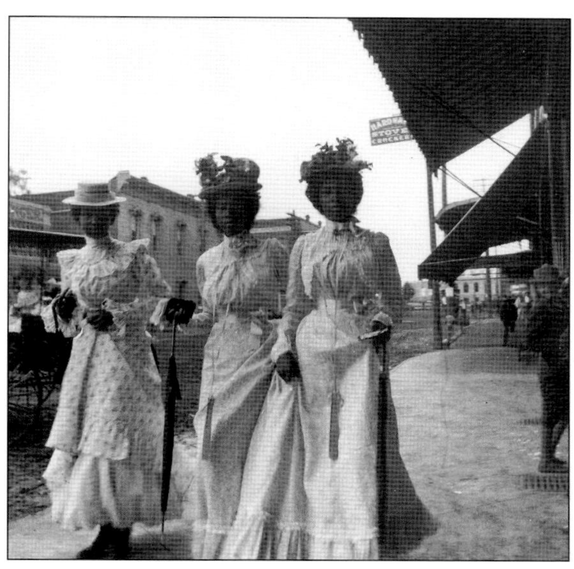

Three women after church in Marshall, June or July 1900. Photograph by Gabriele Münter. Gabriele Münter- und Johannes Eichner-Stiftung, Munich

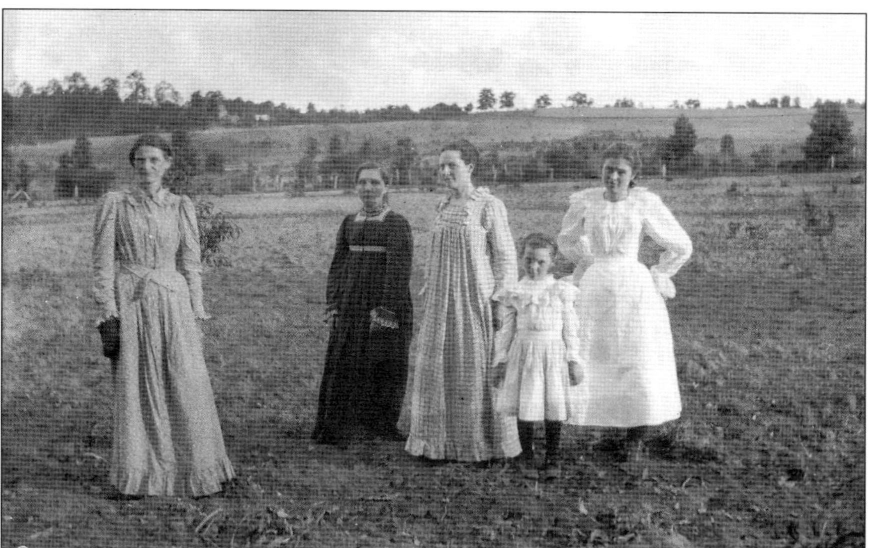

Women and children in the fields, Marshall, June or July 1900. Photograph by Gabriele Münter. Gabriele Münter- und Johannes Eichner-Stiftung, Munich

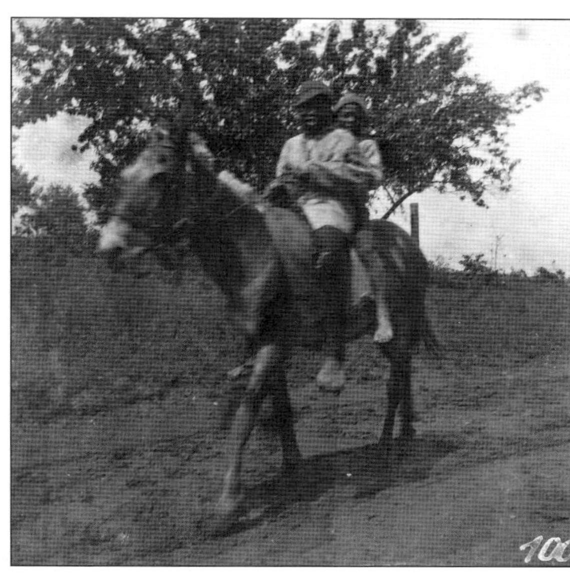

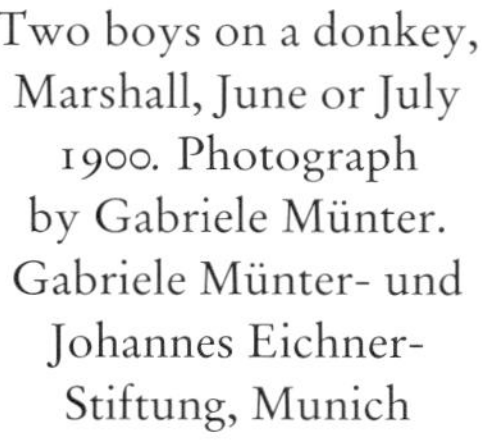

Two boys on a donkey, Marshall, June or July 1900. Photograph by Gabriele Münter. Gabriele Münter- und Johannes Eichner-Stiftung, Munich

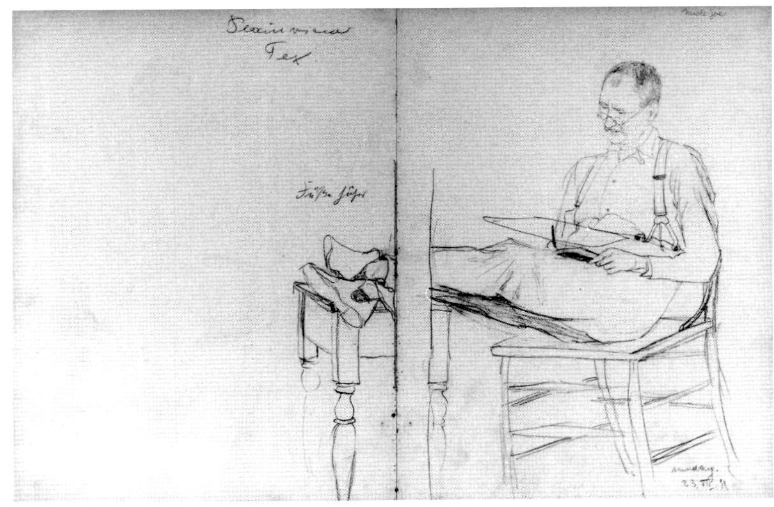

Uncle Joe, Plainview, Texas, 1899. Gabriele Münter- und Johannes Eichner-Stiftung, Munich (Folder 38/4, Sketchbook 1897–99, pp. 50–51)

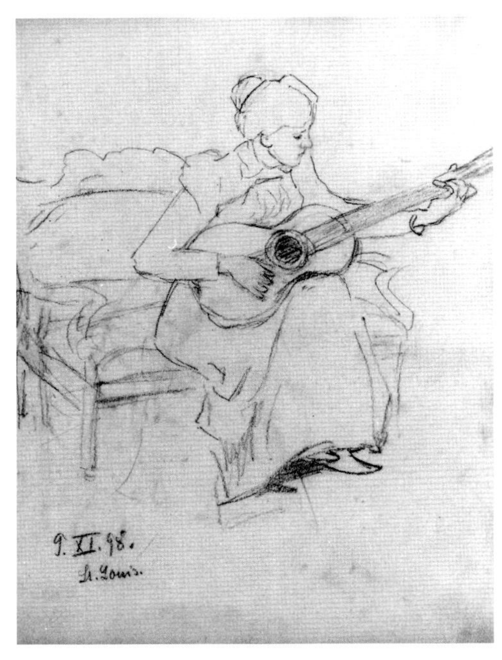

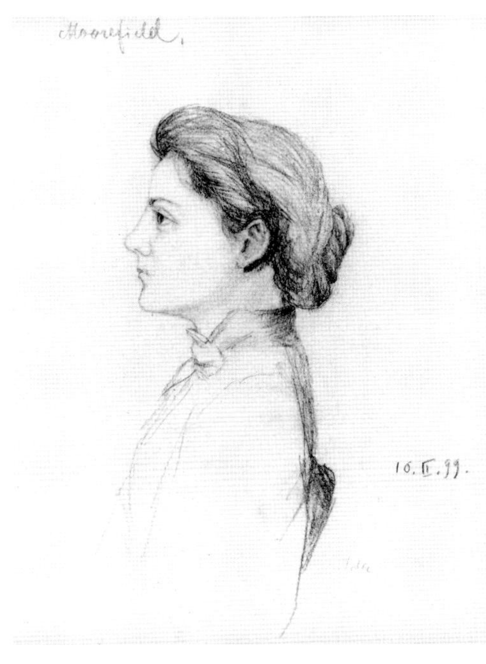

Far left: *Woman Playing a Guitar,* 1898. Gabriele Münter- und Johannes Eichner-Stiftung, Munich (Folder 38/4, Sketchbook 1897–99, p. 27)

Ida, Moorefield, 1899. Gabriele Münter- und Johannes Eichner-Stiftung, Munich (Folder 38/4, Sketchbook 1897–99, p. 41)

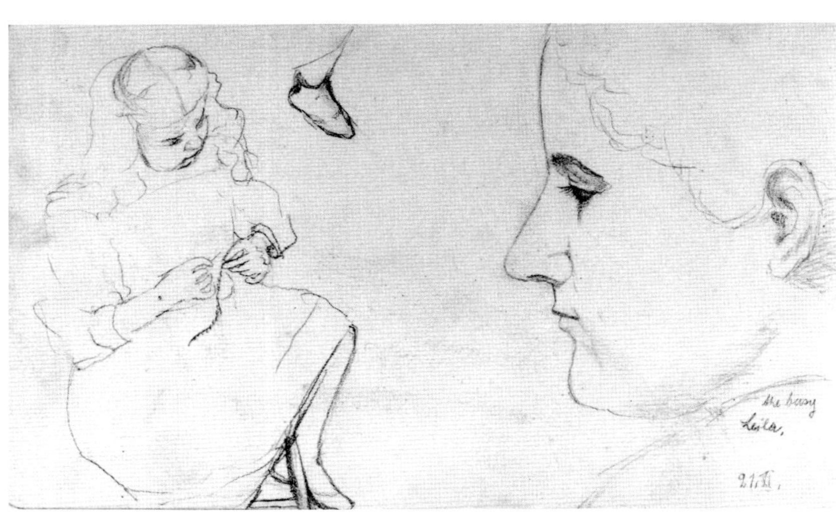

The Busy Leila, 1899. Gabriele Münter- und Johannes Eichner-Stiftung, Munich (Folder 37/3, Sketchbook 1898–99, p. 50)

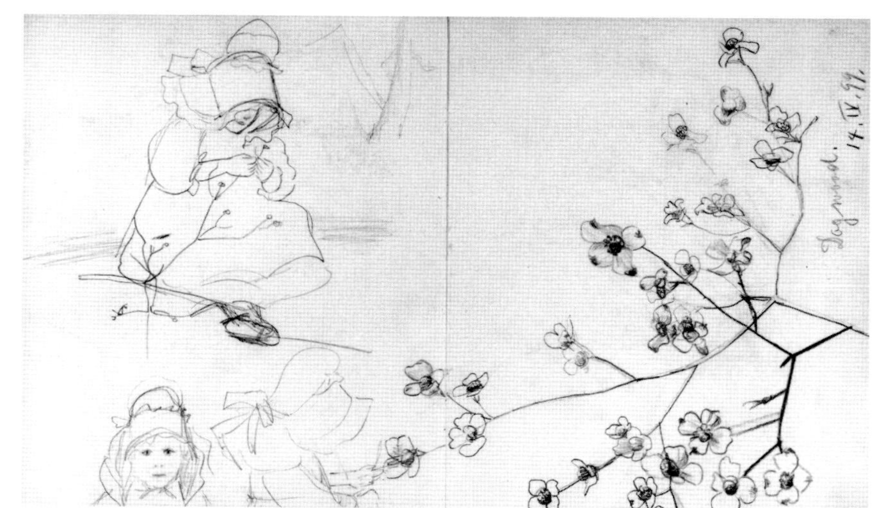

Dogwood, 1899. Gabriele Münter- und Johannes Eichner-Stiftung, Munich (Folder 36/2, Sketchbook 1899, pp. 8–9)

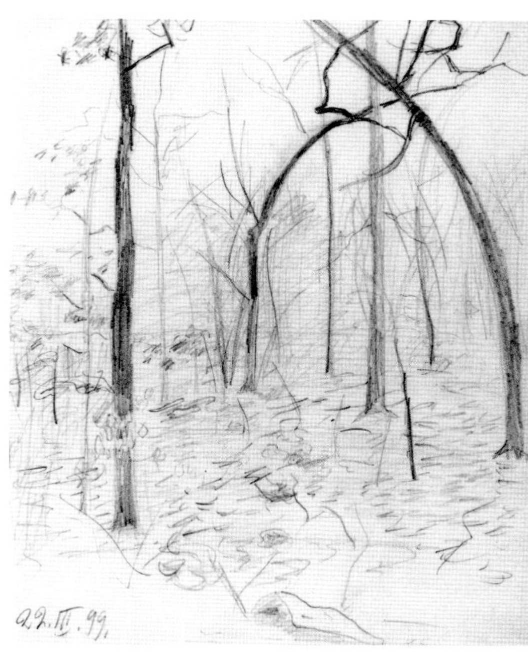

Forest Interior, 1899. Gabriele Münter- und Johannes Eichner-Stiftung, Munich (Folder 36/2, Sketchbook 1899, p. 3)

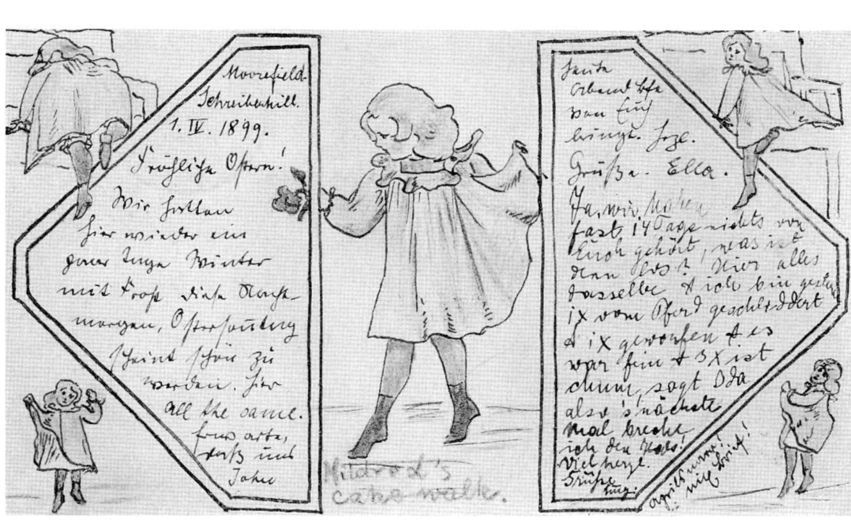

Postcard from Gabriele to Carl Münter: *Mildred's Cake Walk,* 1899. Städtische Galerie im Lenbachhaus, Munich, Gabriele Münter Bequest (GMS 1141)

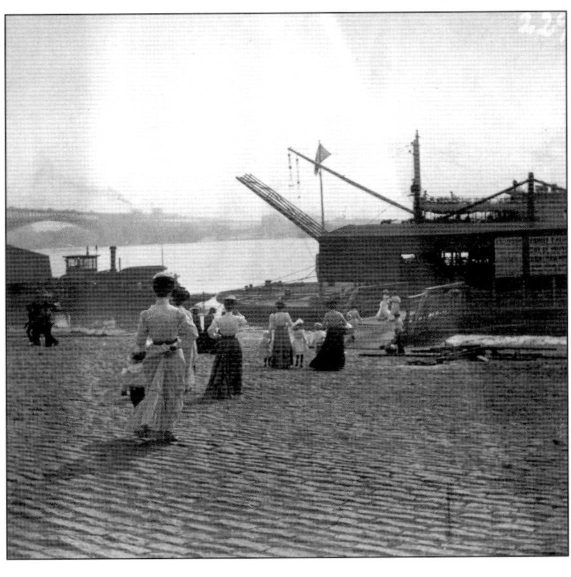

Excursion on the Mississippi River, 1900. Photograph by Gabriele Münter. Gabriele Münter- und Johannes Eichner-Stiftung, Munich

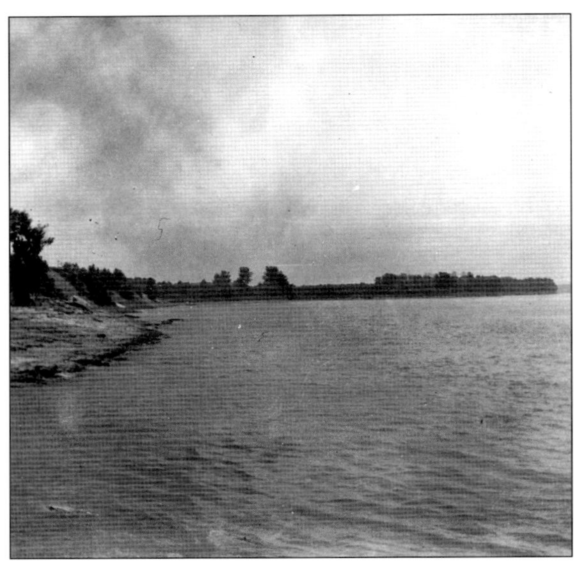

The shore of the Mississippi River, 1900. Photograph by Gabriele Münter. Gabriele Münter- und Johannes Eichner-Stiftung, Munich

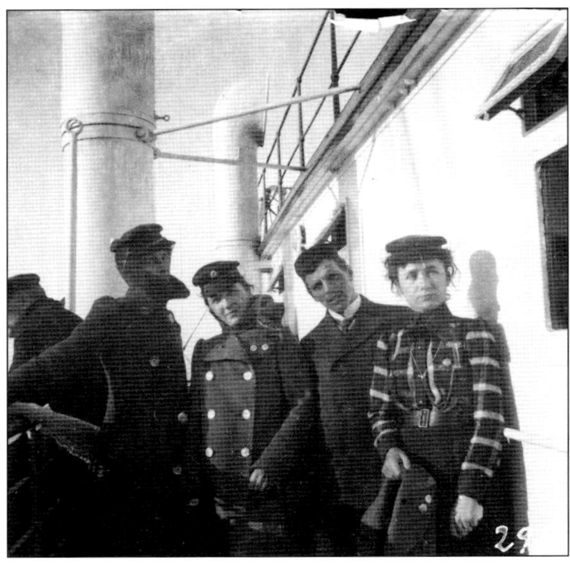

Gabriele and Emmy Münter on the S. S. Pennsylvania, 1900. Photographer unknown. Gabriele Münter- und Johannes Eichner-Stiftung, Munich

Apprenticeship and Travels in Search of a Style

Chapter 1

Gabriele Münter, the youngest daughter of a well-to-do German middle-class family, was raised in the Westphalian city of Herford and the Rhineland city of Koblenz—both of which became part of Prussia after the defeat of Napoleon in 1815. As a young girl, she was encouraged to draw, like other children of her nationality and class, as drawing was considered an appropriate childhood diversion, capable of amusing and educating simultaneously. It provided a valued means of encountering and ordering the visual world, as well as a means of tracking the progress of this process in a child. It also, of course, functioned as a rudimentary introduction to an aesthetic education, notably to the naturalistic judgment of the quality and the degree of illusionistic representation in which a pleasingly recognizable likeness served as the major criterion. This does not, however, indicate an involvement in the visual arts beyond an elementary or even superficial level in the Münter family.

The Münter family had long since been identified largely with commerce and the church. Even the dental practice of Münter's father was an extension of this history more than a turn to medicine as a profession. Trained in dentistry in the United States, he there initially included its practice among the services he provided in his general store in rural Tennessee, and made it his exclusive profession only after returning to Germany in 1864. Practicality and utility marked the concerns of the Münter family, along with the conventional hallmarks of success and material well-being, such as the comfortable new home the family had constructed for itself in Herford before moving there in 1878. The home was tastefully furnished in the opulent style of Neo-Baroque fashionable then, and decorated with reproductions of well-known artworks, such as Arnold Böcklin's celebrated *Isle of the Dead*, an image virtually compulsory in German middle-class homes at the time, around which were clustered several small-scale paintings of the local landscape and of still lifes. It is an inventory of artworks representative of the middle-class German home of the time, where they functioned more as signs of cultural identity, well-nigh invisible in their obligatory presence, than as indices of significant interest in, or fostering of, art as such.

"My early desire to draw came totally from myself," Münter maintained in 1948,[1] and similarly Johannes Eichner, her companion from the late 1920s onwards, maintained in his biography of her in 1957 that "... there was nothing in her family from which one could have predicted Gabriele Münter's profession as a painter, and nothing in her childhood environment that could have aroused and fostered such a talent."[2] Underlying this absolute artistic independence, even in the young girl's initial drawing efforts, is a modernist style favoring originality and freedom over traditional, established forms of expression. Her early works also serve to demonstrate a degree of social alienation resulting from the confines of a bourgeois family and its values, another requisite of the modernist paradigm. A similar modernist template seems to have shaped other childhood memories, which were recalled by Münter late in life. She hid her drawings from her family, she claimed, since art was alien to them. However, a more plausible motivation than the purported puritanical iconoclasm of the Münters would be the child's natural desire to avoid being subjected to the potential criticism or patronizing ridicule of adults who so often find "mistakes" in children's drawings. Only her brother August—who had just returned from America and thus, like her, was an outsider within the family circle—praised and encouraged her continued drawing efforts.[3] But countering these memories is the recollection that she was given a fine set of watercolors for her tenth birthday, surely an indication that the Münter family encouraged more than discouraged the cultivation of her artistic skills. Indeed, they were highly valued in a young middle-class woman as a mark of culture, much as Münter's extensively fostered musical skills—her singing, piano and guitar playing, as well as her composing.

Gabriele Münter's childhood pictorial efforts acquired a more disciplined character when drawing became a formal subject in her school curriculum at the Koblenz Lyceum for Girls beginning in 1890. The Prussian school system included eight hours of drawing a week as an obligatory subject in its syllabus, viewing it as a fundamental skill necessary to achieve "a balanced and comprehensive intellectual, practical and emotional education."[4] Dependent, despite the changes it underwent, on the teachings of the early nineteenth-century theorist of pedagogy Heinrich Pestalozzi, the teaching of drawing to school children emphasized imitation and accuracy by using simple outlines to define forms. In Münter's classes, abstract and ornamental patterns were assigned to be replicated carefully and precisely in exercise books, the pages subdivided into grids to facilitate accuracy in the reproductive process. Münter obediently followed these instructions, but also filled the backs of the assignment pages with free-hand drawings of flowers and portraits in which she applied, perhaps unconsciously, the lessons of simplification, reductivity of line and flattened patterning that were the principles around which her formal drawing lessons were conceived. Implicit in them are the fundamental features of her later art, with its radical reductivity and accented outline. In recognition of her abilities, she was allowed to supplement the drawing of patterns with drawings after portrait paintings and sculptures, predominantly of women, by well-known contemporary German artists. She now incorporated naturalistic elements of shading and modeling to create the illusion of a third dimension. While the standard drawing lessons—with their excessive preoccupation with line and their concern with grid-facilitated, systematic accuracy, which was to be adopted by all students regardless of their individual artistic talent—were considered essential to developing mind-eye coordination but were deemed to have no significant artistic merit, naturalistic drawings employing high-art prototypes were intended to heighten the aesthetic sensibilities and artistic proficiency of talented students like Münter.

These rudimentary lessons given by her drawing instructors at the lyceum—even if she disliked the "boring patterns and models"[5]—proved fundamental to Münter's artistic development. Through them she developed a vision that acknowledged line as the primary determinant of form in an image, linking it with a process of reductivity and simplification to achieve clarity of form, which became the very defining principle of her mature work over a decade later. She also gained both facility and confidence in her drawing ability by means of employing a visual model and a prototype. Firmly established in these childhood drawing lessons as well was the desire to render an interpretation of the visible, to characterize and hold fast the world as visually experienced, giving it in the counterfeited image a permanence and impermeability akin to that of the geometric patterns she once copied. A concept—the Platonic idea—of the visual object rather than the accidentals of the visual world became the goal of her imagery.

"I can report," she wrote half a century later, "that even as a child I practiced with the pencil and, specifically, that I always drew faces. Other children "drew" stories. I made no effort to depict events and actions. Only permanence in appearance fascinated me in a person—the form in which the essence was expressed."[6] Her school exercise books substantiate this remark in numerous renditions of heads, usually in profile, the view traditionally thought best to capture the fundamental character, or essence, of a sitter because it excludes accidental features. Often favored in drawings by children and naive artists owing to its overt simplicity, the profile deindividualizes even though it captures key identifying features. It also readily enables the execution of a two-dimensional rendition, considered to be more abstract or idea-oriented than a three-dimensional picture emphasizing volume, light and shade. It projects a sense of stasis, of immobility that further enhances the quality of the essential and the durable. Münter applied identical principles in her flower drawings, stripping the forms of individuality and reducing them to silhouette-like renderings similar to those in botanical illustrations, which may indeed have served her as models. It was a resemblance she captured in her childhood drawings, whether of persons or of flowers, distanced from the accidental and imbued with the immobility of permanence. "She saw the world as a still life," Johannes Eichner observed correctly, and added: "Therefore, an identifying feature of her work was already determined."[7] The drawing elementals taught to her in rudimentary lessons at the lyceum, usually considered insignificant or even detrimental to her development as an artist,[8] in fact shaped her later attitude towards her art and its means of representation.

What is surprising about Gabriele Münter's childhood, and her artistic activity during that period, is that it was absolutely ordinary. She grew up in the comfort and protection of a well-to-do, German middle-class home during the era of peace and relative prosperity that characterized the first decades of the German Empire. What distinguished the Münter home from others, if anything, was its close ties to the United States: Münter's parents had lived and married there, close relatives—including one son, whom her mother visited at least once during Münter's childhood—continued to live there and American words, sayings, songs and objects were sprinkled among the German ones in the home. Also attributable to the American influence was a lack of rigidity and a greater sense of freedom than was common in the German middle class. As Eichner noted, based on Münter's recollections: "There was no use for force, and little discipline. Social formalities, habitual niceties, superficial appearances, drawing attention to oneself: these were things the child and young girl were not taught."[9] The Münter daughters were allowed unusual freedom, as when they were given bicycles, were allowed to smoke and to read controversial avant-garde literature or were not forced into early marriages. Münter's drawing may not have been accorded special recognition in this milieu, but it certainly was not discouraged, so when she desired formal drawing lessons after completing her lyceum education, the family supported her in her decision to seek the instruction of a professor from the nearby Düsseldorf Academy.

German art academies, with two or three limited exceptions, remained closed to women until after World War I. The demand for art instruction for middle- and upper-class women—the so-called *höhere Töchter* or "higher daughters" of society—as a means of filling their hours of leisure, more than seriously pursuing a profession, however, became sufficiently great during the 1880s and 1890s to inspire many academy instructors to offer private lessons to them outside the academy. Private art schools for women run by such individuals, by groups of artists—including progressive, non-academic artists—or by newly formed women's organizations existed alongside the male-only official academies, and vied with the schools for applied arts, to which women were admitted. The demand for art instruction for women increased, too, when drawing was included in the curriculum of Prussian schools for girls as well as for boys, and the position of drawing instructor became one deemed respectable even for unmarried *höhere Töchter*. Münter's entry into the classes of Ernst Bosch and then the Atelier for Women reflects a trend in German society at the time, even if a somewhat unusual one, and therefore did not significantly break with contemporary social strictures.

The training she received in Düsseldorf was diverse and apparently relatively unfocused and unsystematic as it included not only drawing but also

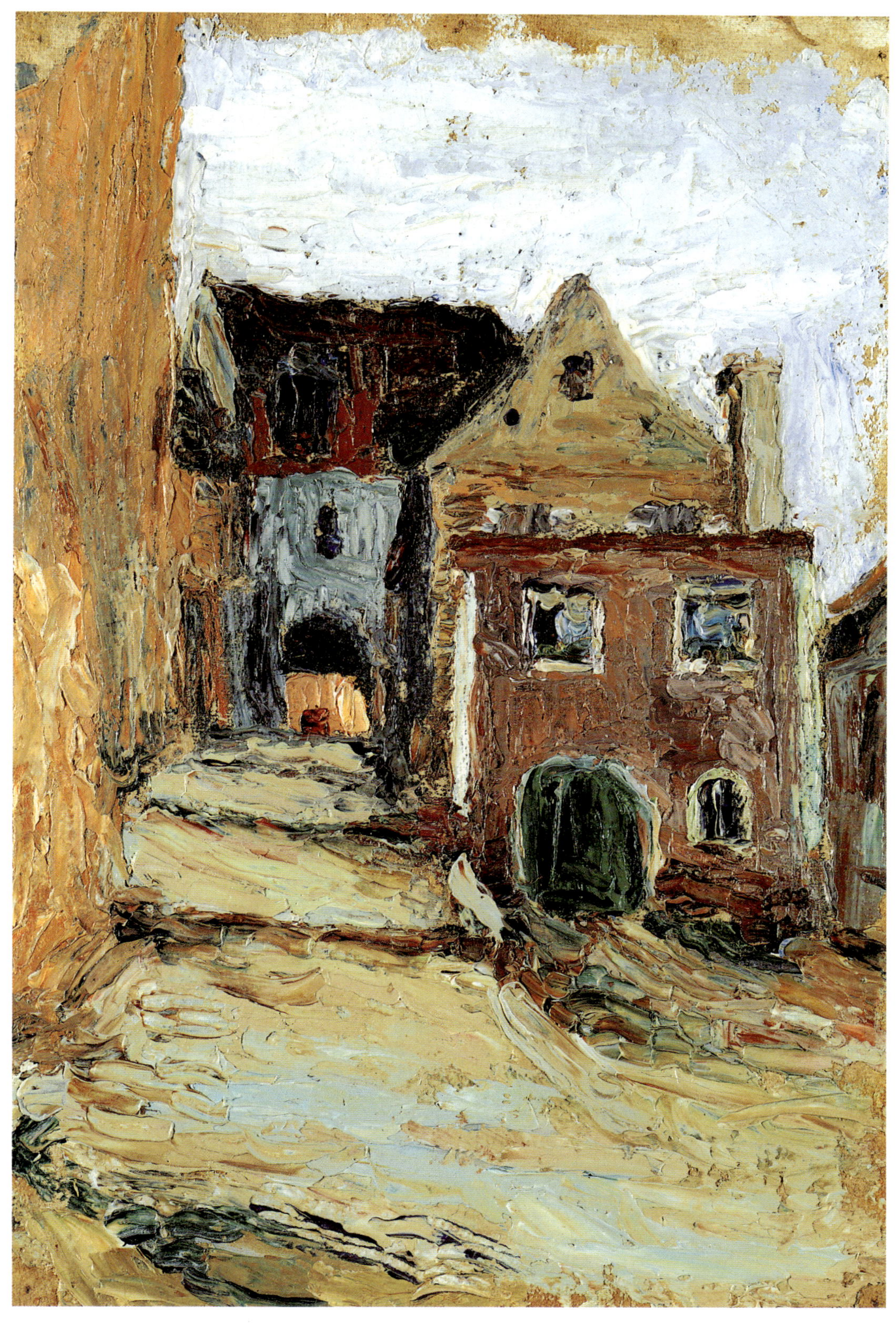

Kallmünz, 1903 (Cat. No. 1)

sculpture, pastels and decorative design. As she later recalled: "I had taken some drawing lessons, as many girls did in those days, but I had also attended an art class for a couple months in Düsseldorf, which still had a great reputation as an art center. I found the teaching at its Academy, however, very uninspiring, still dominated by the ideas and tastes of the late Romantics; besides, nobody there seemed to take seriously the artistic ambitions of a mere girl."[10] A woman with artistic aspirations was an anomaly. Even a decade later, in 1907, the official census identified only 801 women among a total of 4,909 active professional painters and sculptors in the German Empire.[11] For Münter, to train seriously as an artist, beyond the training of an accomplished dilettante, while not censurable, did counter normal expectations, and she hesitated for some time before making the decision to do so. Not until after the death of her mother and the two-year trip to the United States did she finally commit herself to further formal training and study.

Other than a few sketchbook drawings, there is interestingly no surviving material from Münter's interrupted and half-hearted studies in Düsseldorf in 1897–98, as if she or her family, who saved childhood drawings and school workbooks, later rejected its significance. The drawings made after her Düsseldorf training during her America trip, however, show her continual use of outlining devices and simplification of figures, which she had already learned at the lyceum, but now with significantly increased sophistication and facility in much more ambitious compositions. Drawings of her American relatives—usually alone and most frequently women and children—portray them in varied domestic situations and informal poses. Women sit pensively in rocking chairs, recline in hammocks or play the guitar; children carry dolls or a bunch of freshly pulled carrots. Their bodies often turn or are foreshortened, and they are seen against plain backgrounds or with a minimal indication of their surroundings. Likeness is achieved with few lines. Boldly drawn, accented outlines define the figures and faces, while limited modeling suggests texture, color, shading and volume. But, largely, it is only the surface of the empty page, between the outlines that curve and meander, that is permitted to identify the figures' presence. While Münter still avoided multifigured scenes, preferring the simplicity of the single figure, the surety of placement, cropping and balance on the various sketchbook pages is the result of a by now well-developed sense of composition that avoids overly predictable centering as well as disconcerting crowding.

Indeed, the devices she employed, when seen in their totality, suggest she looked hard at progressive contemporary illustration in periodicals, such as *Die Jugend* or *Simplicissimus*, in which there appeared drawings by the major German artists associated with the innovations of *Jugendstil*, the German variant of *art nouveau*. Clearly, Münter went beyond the lessons taught to her by academic teachers, and independently sought out, observed and studied the works of German artists striving to define a new modern style, released from the naturalistic traditions of the academy and of conventional taste, and in concert with artistic developments in other countries. Although later Münter maintained, not without justification, that she remained a "humble dilettante without artistic intentions" as she filled her sketchbooks during the American trip, and that the sketches were "private notations of visual experiences which I wanted to fix on paper as a personal memento," her works were far from untutored or "... simply inborn."[12] While they undeniably reveal awkwardness in their rendering, a certain stiffness in the poses and inaccuracies in the proportions of the figures, her American drawings were learned, disciplined and practiced—the products of someone cognizant and emulative of contemporary artistic innovations, especially those of *Jugendstil* and artists related to it.

In the transformation of Gabriele Münter from artistic dilettante to professional artist, the American experience was fundamental. With the exception of one trip taken to the Metropolitan Museum of Art in New York, where she was confronted by models of European architectural monuments as well as by the museum's incipient collection of works by distinguished European "masters," and where standard European values were thus enshrined and reconfirmed, she encountered little that would commonly be recognized as art during her visits to Missouri, Arkansas and Texas. The St. Louis Exposition, which she visited on 27 October 1898, included a collection of works by American—predominantly local—and a few European artists. In *The St. Louis Post Dispatch*, the director of the Exposition's art department was cited as remarking that the display was "... more extensive than ever and of great merit.... Lovers of art will surely find enough and more than enough to interest them during the forty days of the Exposition."[13] Watercolorists were especially well represented so as to form a "remarkable feature" of the Exposition, and perhaps induced Münter to produce the several watercolors she did while still in St. Louis. The works displayed included a variety of portraits, still lifes and genre scenes as well as landscapes that would not have been out of place in European academic art exhibitions but for the dominance of American motifs. Director Kurts also observed, however, that in contrast to Europeans, "St. Louisans did not buy many of the pictures exhibited here last year," with the result that "artists are not putting much energy into their work, and are not producing many pictures, because there is little demand for them." In the midwestern and southwestern United States visited by Gabriele Münter, an art market had little significance and little place. The years spent among her American aunts, uncles and cousins were devoid of art. She filled that vacuum with her own images, the highly skilled but dilettantish sketches of the novel, mixed milieu she found in the households of American bankers, cowboys and cattle dealers. The drawings were shown to them, allowing them to marvel at their own likenesses, but most of these works she made for herself, as she later contended. Renditions of personal memories of her American experience were shaped according to the principles of *Jugendstil* illustration, its practice of simplification and reduction as well as its preference for the accented, stylized contour and silhouette—an art in which allusion prevails over naturalistic illusion.[14]

Drawing in an artistic void, without guidance or reinforcing models, Münter was forced to depend solely on her own artistic memory, her own previously taught and continuously developing skills, and her own judgment. The only means she could employ were the ones she herself supplied. Fostered by her isolation were unprecedented self-reliance and independence of spirit. However, these were also linked with Münter's recognition that she remained a dilettante and that her drawings had no greater seriousness of purpose than did the writing of a diary. Her formal training was both rudimentary—the less rigorous classes reserved for women—and interrupted, and this recognition induced uncertainty and self-abnegation. Her attitude towards her own work would remain forever marked by this conflicting, persistently linked duality, which first became manifest in America. Dependence on the self and rejection of external authority went hand in hand for Gabriele Münter then and in the following years with a lack of faith in her own work, which she viewed as being subordinate, as less sophisticated or ambitious, indeed as inferior, to the work of other artists with more formal training or greater familiarity with art theory.

From her two-year sojourn in the United States, Münter returned to Koblenz in October 1900. Apparently, she had already decided by then that she would continue her education as an artist, since that month she was in contact with the successful portrait and monument sculptor Hermann Küppers in Bonn. Private lessons were arranged, but they must not have satisfied her, as on 15 January 1901 she noted succinctly in her pocket calendar: "Küppers finished," followed on Sunday, 24 February with an entry in English: "at home!"[15] Still intent on becoming an artist, she therefore resumed her search for a school or studio where she could continue her formal training more satisfactorily. However, in Germany she had few alternatives outside private lessons or private studios, such as Küppers's, which she found inadequate.[16]

The refusal of the art academies to allow women to enroll in them was the legal and pedagogical manifestation of the widespread belief that women, deemed essentially different from men and considered to be focused by nature on nurturing and on giving birth, lacked the capacity for significant artistic productivity such as men were proven historically to possess. "Atrophy, sickliness or hypertrophy of sexual feelings, perversion or impotence" were the prices women paid who attempted to break with their biologically-determined limitations and sought to be serious artists, according to the study *Woman and Art* by the respected German art critic

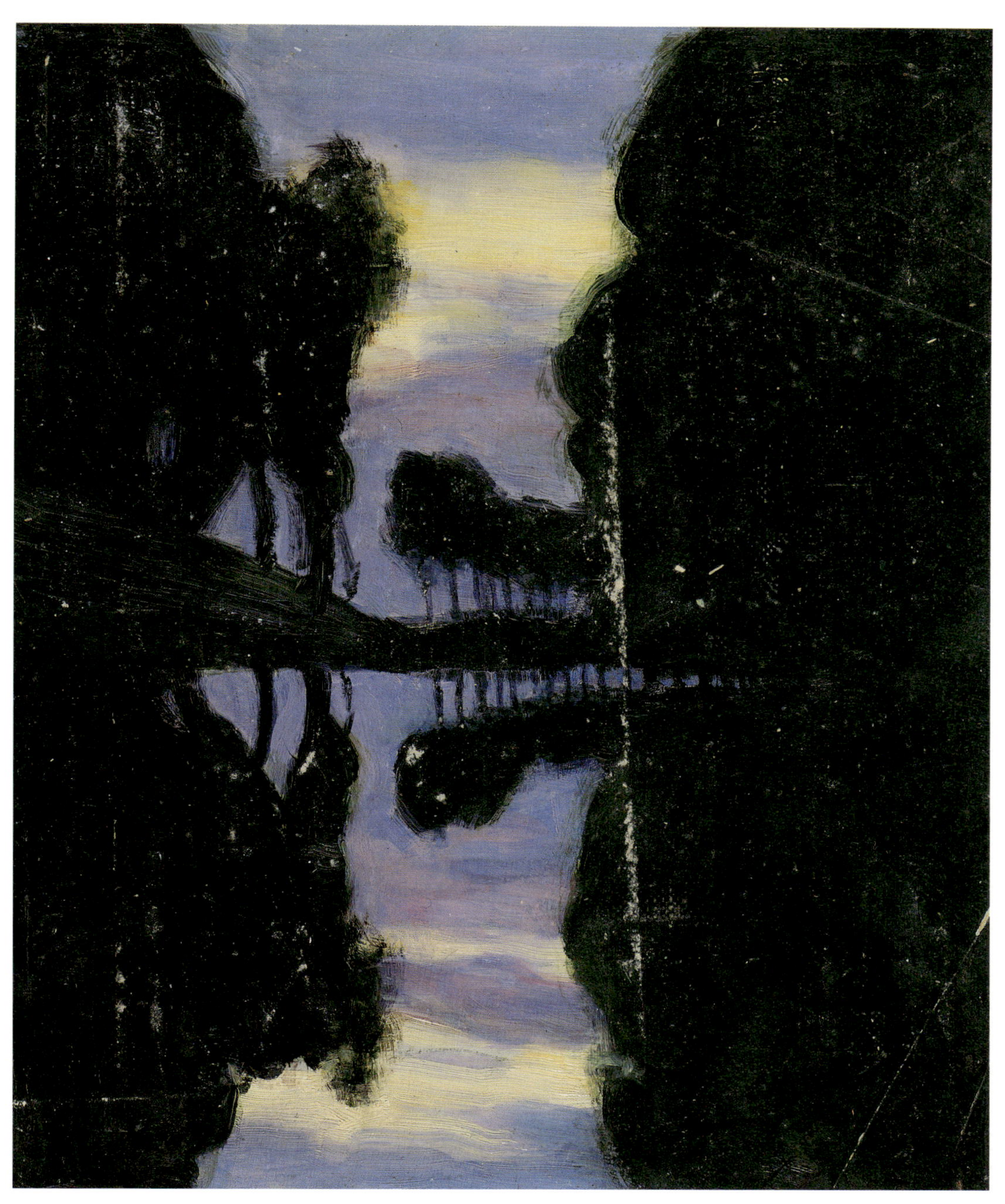

Study from Holland, 1904/05 (Cat. No. 2)

and publicist, Karl Scheffler, an early champion of Impressionism and other progressive modern art movements.[17]

In their judgment of women and of women's artistic capacities, the progressive and reactionary camps of German ideology, sciences and art largely agreed. The Conservative Party of Prussia thus wrote in its program that the "norm is that girls marry and acquire their education [Bildung] through their marriage, but nonetheless something can also be made of sisters, daughters, nurses through brothers, fathers, the sick and the aged if they serve these men with a warm heart."[18] Similarly, Scheffler fundamentally viewed women as empty vessels, as passive shells needing fulfillment through a man, providing the harmonious "other half" to his creative, isolated individualism. Once a woman breaks with her natural passivity and seeks originality, she turns into a defeminized "third sex," unhappy and bitter, the monstrous and unproductive mixture of a woman with man-like attributes:

> If she forces herself to be artistically creative, then she immediately becomes mannish. That is to say: she cripples her sex, sacrifices her harmony and with that surrenders out of hand every possibility of being original. Because true originality can only be found there where inner necessity reigns.... Therefore, since woman cannot be original, she can only attach herself to men's art. She is the imitatrix par excellence, the empathizer who sentimentalizes and disguises manly art forms. In Goethe's words, she "is not capable of a single idea" and she "takes the knowledge and experience of man as ready-made and adorns herself with it." She is the born dilettante.[19]

The denigration of women's artistic ability, a component of a larger social antagonism to women's emancipation generally and to the entry of women into other previously exclusively male-dominated professions, such as law or medicine, was readily accepted by popular culture. Directed to the educated middle-class readership of the periodicals *Die Jugend* or *Simplicissimus*, otherwise progressive in their social and artistic stances, cartoons proliferated that ridiculed the "third sex" woman professional, especially women artists, as when a cartoon by Bruno Paul bore the caption: "You see, miss, there are two sorts of woman artist: the ones who want to marry, and the others who likewise have no talent."[20] Artistic talent was a male monopoly and if women claimed it, it was a mark of perversity according to the prevalent convictions of the German people around 1900.

Despite such general public disdain and ridicule of women artists, extraordinarily, in 1901, Gabriele Münter's family supported her determination to be one. Her studies, it was felt, would be a means to bring direction and order into her life as she approached her mid-twenties, rescuing her from aimlessness, granting her greater satisfaction, making her more self-confident.[21] Indicative of the family's non-conforming attitudes, marriage, the

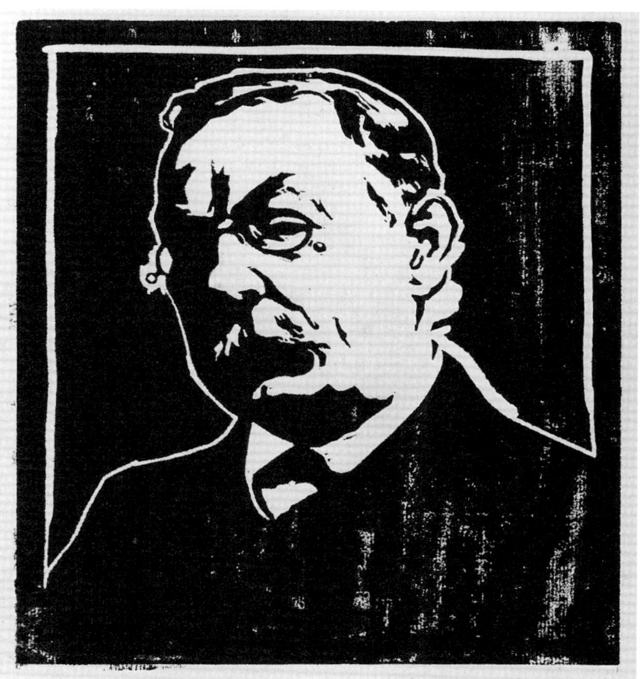

M. Vernot, 1906 (Cat. No. 4)

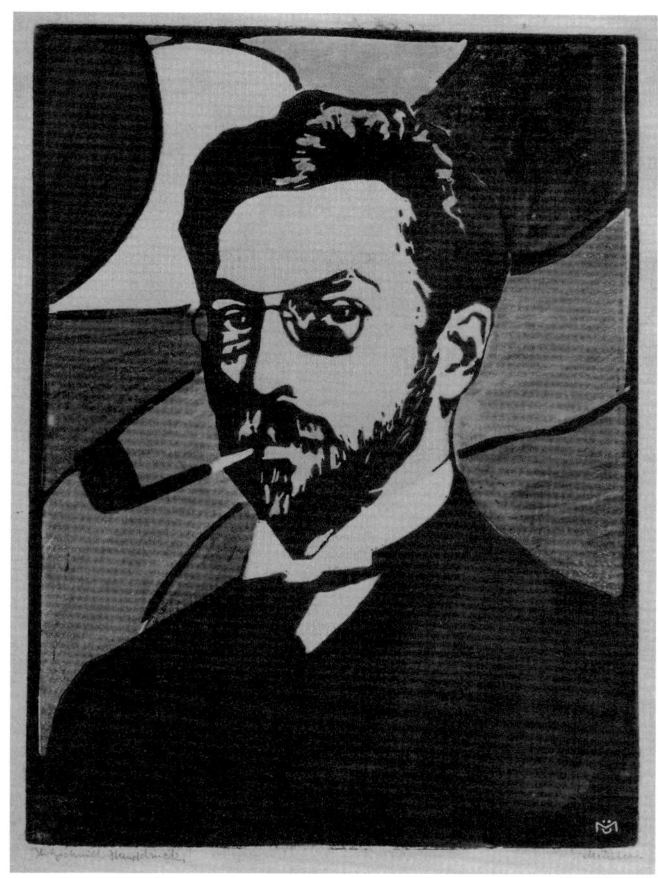

Kandinsky, 1906 (Cat. No. 3)

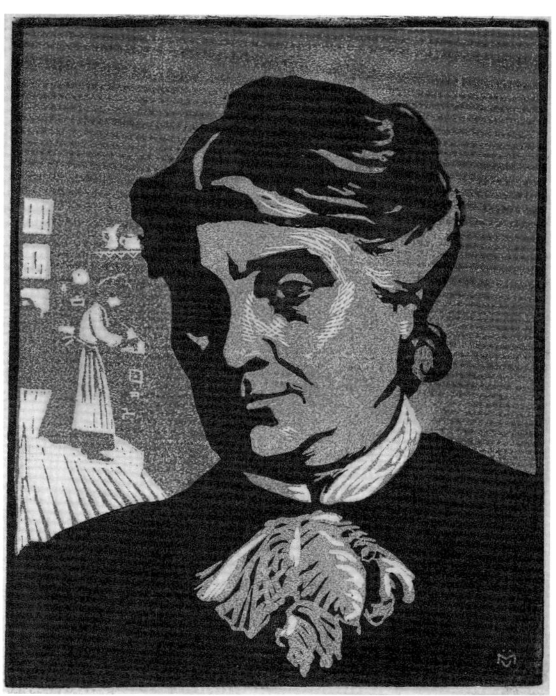

Mme Vernot with Aurelie, 1906 (Cat. No. 5)

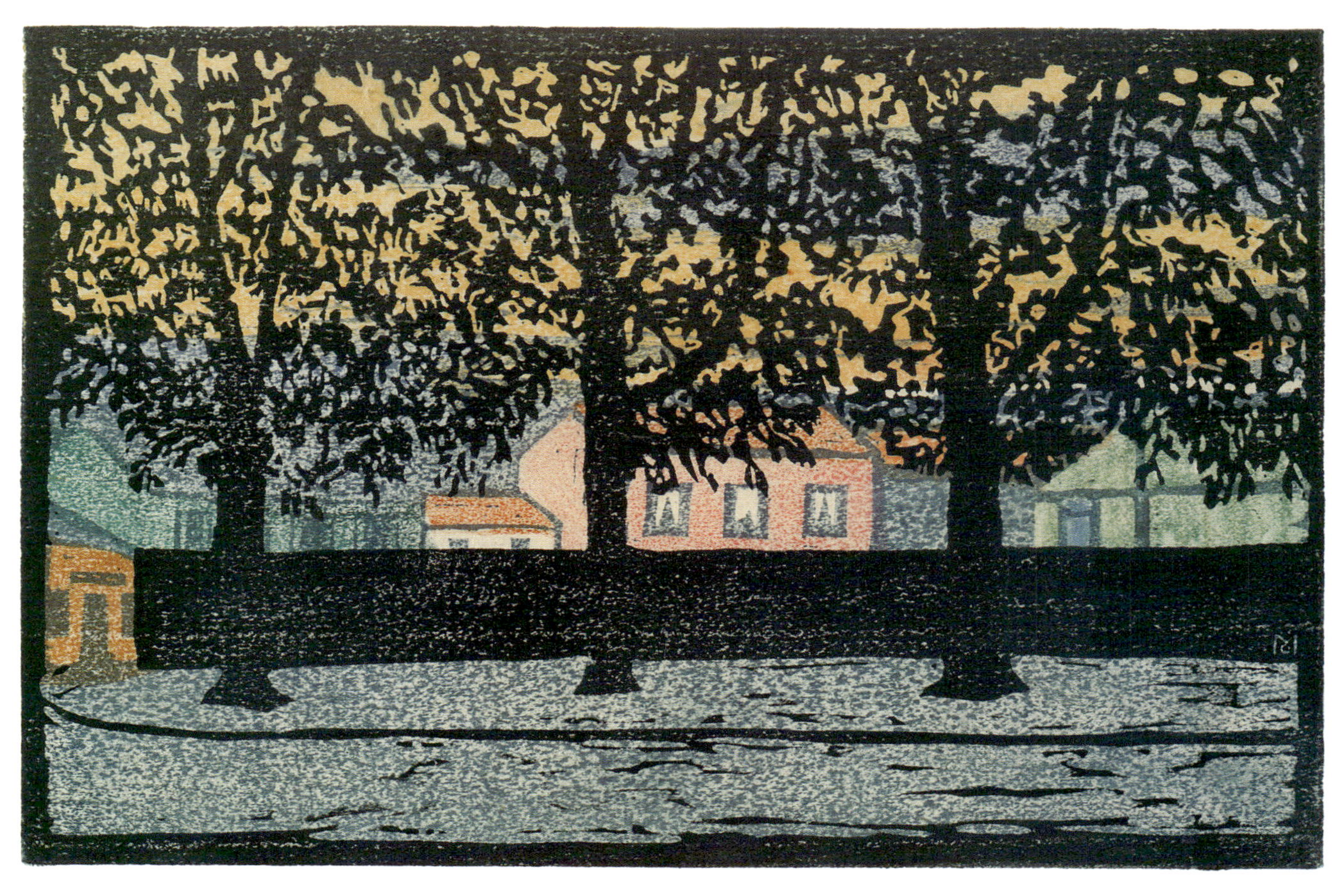

Fall Evening — Sèvres, 1907 (Cat. No. 8)

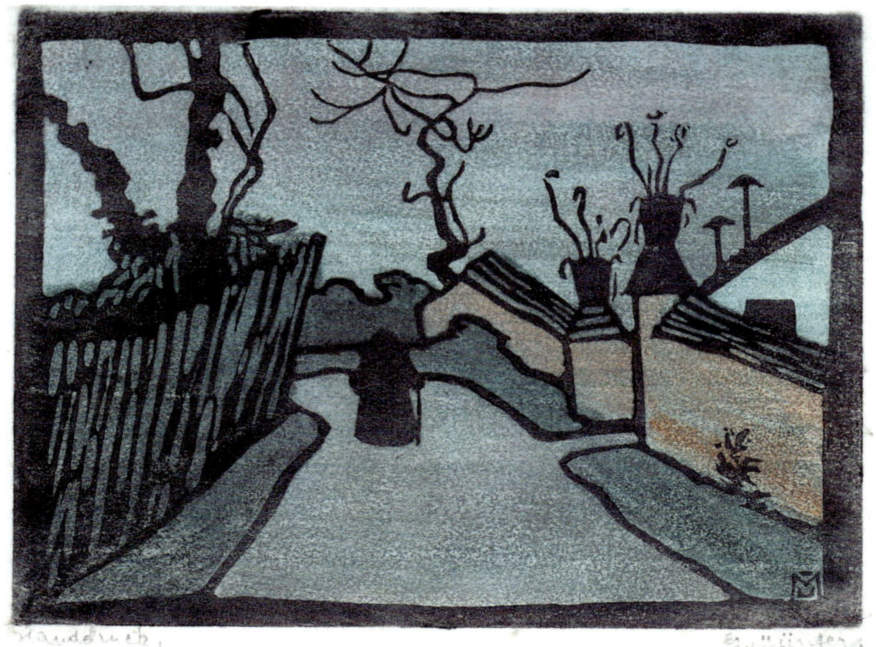

Path, 1907 (Cat. No. 9)

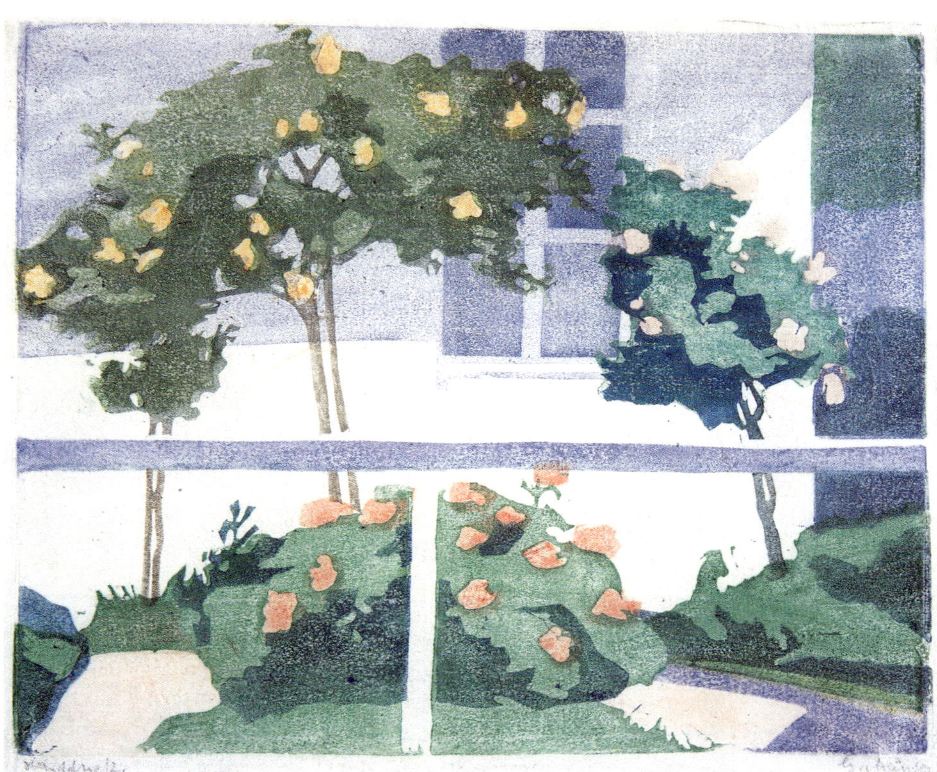

Rose Garden, ca. 1907/08 (Cat. No. 11)

common solution to a young woman's "aimlessness" in German middle-class society, seems not to have been contemplated, even though it was sought for Münter's elder sister Emmy. After considering alternatives available to her and discussing them with her family, Münter decided to study in Munich, widely considered to be Germany's preeminent art city, even if that designation was being challenged by Berlin.[22] What made Munich preferable over Berlin for Münter and other women artists, however, was the establishment of several studios specifically to train women artists there.

Encouraged by Margarete Susman, a fellow student three years earlier in Düsseldorf, Münter enrolled at the Ladies' Academy *(Damen-Akademie)* of the Association of Women Artists, one of only three such schools formally organized in Germany for women by women. Aimed especially at the *höhere Töchter*, the "elevated daughters" of the middle class—like Münter—who were seeking artistic training in increasing numbers as of the 1880s despite social disapproval, the Ladies' Academy modeled its curriculum and pedagogy on the men's academies. The teachers were men, often young artists who soon "graduated" to the faculties of the official academies, leaving a high degree of instability and fluidity among the Ladies' Academy staff. Nonetheless, after surveying the art pedagogical possibilities for women in the city, the Munich Ladies' Academy boasted with justification that Munich was the equal of Paris in "offering the most for women's studies in the area of fine art."[23] It fostered an attitude of support, seriousness of purpose and a community such as few private studios provided for their women students. Side by side with other women, here, Münter ceased to denigrate her own work as dilettantish, but rather identified it as clearly professional in intention

When Johannes Eichner described Münter as an artistic *tabula rasa* when she went to Munich at the age of twenty-four, "not burdened by the prejudices of tradition or by the passing taste of the times," he exaggerated in order to emphasize his construct of her as someone who worked totally from the "characteristics of her being," a natural-born artist, not one shaped by academic teachings or by emulation of others.[24] Indeed, the studies she had undertaken under academy professors in Düsseldorf and Bonn did little to mark her manner of drawing, but her earlier lyceum lessons and her high regard for *Jugendstil* illustrations fundamentally informed her manner of seeing and rendering the world she experienced as an essentially linear construct. Far from artistically naive, she had developed, largely autodidactically, a sure perception of art, especially of drawing and illustration, in clear accord with the progressive models of the time. She indulged her ability to draw quickly in this fashion with sketchbook renderings of the other women at the Ladies' Academy as they drew after the model, but the lessons being taught demanded a more three-dimensional rendering, accenting volume and mass, light and shade, as well as detail.[25]

The initial class, taught by Maximilian Dasio, concentrated on portrait drawing, in particular, on "character heads" of working-class women and peasants who posed for the students. The effort was fostered not only to produce portraits that displayed a recognizable likeness but to search for the "type" represented by the individual, to seek commonality beyond the accidentals of personal appearance. Significantly, for Münter, this lingering neo-idealist underpinning of German academic training remained in accordance with the universalizing principles that formed the basis of her lyceum drawing classes. Therefore, even though the manner of drawing countered her prior habits, the intent of the drawing classes continued to reinforce them. Her practice of searching for the characteristically defining essential, or representative features, of an object or person here found further support and justification.

Dasio also taught a class in landscape drawing during the summer, which Münter took, thereby submitting that interest developed during her American trip to more formal critique and practice. By 1900, *plein air* painting was included in the curricula of even the official academies in Germany. Munich painters in particular sought out nearby villages and towns, such as Fürstenfeldbruck where Dasio's class went to draw, often spending entire summers there. Since landscape and village scenes were among the most readily marketable motifs, especially in relatively small formats, Dasio's class served also to introduce its students to one of the most widespread subject matters and practices in contemporary art. These formal art lessons and their moderately conservative outlook apparently did not meet Münter's demands, however. As soon as the landscape class ended, she stopped on her way home to Bonn for several days at the Mathildenhöhe in Darmstadt to investigate the newly founded artists' colony there. Under the patronage of Grand Duke Ernst Ludwig of Hesse, with the opening of the Mathildenhöhe artists' exhibition hall and studios as well as their exhibitions in Munich, Berlin and Dresden in 1901, which gave them considerable publicity, the Mathildenhöhe artists set out to reform German art according to *Jugendstil* principles, to create a "...healthy German art standing in the midst of life, supported by the people."[26] Her interest in the controversial innovations of the architects and designers of this colony indicates Münter's continued concerns with contemporary, progressive directions in art. It seems probable that the search for a more innovative training may have inspired her three-day visit in Darmstadt as much as curiosity about the "Document of German Art," the colony's exhibition held there.

Perhaps because Darmstadt failed to offer any significant alternatives to what Munich offered, Münter returned to the Ladies' Academy for the 1901 winter semester. Dasio had been appointed to a professorship at the Royal School of Applied Arts. The portrait drawing class was now supervised by Angelo Jank, who published his illustrations in *Simplicissimus* and *Die Jugend*—whose 1901 cover of the 300th issue featured a Jank image of a robust Munich beer-hall waitress carrying seven large, overflowing steins of beer, a motif otherwise frequent in Munich's popular and souvenir art, here lightly stylized with an overlay of *Jugendstil* linearity. He was also allied with the artists' group "Scholle" (The Soil) that advocated a new monumentality while opposing both academic and *plein air* painting. Münter was quickly promoted to the life drawing class at Jank's recommendation, but despite this recognition of her ability and achievement within the strictures of the Ladies' Academy's curriculum, she was dissatisfied with her instructor and her progress. Early in 1902, Münter therefore began to participate in classes at the recently founded school of the Phalanx artists' society, although she continued to be registered at the Ladies' Academy until 1904.[27]

Phalanx was organized in May 1901 as an artists' exhibition society that wished to work outside the jury system of the Munich Artists' Association and of the Munich Secession, and to introduce progressive foreign artists to the city who otherwise had no forum there. Founding members were the sculptors Waldemar Hecker and Wilhelm Hüsgen, who also worked at the avant-garde political cabaret "The Eleven Executioners," the medical student Gustav Freytag, the painter and illustrator Rolf Niczky, briefly the small group's first presiding officer, and Vassily Kandinsky, the driving force behind the organization, who became its chairman in the early autumn of that year.[28] Shortly after Kandinsky formally assumed the role of Phalanx's leader, in the late winter of 1901 or early in 1902, he joined with Hecker and Hüsgen to open a private art school with six studios in a three-story building at Hohenzollernstrasse 6. Kandinsky taught the drawing and painting classes, according to a schedule not unlike that of the academies: three hours of portrait drawing in the mornings, two hours of drawing after the nude model in the afternoons and in the evenings rapid sketching after the nude, in which the sitters posed for four twenty-minute periods; in addition, every eight days there was a still-life painting class. A major distinction from standard art school practice, however, was that both male and female students were integrated into the same classes and had the same curriculum. While at the Ladies' Academy the women students practiced life drawing under "protected circumstances" with semi-nude models—the women's pubic area was covered, men wore bathing suits—the Phalanx School models were nude and the classes were coeducational.[29] Greater freedom generally and a stylistically more progressive aesthetic characterized the Phalanx School in comparison with the official Academy as well as the Ladies' Academy. Variations on Impressionism and Neo-Impressionism were the favored modes of painting, students were encouraged to take part in other classes in addition to those in which they were enrolled and class sizes remained small—photographs of the sculpture class in 1902 show three students, of Kandinsky's evening nude drawing class, five students, while over 260 registered for crowded classes at the Ladies'

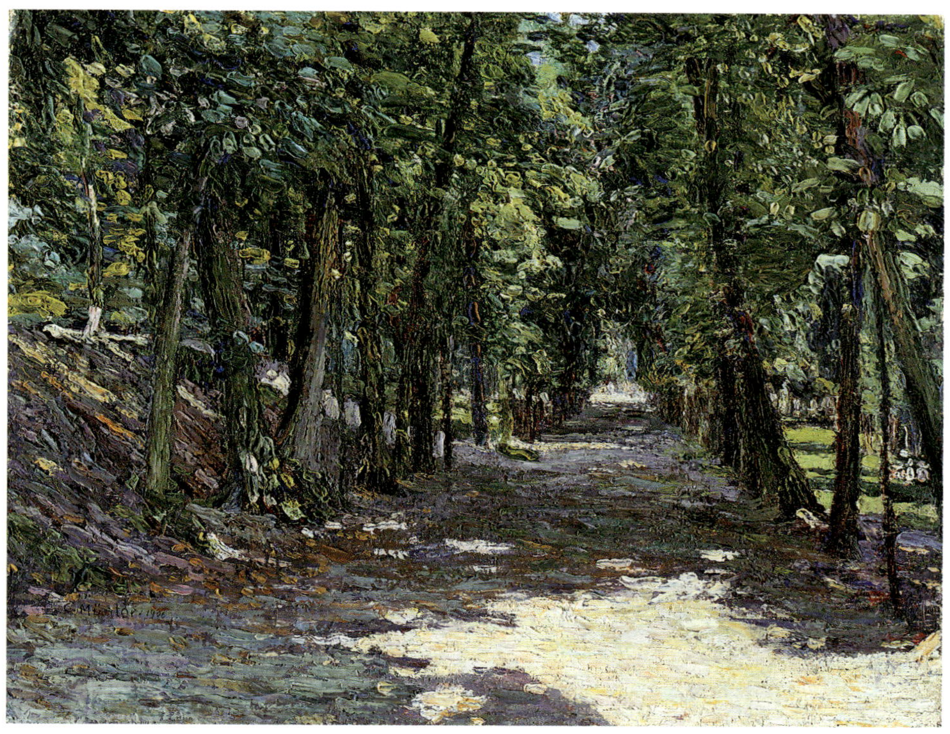

Path in the Park of St. Cloud, 1906
Oil on canvas, 15 7/8 x 19 3/4 in. (40.5 x 50.5 cm),
Munich, Städtische Galerie im Lenbachhaus (GMS 651)

Academy. Hence, individual interaction between the instructors and their students was greatly facilitated.

Asked about the Phalanx Society in 1950, Münter concisely summarized its history and activities:

> *Phalanx* was an association, founded by K. and other young artists in 1900 or 1901 in Munich, that had the purpose of providing these artists with exhibition opportunities since the Munich Secession shut out all the young, and in order to bring modern (i. e. at that time, predominantly Impressionist) foreign artists to Munich.... Generally, however, the exhibitions were not well attended and a deficit constantly had to be covered by K., the president [of Phalanx], and by the secretary and treasurer, a young medical student, Dr. Gustav Freytag, the son of the famous writer. The other members had no money. An art school was opened right away as well on a much too ambitious scale in which the members of the association would serve as teachers. But the classrooms remained empty, and after reducing the size of the school in 1902, only Wilhelm Hüsgen's sculpture class (which I entered and which was not run well) and the classes in which K. served as an outstanding teacher remained: portraits and still life, drawing and painting class and evening nude. Even then, all that one spoke of was the "Kandinsky-School," and not the Phalanx. The students were mostly foreigners and, the majority, women. In 1902, I went to study landscape in Kochel with

> this school... and in 1902 to Kallmünz in Upper Franconia. Both times the number of participants did not exceed ten. When, in 1904, K. began traveling with me for several years Phalanx was definitively ended.[30]

The exact date of the Phalanx School's opening remains unknown, but must have been no later than January 1902, at which time Gabriele Münter learned of it when she attended the second of the Phalanx-sponsored exhibitions, which featured the Darmstadt artists whose work she had sought the previous summer.[31] What attracted her to the school was not Kandinsky, however, but the possibility of studying sculpture, which had been her interest since she returned from America. She signed up, therefore, for the class held by Wilhelm Hüsgen, whose portrait masks of participants in the Eleven Executioners cabaret she admired at the Phalanx exhibition. Under Hüsgen's direction she completed several sculptures of nudes, naturalistic in appearance and conception—one photographed by her next to the model as if to demonstrate its imitative veracity—none of which survive today.

More significant for her future, as her recollections confirm, was the life drawing class taught by Kandinsky, which was the obligatory adjunct to the sculpture course in the curriculum. Unlike her previous teachers, Kandinsky critiqued carefully, spent time with his students to discover their strengths and encourage them, and—most unusually—took seriously the artistic ambitions of the women students.[32] "He valued my talent highly, and it upset him that the others did not understand it as he did," she later claimed.[33] When Kandinsky set up a still life for his painting class, she took the opportunity to make her first oil painting, which he praised as "fresh and colorful." Where the Ladies' Academy would still have required further drawing study before permitting her to turn to painting, at the Phalanx School she now began to learn the rudiments of painting technique directly under Kandinsky's supervision. Her transformation from dilettante to professional artist accelerated dramatically as her loyalty to sculpture faded, to be replaced by an interest in painting.

The next steps in Münter's training took place during the summer landscape painting course Kandinsky taught in the Bavarian town of Kochel, dramatically located near Lake Kochel in the foothills of the Alps. Kandinsky had painted there two years earlier, and now added his class to the many other *plein air* landscape courses being taught to serious students and dilettantes alike in the Bavarian countryside that summer. Each student worked individually, painting and sketching in different locations, with Kandinsky moving among them to offer his critique. "Once," Münter later recalled, "I was painting at the lake and K. came for the critique. He looked at my paint box and found bad colors there, e.g. Schweinfurt green and others. He threw them all onto the grass, as forbidden. And I used only good colors that he permitted after that. On walks he talked of colors and color mixtures."[34] It was into the use and application of color that Kandinsky further initiated her, building on the introduction provided by the previous still-life painting exercises. He limited the premixed colors to be used, preferring to blend a few colors and to apply them in Impressionist-derived, distinctive touches of the brush or—as he was beginning to do in his own work—with the palette knife, and sometimes simply squeezing the paint directly from the tube onto the canvas.

Münter, still timid, painted little. She did, however, fill sketchbook pages with landscape drawings, sketching with assurance, either rendering atmospheric effects of dusk, for example, with carefully modulated shading, or transforming even the clouds into sharply linear motifs. The spectacular alpine vistas from mountainsides onto lakes and across valleys, the views of clouds in majestic sunsets and of fir trees grouped and silhouetted against the clear sky attracted her interest as no other landscape had since she experienced the antithetical flatness of the Texas prairies. The persistent drawing exercises in the Ladies' Academy and the Phalanx School instilled in her a new refinement of technique, a diversity of touch and line not present in her earlier work as she drew with charcoal pencils. Greater sophistication emerged in her compositions, where multiple elements were balanced against each other rather than maintaining the focus on a single figure or central object as had been her wont previously. Kandinsky may have inspired this in her, as she also took up the practice of making small thumbnail sketches of motifs, an inch square or smaller, drawn with surrounding dark frames like miniature paintings, to render the main forms of a landscape scene so as to enable her to recall them from memory for development in later paintings. The repetition of small compositional sketches, therefore, was designed to further ensure her ability to render the images rapidly and confidently from memory. Kandinsky offered her a synthetic approach to painting in this way at Kochel, encouraging small oil sketches to be painted in the open air, but also promoting pencil sketches, sometimes with color notations, to enable the later creation from memory of larger images away from the immediate impression of the motif. Techniques of naturalism and Impressionism combined with devices to counter their dependence on the model and to approach an art more independent of nature.

Münter's progress as a painter was interrupted, however, as Kandinsky pressed her for a romantic relationship and she acquiesced. When Kandinsky's wife, Anja, arrived in Kochel and he requested that Münter leave, she complied. Returned to Bonn, she continued to practice what she had learned in Kochel as she sketched studies in oil, using the palette knife as Kandinsky had taught her rather than a brush, on small pieces of canvas tacked to the lid of her paint box during a bicycle tour along the Rhine River. She wrote to him that she was continuing to paint and to find numerous motifs; in response, he sent a postcard from Kochel with a view of Moscow, included greetings from his wife and teased her—in Bavarian dialect to mark the levity of tone—about her frequent lack of ambition: "I'm very glad that you are having so much success and fun in using the palette knife, it's very ... satisfying to me. I've always thought, after all, that our lazy M. would do something good sometime. She just has to have some patience."[35] But Münter's desire for more instruction and criticism through his letters—certainly a difficult task—he did not fulfill.

When Münter returned to Munich in October, Kandinsky immediately sought her out again, leaving her extremely agitated emotionally as she tried to come to terms with her conflicting feelings: her sense of shame at being intimately involved with a married man, her desire that he file for a divorce and marry her and her admiration for Kandinsky as an artist and a teacher. The two met secretly, exchanged notes, and she enrolled in Angelo Jank's drawing class at the Ladies' Academy rather than return to the Phalanx School with the difficulties that encounters with Kandinsky in class would entail. The decision was one she regretted immediately, as she wrote in a diary-like note on an envelope originally intended to hold a letter to Kandinsky:

> Why in the world didn't I go to Kandinsky for drawing instead of to Jank? When I finally enrolled formally for three months today, I immediately regretted it. I've already had a year with Jank, after all; it would surely be better to change sometime—I simply don't seem to be making any progress—it's as if all the others were passing me by.[36]

She continued to see Kandinsky, and their relationship intensified, but she also brought her drawings to be critiqued by him. By November, however, he was getting impatient with the arrangement, and in response to her suggestion that either he leave his wife or they be "friends—but certainly completely differently than we started out now," he argued:

> It is not the kissing alone that I need. "That is not part of it," you said about our friendship. And that is indeed true: I do not kiss my other friends. But it is not my fault if my feelings for you are more than friendship. And it will always be this way. I can control my behavior, of course, if you absolutely insist.

But then he added a condition, recognizing the strength of his position as teacher and critic in her eyes, as well as her dissatisfaction with Jank:

> There is one more thing I want to say. Do not be angry with me if I stop saying anything about the drawings you make for Jank. He has his viewpoint, I have a different one. You don't know about these things, and misunderstandings are the only result. In the end you will not really believe either one of us anymore, something I do not want to happen.

In your other work I will gladly help as much as I can. So, until Tuesday—a long time! Have faith in me, please. Won't you?[37]

The maneuver worked. Münter's dissatisfaction with Jank increased. In December she enrolled in Kandinsky's Phalanx class for the winter semester. Their "engagement" occurred half a year later as she participated in his summer landscape painting class in Kallmünz.

Located in northeastern Bavaria at the edge of the Bavarian Forest, where the Naab and Vils rivers converge, and reachable by river steamer from nearby Regensburg, Kallmünz is a medieval market town, much of whose ancient walls and ruined castle are still preserved. From the heights of a limestone cliff on which the latter was built, a vast vista opens onto the surrounding valleys, while the town itself offers numerous picturesque views with its old houses and narrow streets, bridges spanning them to link houses on opposite sides of the road, juxtaposed stuccoed facades, intersecting and overlapping in abstract studies of planes and volumes. The medieval setting particularly appealed to Kandinsky, as it fed the visions of a bygone utopia whose knights and ladies he so frequently depicted in his pictures of the streets of Kallmünz the following year. Münter enthusiastically sketched, photographed and painted the streets and houses she saw. Her works, however, were largely unpopulated, studies in masses and surfaces rather than the atmospheric and light effects common to *plein air* painting.

Sketchbook drawings and photographs accompany the small painting *Kallmünz* (Cat. No. 1), the same motif rendered in triplicate in the varied media she employed, but without a particular sequence that moves from photograph and sketch to painting. If they preceded the painting—and they need not have—the penciled and photographed images served to fix the image in her memory and to facilitate the return to painting. In fact, with its paint applied by varied strokes of the palette knife in emulation of Kandinsky's method, painted on a small, readily portable, canvas-covered artist's board, *Kallmünz* has the appearance of being executed quickly, on the site and in the open air, not painstakingly rendered from exact preparatory studies. Repetition was a means towards achieving a quality of spontaneity; it disguised the effort and thought of painting to offer an illusion of uninterpreted immediacy. "You have probably understood that I had always been mainly a *plein air* painter, ..." she remarked in her interview with Edouard Roditi in 1958.

At first I experienced great difficulty with my brushwork—I mean with what the French call *la touche de pinceau*. So Kandinsky taught me how to achieve the effects that I wanted with a palette knife.... My main difficulty was that I could not paint fast enough. My pictures are all moments of life—I mean instantaneous visual experiences, generally noted very rapidly and spontaneously. When I begin to paint, it's like leaping suddenly into deep waters, and I never know beforehand whether I will be able to swim. Well, it was Kandinsky who taught me the technique of swimming. I mean that he taught me to work fast enough, and with enough self-assurance, to be able to achieve this kind of rapid and spontaneous recording of moments of life.[38]

Münter's comments echo those in the monograph entitled *Kandinsky und Gabriele Münter*, published the year prior to Roditi's interview, by Johannes Eichner, who likewise contended that "... creativity in Gabriele Münter bursts forth from her naturalness. She is committed to no rules. Logic offers no directions. She submits to the demands of the motif and the stirrings within herself."[39] The emphasis on Münter as a sort of medium of nature, recording the dictations of nature without the interference of rationality follows a topos often applied to the art of women, and already posited by Kandinsky in 1913 as characteristic of Münter's art "... produced from a pure inner instinct."[40] In an often cited recollection, first published by Eichner, Münter quotes Kandinsky as saying: "You are hopeless as a student—it's impossible to teach you anything. You can do only what has germinated within you. Nature grants you everything. What I can do for you is protect your talent and nourish it so that nothing false disturbs it."[41] In all such evaluations, Münter is presented—or, late in her life, presents herself—as an artist who possesses a mysterious inherent talent, one granted by nature, which defies and indeed is destroyed by rigorous discipline or a thoughtful, determined approach. Münter's art is presented as something generated from within, growing and emerging much as a child might in and from a woman's womb, without conscious intervention on her part; it is accordingly a product of nature rather than of learning.

Several different perceptions of art, artists and women shaped these analogous conclusions.[42] For Münter in the 1950s, when she positively rather than—as earlier—negatively interpreted Kandinsky's remark, the suggestion that she painted without effort according to the dictates of an inner drive guaranteed the sincerity of her work—in part, as a lingering desire to counter Nazi arguments of modernism's degeneracy, in part, to link herself to the abstract art of the 1950s that emphasized the artist's unconscious as the source of art—thereby granting it definite contemporary relevance as well as historical significance. Eichner, in turn, by suggesting that she worked without a preconceived image and that the paintings corresponded to Münter's personal psychological makeup, vouched for their sincerity, but this also granted them an existence as a particular woman's work outside the constructs of male-dominated art movements, such as Expressionism or Cubism. It was a tactic he first employed defensively on her behalf during the 1930s to avoid her being linked to the modernism despised by the National Socialists, but when employed later it accentuated her isolation as a woman artist, not an integral part of the pioneering work of men, even as it confirmed the psychological determinism of Eichner's book. Kandinsky, whose further comments on Münter's work I shall discuss later, and who saw her as incapable of being taught because "nature" had given her abilities outside the realm of pedagogy, equally insisted on her status as a fundamentally passive instrument of artistic volition and of nature, a specifically female-associated characterization that denied her the sort of determination and vision attributed to male artists, such as Kandinsky, in their quest to shape the art of the future.

The notion of Münter as a simple, naive artist painting, as she herself insisted, "with the certainty of a sleepwalker..." ("I do not compose. I saw something that appealed to me, took notice and painted it"),[43] has dominated the reception of her work. It suits varied purposes, but has also worked against a proper historical evaluation of her contribution to German modernism. Unlike Kandinsky's similar small landscape studies, which are analyzed as evidence of his serious confrontation with the nature/art dichotomy, hers are described as "carefree improvisations" of "female creativity," allowing their historical significance to be dismissed or ignored.[44] Furthermore, this cliché contradicts the evidence of her working habits in which she consciously and deliberately impressed a motif into her memory, letting it become natural to her hand through repetition so as to allow the final painting to take on the appearance of spontaneity and immediacy. The painting *Kallmünz* thereby transmits not only the intensity of its execution as it accents the individual touches of Impressionist-like strokes, but also the artist's involvement with the scene, her assumed position within or before the motif depicted. By limiting her palette, moreover, to shades of brown and green, Münter adopted synthetically descriptive colors for the Kallmünz townscape. These are the tans of limestone cliffs and stuccoed houses that compete with the greens of grassy plains and trees as they might be recalled, without other local colors that distract from a coloristic characterization of the town and without the confusion of detail and multiplicity. Memory and its reductive filters are represented by her with the means of *plein air* painting's facture of rapidity and direct confrontation in a carefully manipulated personal amalgam modeled on Kandinsky's techniques.

Münter took up the motif of the Kallmünz street and its intriguing juxtaposition of gate and overlapping house facades again during the winter of that year in her newly rented studio in Munich, not as a painting but as a woodcut, one of her first attempts in this print medium.[45] Again, she followed the example of Kandinsky, who had worked intensely on woodcuts during the time in Kallmünz, but she did not adopt the imaginary rococo and medieval scenes he favored, and instead chose motifs that "told no stories," as was her consistent practice. Nor was Kandinsky her sole inspiration. Since the 1890s, woodcuts were a favorite medium for *Jugendstil* artists and others, especially in Munich, seeking a way to reform German art and to move away from the perceived dead end of naturalism. When

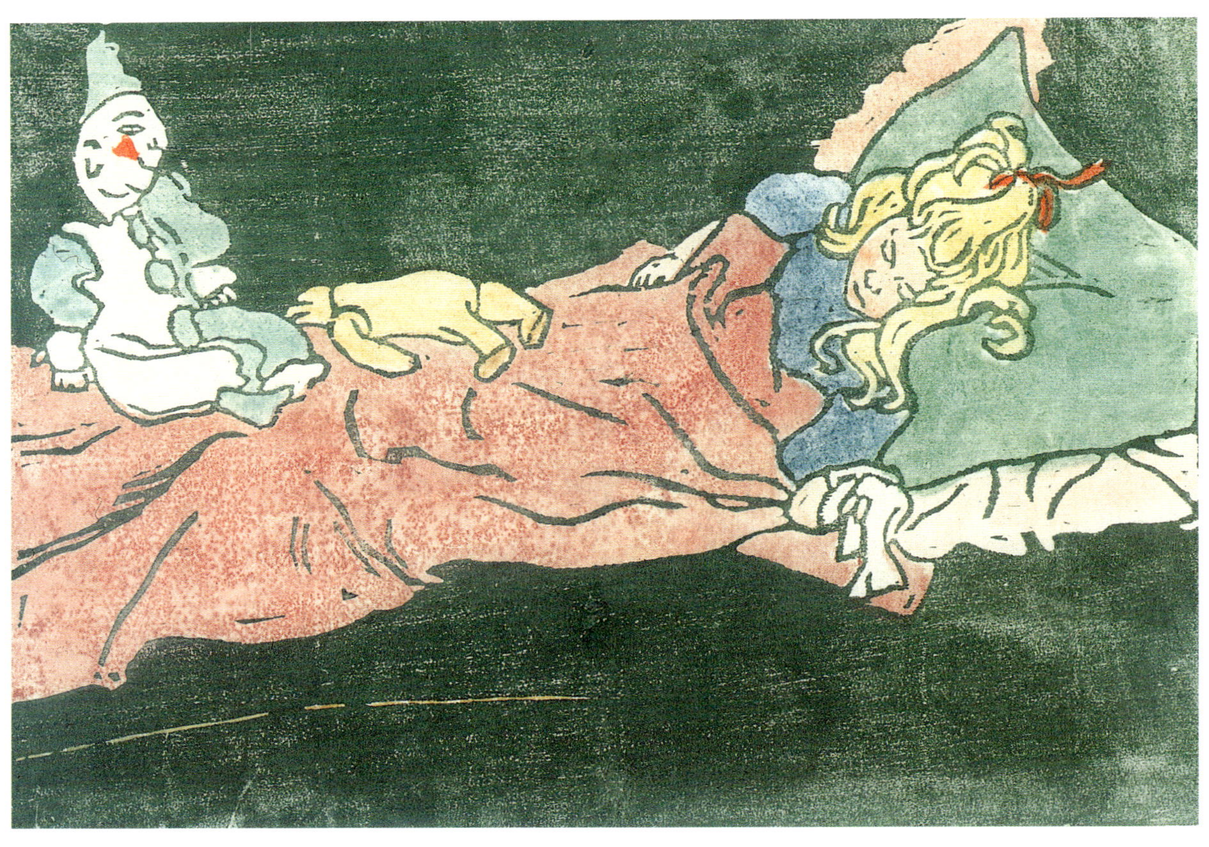

Sleeping Child, ca. 1907/08 (Cat. No. 13)

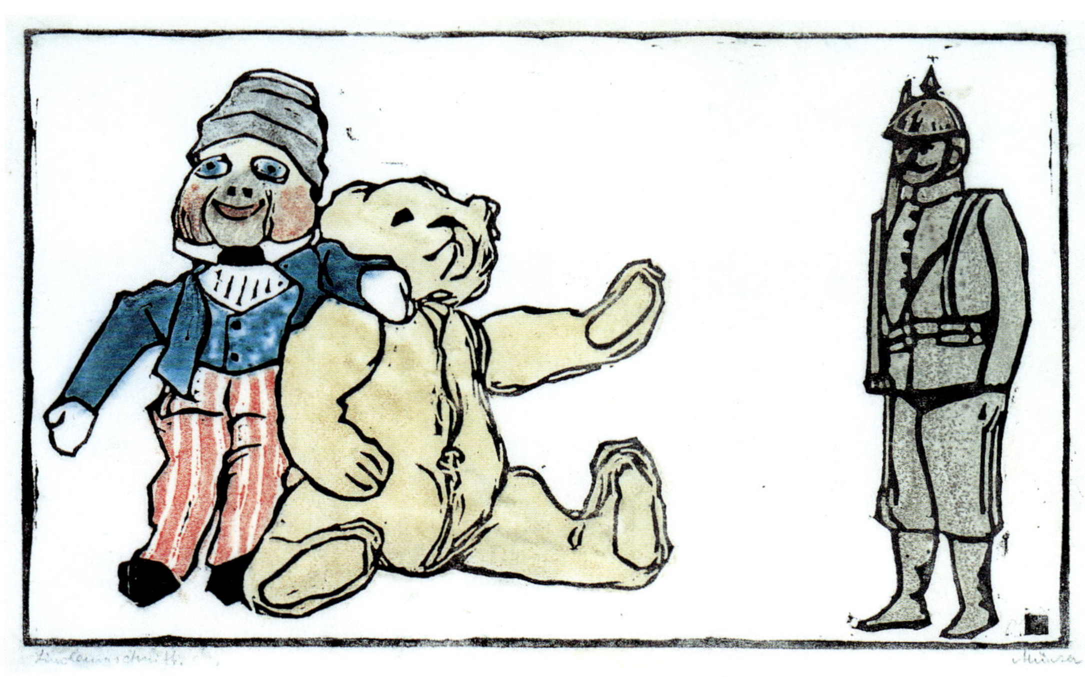

Uncle Sam and Company (Toys, No. 2), 1908 (Cat. No. 14)

Münter and Kandinsky in 1903, therefore, began experimenting with the woodcut, they added their voices to an already sizable chorus of progressive artists in a plea for artistic and cultural reform.[46] Kandinsky encouraged Münter as he wrote from Vienna to cajole her and urge her on to new experiments: "Say, what do you think of the woodcut? Does it interest you? Won't you try it? It is truly something remarkable. Yes, indeed! But a significant effort is necessary, much too much for the small, poor (lazy) Ella."[47]

This time, a photograph served to initiate the view of the gate and houses; she traced its lines onto tissue paper, then transferred the reversed image onto a woodblock, from which it would then print the image the right way around. She complained, however, about the labor of printing and the difficulty she had with the inks as Kandinsky failed to instruct her on their proper mixture and use:

> [I] spent all afternoon grinding and mixing and printing colors until it became too dark, and in all that time finished only three prints. Two hours...[48]
>
> This morning [I] was still carving woodblocks and this afternoon until it got dark made three moon[light] prints and let the stove go out in my enthusiasm.... Yesterday and today I did not touch a single key of the piano since it is covered with wet prints. And when I stopped today, I thought, I don't want to make woodcuts anymore, why should I torture myself with the discovery of things and lose time in the process if others already discovered them a long time ago. Slowly I'm starting to figure out how one has to handle the colors so that they are absorbed evenly and thinly by the paper and do not lie on top of it in clumps as has always been the case with me so far. Why did you not tell me any of this?[49]

The multicolored print that resulted, each color printed separately, with its moodily suggestive, muted coloration, adheres to *Jugendstil* style as it flattens forms and offers a gently balanced composition within a clearly enunciated frame. Seen in conjunction with its nearly square format, these qualities bring it particularly close in appearance to contemporary prints from the Vienna Workshops (*Wiener Werkstätten*), as Münter modeled her print technique on some of the most successful and innovative contemporary work available to her, distancing herself in the process significantly from Kandinsky's example.

"From preliminary studies and the manner of the then current naturalism, I soon arrived at the liberating brushstrokes of Impressionism and at woodcuts that represent an initially technically determined attempt to achieve a simplified presentation of form and a flat extension of color," she observed in a short autobiographical statement in 1948.[50] The woodcut and its stylized vocabulary enabled her to distance her imagery from a naturalistic prototype, to enhance its autonomy and its function as a mood-inducing image of memory. Kandinsky persistently encouraged her to paint "from the head" because "memory and inner sight must be practiced intensely,"[51] and she obeyed this aspect of his teachings willingly, with enthusiasm. When the two went together to Holland in 1904, she made drawings of Dutch costumes, but also several small painted nocturnal studies of Dutch canals (Cat. No. 2). The trees silhouetted against an evening sky, their dark forms duplicated in reflections in the waters of the canal, their colors applied in broad, unmodulated patterns of dark blue-greens that are set off against sky and water in pale violet, pink and yellow, once again appear as a pronounced *Jugendstil* statement of decorative flatness and broodingly lyrical mood, silent, deserted and still.[52]

To achieve these effects, Münter forgoes the palette knife and the late Impressionist paint application of her prior work, and instead applies a smooth, brushed surface significantly unlike Kandinsky's Dutch landscape paintings in which a bravura palette knife technique is employed, laying on viscous pats of paint to render color effects, leaving large stretches of canvas bare in the manner of late Neo-Impressionist painting.[53] If she appears to be turning her back on such virtuoso demonstrations of color and technique, she simultaneously recalls the qualities of Kandinsky's woodcuts of 1904, such as *Moonrise*.[54] However, the similarity here is indicative of the artists' close relationship, more than it is a demonstration of true influence, since both Münter's painting and Kandinsky's woodcut date from July or August of 1904, after their trip to Holland, when the two were apart, she in Bonn and he in Munich. By this time, instead of one being dependent on and subordinate to the other, they shared concerns for and solutions to different media, continuing to work as if side by side even when separated.

Münter, however, put herself in the position of apprentice to Kandinsky even as she gained the powers to work independently. She copied, indeed traced and then painted, at least one of his landscape studies,[55] and she carefully examined the woodcuts he gave her, trying to construe the principles according to which they were produced, asking Kandinsky about them in letter after letter. In order to work together even when apart, the two also collaborated on a number of pearl stitchings, appliqué wall hangings and dress designs. Though most of the designs were his, Münter carried out the stitching and sewing, and wore the reform dresses, carried the purses and hung the wall hangings in her room. It was a collaboration, but one in which she was subservient as she applied herself in traditionally womanly crafts—sewing and stitching—to the original inventions of the man. "My dearest, my golden one," she wrote to him in July, "your letter is so very wonderful. As I said, with time I have been able to obtain better effects by myself in my painting efforts. But I thank you for your advice. I am sad that you are in such a bad mood. Don't be like that, please! And make something of your Dutch impressions! I look forward to the time when we will be together and can work together—then I'll even help you with your prints. If I could find time for it, I would like to stitch a pearl purse from a design by you—dark colors on white, maybe.... Would you design something?"[56] She flatters and cajoles, indicates her independent progress, but immediately modifies it with thanks for his help and with plans to work together in which she aids him, her own work left unstated by then, a careful adjustment to Kandinsky's attitudes in which she offered help but also sought his continued primacy in their artistic as well as personal relationship.

It was with such ambivalence as to their being and working together that Münter and Kandinsky set off on their extended trips to Tunisia and Italy in 1904, ultimately, to reside outside Paris in Sèvres until June 1907. Münter, perhaps inevitably, continued to closely emulate Kandinsky's work, painted the same landscape motifs and reverted to his modified Neo-Impressionist painting manner. Both underwent changes in their technique during these years, and it is difficult to determine who was the first to try to bring about a particular effect, but it is Münter's work that demonstrates a clear developmental process as her painted landscape studies become more fluid and less rigidly composed. She became so adept in their shared approach, in fact, that her paintings of the park in St. Cloud from 1906–07 are nearly indistinguishable from his (see illus., p. 53)—perhaps slightly less bold in their paint application with both brush and palette knife, but employing the same color harmonies of violet, yellow and green—although he liked to mix in individual touches of intense red and orange as well. Fundamentally, their paintings of Sèvres and St. Cloud speak the same language, with his intonation only slightly louder and brash, with a more overt display of virtuosity.

For Münter's later development, this time spent with Kandinsky and their shared experience of foreign lands most significantly impacted her sense of color. Even if based on or accompanied by sketchbook drawings, the paintings strove increasingly to devalue and eliminate line in their representation to become, like Kandinsky's, studies in color itself, in the visual and material interactions of varied but limited hues. "One cannot paint what one cannot draw," she remarked to him, however, in affirmation of the primacy of drawing for her.[57] She restricted her palette even more than Kandinsky did, to make use of only Prussian blue, ultramarine, pale ocher, terra-di-Siena brown, crimson-lake red, cadmium red, cadmium orange, cadmium yellow, chromoxide green, burnt umber, ivory black and zinc white, and she developed a numerical code whereby she could insert color codes into her sketches.[58] A significantly refined and sophisticated sense of the material and emotive qualities of color was the remuneration she received for her four-year submission to Kandinsky's teaching and example in painting.

Far from satisfied with being a simple Kandinsky epigone, Münter established her own imagery in wood- and linocuts during their stay in Sèvres, where she took up printmaking again three years after completing her Kallmünz woodcuts. To revive her discipline in drawing as well as to gain distance, both physical and professional, from Kandinsky, she left him in Sèvres and rented a room for herself in Paris in November 1906. At the same time she signed up for classes taught by Théophile Steinlen, a frequent contributor to German *Jugendstil* periodicals, at the Académie Grande Chaumière. Steinlen praised her drawing inordinately, she later recalled,[59] and she began work on a series of linocut portraits—the owners of the Paris and Sèvres pensions where she lived, other guests and servants there, and Kandinsky (Cat. Nos. 3–5)—that were also her first major independent efforts in portraiture, far removed from the "character head" assignments during her studies previously. Conceived in simple, broad, black-and-white planar configurations with only sufficient detail to render an identifiable likeness, they reflect the methods of Felix Vallotton and William Nicholson, which were also employed by numerous other *Jugendstil* and *art nouveau* artists internationally.[60] In effect, it brought her technique into the context of the most widespread progressive contemporary printmaking practices.

Not satisfied with solely black-and-white impressions, Münter also injected color into her wood- and linocut images in emulation of Kandinsky's practice but also necessarily in competition with it, suggesting a different content than the fantasies he invented and which she continually criticized, positing her work as interpretive of the world she inhabited. She set her portrait of Kandinsky against a patterned background of muted green, yellow, blue and red (Cat. No. 3); M. Vernot is softly rendered in a Parisian street scene (Cat. No. 4), and his wife is seen with the servant Aurelie working in the background (Cat. No. 5). In intricate patterns of black, she provides a frieze of trees in *Fall Evening—Sèvres* (Cat. No. 8), the silhouettes of an evening landscape, with washes of orange and violet to suggest autumnal foliage and dusk, as houses glow in white-yellow beneath. Though this print retains traces of emotive symbolist and *Jugendstil* landscape imagery, more drastically simplified and aiming at a radical stylistic vocabulary is *Path* (Cat. No. 9), in which broad black outlines define forms and all shapes are severely reduced to stylized, suggestive constructs, and colors—playfully varied from one print impression to the other, suggesting different times of day and various emotive projections—appear as large unmodulated, uninterrupted planes. While relatively small in scale, the print anticipates the transformations Münter's painting would soon undergo, once she and Kandinsky had returned to Germany, finally to settle in Munich, albeit in separate residences.

With her prints, over twenty of them completed during the few months she worked on them in Paris and absolutely distinct from Kandinsky's work, Münter entered the realm of professional artists as she exhibited them in Paris at the Salon des Indépendants, once again encouraged by Kandinsky. "Thus Gabriele Münter's student years had slid away..." Eichner wrote. "After years of indecision, her call to the profession of artist was now firmly established."[61] His emphasis on a passive Münter being impressed with artistic training without active effort is fundamentally misleading, but the conclusion about the termination of her artistic apprenticeship is correct. During the following year, she entered into a renewed collaboration with Kandinsky that became one of the premier chapters of the history of German Expressionism.

Modernity, Munich and Murnau

Chapter 2

Gabriele Münter returned to Germany from her travels just in time to be counted in the occupational census of 12 June 1907. If she qualified as a "working artist," she was among the 801 painters and sculptors of "female sex" registered then, with the greatest number, 202, in Munich, where some 1,447 artists resided.[1] Though the work Münter brought back with her distinguished her from the great majority of these artists, whether women or men, she readily fit into the small subgroup of artists active in progressively transforming late Impressionist, Neo-Impressionist and *Jugendstil* painting into the more radical, non-naturalist art we today identify as Expressionism.[2]

In 1907, Münter's art divided into two seemingly diverse categories: the paintings she completed in Paris that represent a modified, coloristically enriched Impressionism and her prints, which employ a radical *Jugendstil* simplicity and a suggestive Symbolist mood with softly muted colors, collapsed pictorial space and flattened forms often outlined in black. She seems to have painted little, if at all, immediately after her return from Paris, as she first visited her family in Bonn, and then moved to Berlin with Kandinsky. She used this time, however, to work on additional color linocuts that took up motifs from her travels, derived from earlier sketchbook drawings, or from the domestic milieux of her brother's family in Bonn and her sister's in Berlin.

What interested her most was the world of her young niece Elfriede, nicknamed Friedel. A color woodcut (Cat. No. 12)— kept simple but emulating a pencil study with short, broken lines defining the scene of the little girl, contented and plump as she reclines with her head on a cushion, sucking happily on a bottle—recalls the image of a sketchbook drawing dated 25 September 1904, a few months after Friedel's baptism. Allied to this recollection, whose sketchy manner suggests the imprecision of memory, is another woodcut that employs a network of more gently curving lines for its rendition of the four-year-old Friedel sleeping (Cat. No. 13). *Jugendstil* children's books as well as those by the English illustrator Kate Greenaway, Carl Larsson's highly successful series of watercolors entitled, "A Home," popular in Germany since 1898, with frequent representations of the artist's daughters, but also Münter's own numerous drawings of her American cousins served as conceptual prototypes for the print. Friedel is shown at a slight diagonal while she rests on her bed, her shock of blond curls framing her face. The peacefulness of Friedel's childhood sleep and dreams is metaphorically represented in the way she seems to float weightlessly on wave-like fields of color, different in each impression of the print. At her feet sits a smiling clown doll and a teddy bear resting facedown, as if carelessly dropped by its sleepy playmate.

Münter's exploration of the world of children continued in a series of five linocuts devoted to toys (Cat. No. 14). As in the woodcut *Sleeping Child*, no overt anecdote characterizes these images, no story is told. But the juxtaposition of dolls and other playthings offers scenes alluding to meaning, a common practice in Symbolist and Neo-Romantic art, here present in a seemingly mundane collection of toys. Across the divide of a large empty space, an Uncle Sam doll and a teddy bear, joined together in an expressive grouping of friendly companionship, confront a toy soldier, sharply erect with arms at his sides and topped by the prickly points of his bayonet and helmet, to draw a visualized antithesis between two gendered worlds of play.[3] Dolls and teddy bears become anthropomorphized; they acquire a semblance of life and personality. Simultaneously, however, they also are representative still lifes in which inanimate objects project the personality and presence of their owner, acting as Friedel's substitute, suggesting an idyllic childhood world focused on playthings, whimsy, imagination and harmonious companionship. The world of the child, a constant source of fascination for Münter and first apparent in her American drawings, is presented as a repeated motif, capable of innumerable variations.

If the prints with scenes of children and toys marked the first mature exploration of these themes by Münter, the more radical stylistic vocabulary she explored in Bonn and Berlin through her wood- and linocuts reached its most incisive presentation in the print *Washing at the Shore* (Cat. No. 10). Based on a sketchbook drawing from Rapallo dated 27 December 1905, the print depicts laundry as it dries on a mast's spar extending from a fishing boat. The motif is simple, a picturesque reminiscence of Mediterranean warmth and Italian mores, but is translated into a sequence of highly abstracted shapes. The multicolored pieces of laundry and their corresponding blue shadows, the blue bows of the boats and the broad blue band of the sea interact with the shapes of sand and sky articulated in orange-yellow. The single figure of a small girl gazing at a distant sailboat adds a final playful note, but is also a referential anchor in visual reality that prevents laundry, boats, beach and sky from becoming fully abstracted inventions.

In her sureness and precision of drawing, in her capacity to drastically simplify forms into hieroglyphs of representation without diminishing their ability to act referentially, in her insistence on a vision of the contemporary environment and in her rejection of emblematically symbolic content, Münter's prints continued to contrast almost diametrically to Kandinsky's contemporary ones. Only in their use of similar soft color harmonies do the two artists betray the bonds of their companionship and mutual interaction. Despite Kandinsky's continuing criticism of her work, Münter maintained a remarkable independence in her drawings and prints.

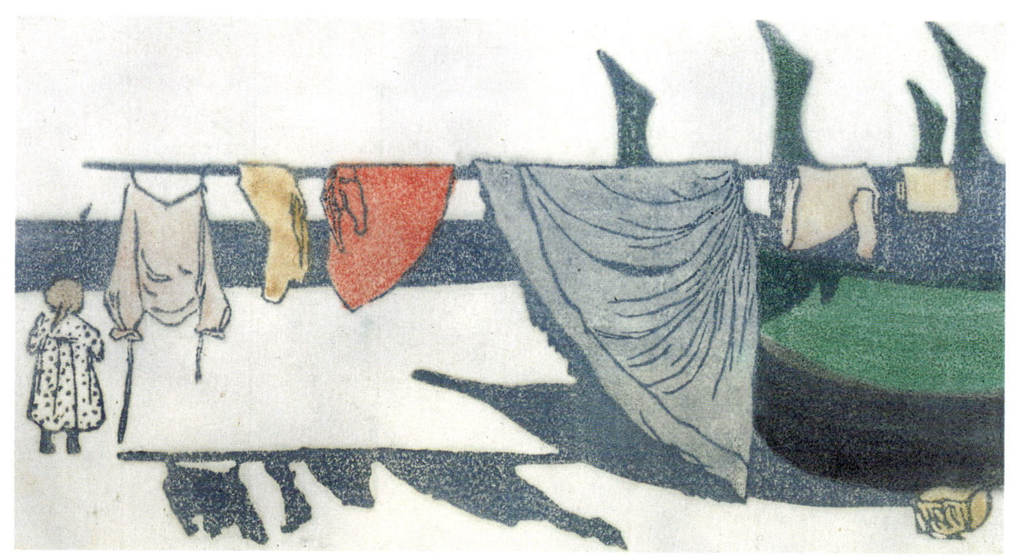

Washing at the Shore, ca. 1907/08 (Cat. No. 10)

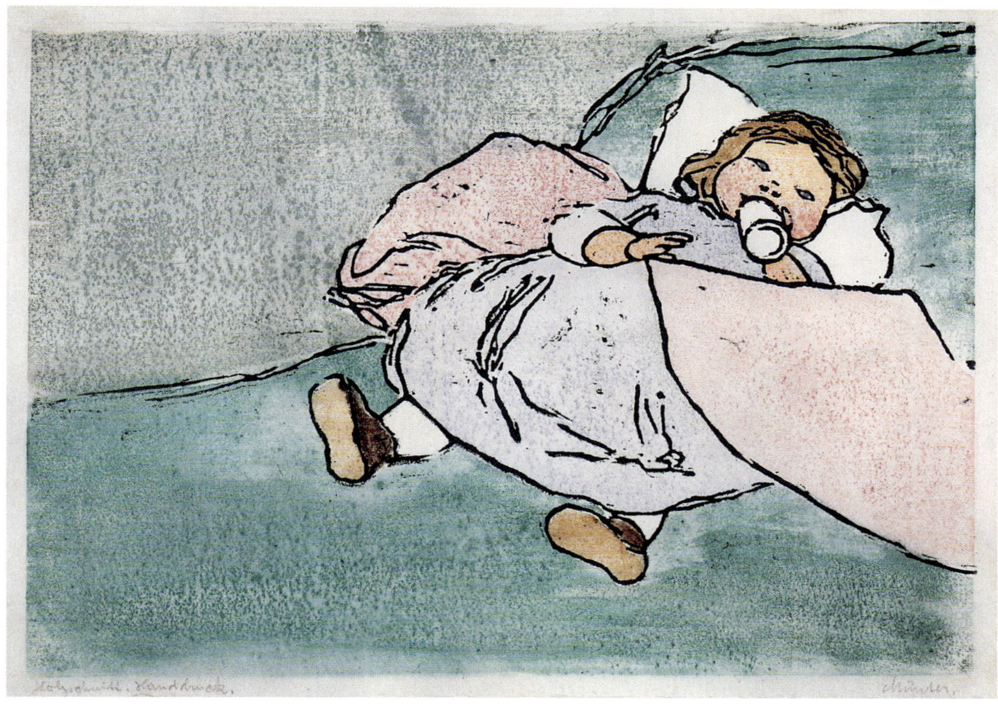

Child with Bottle, ca. 1907/08 (Cat. No. 12)

Her paintings, however, continued to employ Kandinsky's palette knife and impasto technique with a late Impressionist method that permitted little individuality in its approach, especially as the two painted landscape studies together. What is surprising is that they both maintained their allegiance to their modified Impressionism for as long as a year after they left Paris, where despite their rather isolated life-style they came into contact with works by much of the Parisian avant-garde.[4] In a sketchbook, Münter recorded a virtual inventory of the major Impressionist, Symbolist and Fauve artists—Gauguin, Van Gogh, Monticelli, Redon, Bonnard, Cézanne, Matisse, Morisot, Degas, Signac and Renoir—but offered no rationale for the list.[5] As Kandinsky remained associated with the late Symbolist periodical *Tendances Nouvelles*, which also reproduced several of Münter's works in 1908, neither their paintings nor their prints took any notice of the innovations of Paris' progressive artists.

Ironically then, the memory of Matisse and Fauvism, of Gauguin and Van Gogh, began to shape Münter's and Kandinsky's painting only after they moved back to Munich and visited the small Bavarian market town of Murnau during August 1908, over a year after they had left Paris. Joined by the Russian artists Marianne Werefkin and Alexei Jawlensky, both also living in Munich, Münter and Kandinsky suddenly altered their style radically, as if conceptually they had already changed it and were only waiting for the physical opportunity to execute the change in the actuality of painting. It is useful to recall Gabriele Münter's description of her work during the summer of 1908, written as she became aware of the art-historical significance of their group and began to act as its unofficial scribe, as a "major leap" from Impressionist nature studies to "the presentation of an extract."[6] Concisely, but almost as if in disbelief at the swift transformation in her art, Münter outlined the emergence of her radical new style, its fundamental features shared with Werefkin, Jawlensky and Kandinsky. The development was communal, with no single voice absolutely dominant; no one alone served as leader or guide who called to the others to follow. The artists collaborated, frequently painted identical scenes and, together, discussed the remarkable transformations their work underwent.

Long, if not always deep, friendship made such interaction possible. Kandinsky, Werefkin and Jawlensky had known each other since at least 1897, and had been neighbors in Gisela Strasse for several years; Münter had met them by 1905. This close association also sought to fulfill the frequent arcadian modernist vision of a utopian community of artists unrestrainedly outside the urban confines of cities. With ideals based in Romanticism, and with France's Barbizon painters as models, numerous German artists "discovered" the rural charm of small villages throughout Germany and established artists' colonies in them in order to focus on landscapes of the nearby moors and mountains.[7] Murnau was particularly well suited to such a venture. Located in Upper Bavaria's subalpine plains, with some

2,500 inhabitants, Murnau was an old market town to which farmers still brought their wares, but that also fostered a significant tourist industry, attracting about 1,700 visitors each summer and easily reachable with the Munich-Garmisch railway line. Before Münter and Kandinsky settled there, it was featured in the popular illustrated periodical *Velhagen und Klasings Monatshefte*[8] in 1908, where its location was enthusiastically described:

> Towards the south lies a former lake bed, the Murnau Moors, behind which rise magnificent mountain massives, towards the left Herzogstand and Heimgarten [alpine peaks], further to the right the Krottenkopf; to the right the Ettaler Mandl protrudes, and from the south one is greeted by the Zugspitze, Germany's tallest mountain peak. Staffelsee, with its seven islands, offers an unusually beautiful view. From Murnau an hour's ride on the electric train takes you to the famous Passion village, Oberammergau. To the east and north, the countryside gradually begins to flatten out.

Moreover, beginning in 1906 the town, destroyed by repeated fires, had undergone a major transformation, an "urban renewal" that brought greater cohesion to the central market area, as the article reported:

> The initiative for this rebirth of Murnau by means of a folk art once common in the entire Bavarian foothills derives from Professor Emanuel von Seidl.... And with what economy of means does he obtain an often remarkable result!... [He] gave himself the task of supplying all houses of Market Street, indeed of the entire market area, with original house decorations, or at least with a sound coat of paint, and to submit them to the unity of the total scene with simple tasteful renovations. While some of the facades are equipped with only colorfully enframed windows, others are accented with rich figurative decoration.... There are always multiple dominant tones with which the architect works, here a saturated red, there yellow, here blue and there again violet tones govern the facades.[9]

Employing *Jugendstil* concepts in conjunction with a historicist effort to revive Bavarian traditions of domestic village architecture and architectural decoration, Seidl's renovation gave the town a picturesque cohesion and colorfulness that were fundamentally modern, creating more than preserving the appearance of an archetypical alpine town. It appealed especially to the bourgeoisie of Bavaria's cities, who by 1914 nearly doubled Murnau's size with the summer homes they built. The villagers and farmers from nearby continued to dress in *Lederhosen* and folk costumes, but the "unspoiled" Bavarian village in which they now lived was a stage shaped according to a sanitizing modernist ideological celebration of rural authenticity. Guide-

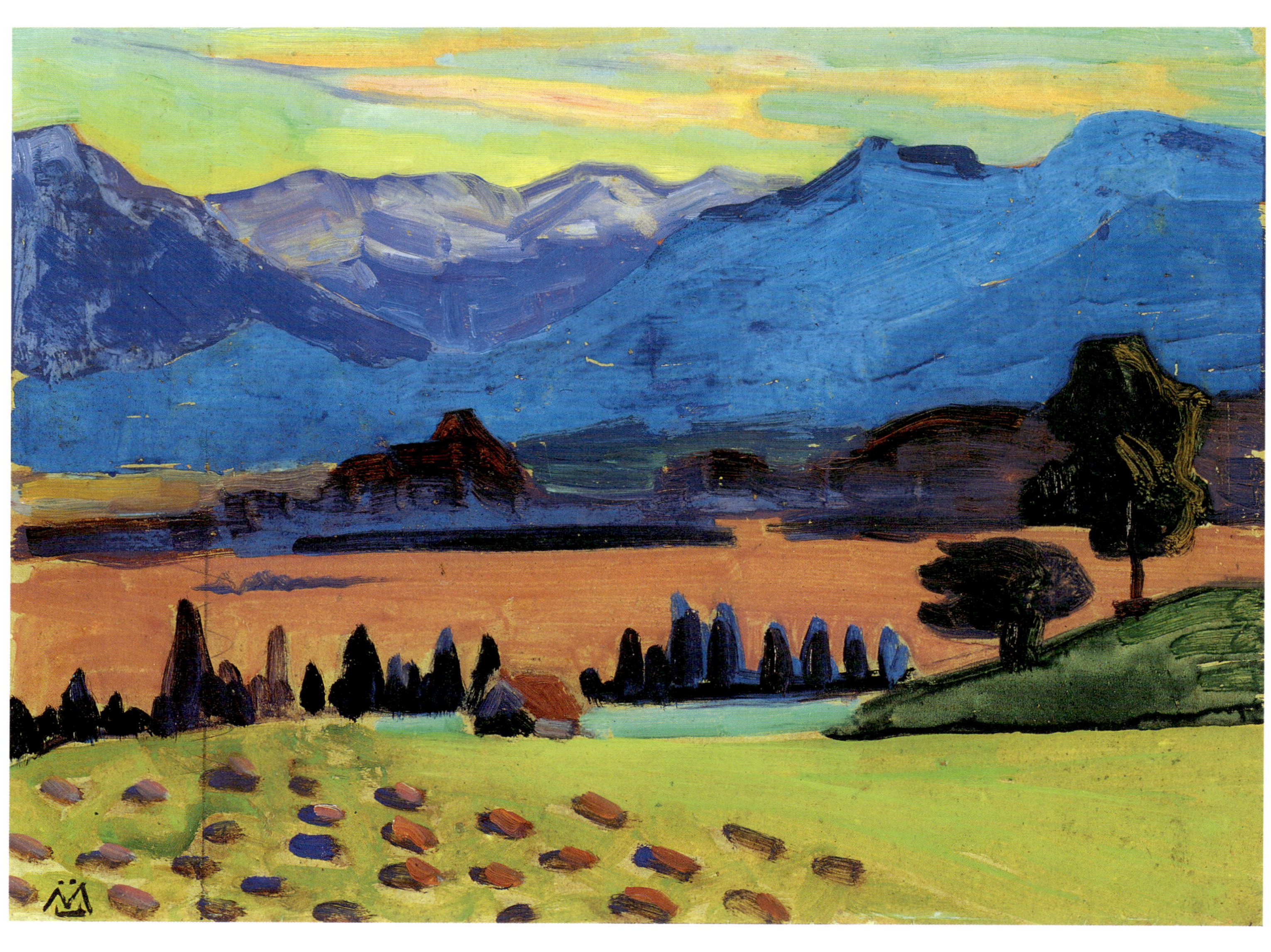

The Murnau Moors, 1908 (Cat. No. 18)

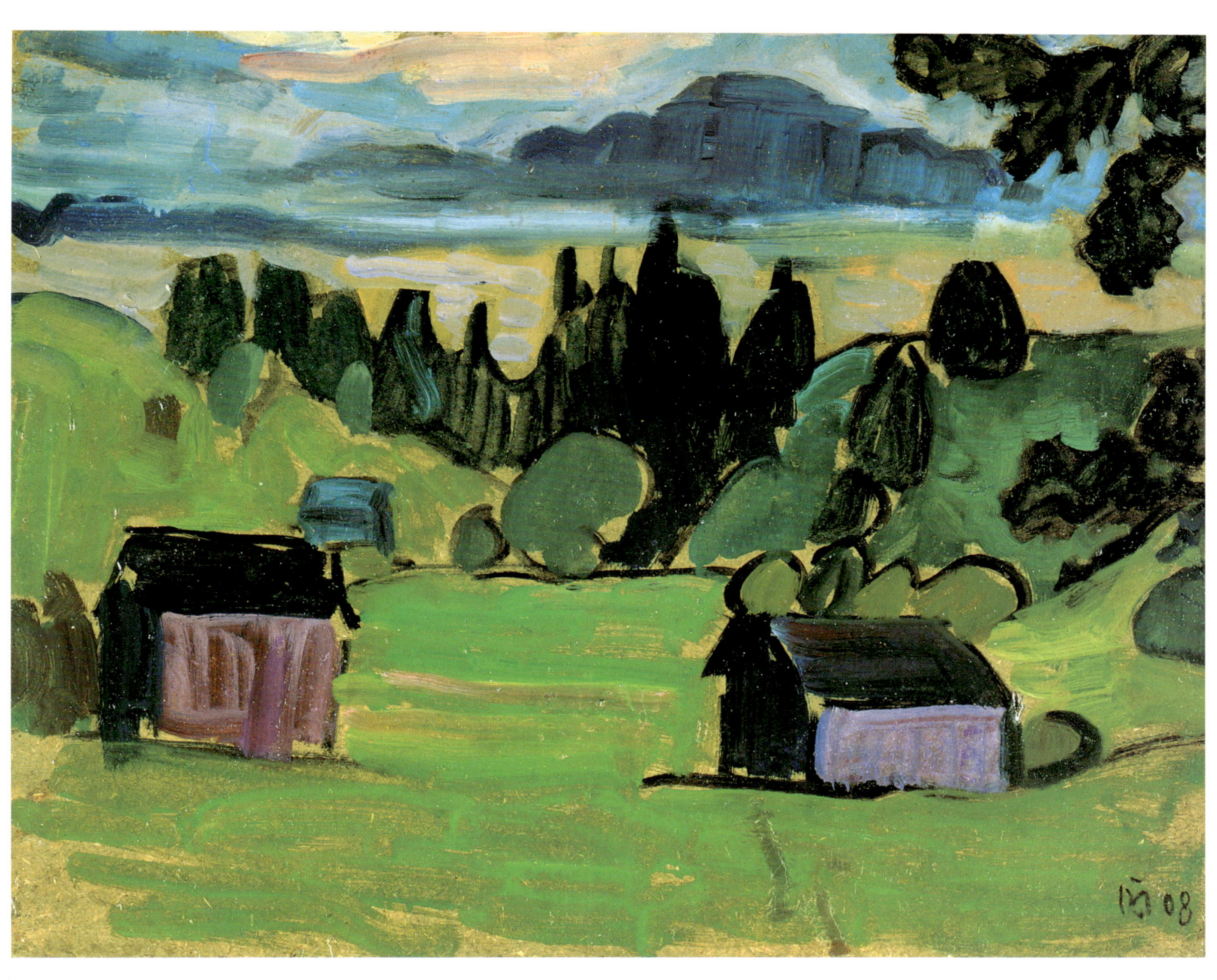

View of the Murnau Moors, 1908 (Cat. No. 19)

books today continue to reach for superlatives: "Here one is surrounded by a sense of well-being; whoever establishes residence here will certainly never leave again."[10] With a white, Baroque, onion-domed church rising above it on a central hill, with several chapels and a small Gothic fortress, it appealed to Kandinsky and Münter precisely because it corresponded to their preconception of what Bavarian village life should be.

The idyllic town, moreover, lay as if on an extended terrace between Staffelsee and the Murnau Moors, while the southern horizon offered a spectacular ring of massive, tree-covered alpine peaks that "... lent the almost too dramatic landscape a particularly pictorial tone," as the Kandinsky scholar Peg Weiss sensitively observed. "The pure air and the glowing light typical of the subalpine climate seemed to compress the perspective so that the hills and mountains appeared to spread out over an indeterminate distance as if on a small, crystalline plain."[11] In effect, the flat expanse of the moors and the unique properties of atmosphere and light subdued the overpowering grandeur of the Alps into a series of relatively flat, monochromatic forms. This made the landscape readily translatable, without succumbing to a sense of miniaturization, into the small-scale studies Münter and Kandinsky preferred. It was as if the landscape itself had fulfilled the modernist transformations their art was about to undergo.

"I learned much from you then and will be eternally grateful to you for it," Kandinsky wrote to Jawlensky in the 1930s as he recalled the time they spent together in Munich and Murnau.[12] Münter likewise repeatedly acknowledged Jawlensky's early guidance in the summer of 1908; Eichner summarized: "Without a doubt Jawlensky was the most advanced when the group began its work in Murnau. He already knew how to paint in a 'modern way.' He had learned the School of Pont Aven's method of harnessing color planes to linear contours."[13]

Far more than Münter and Kandinsky, Jawlensky was attuned to recent developments in progressive French art. After he exhibited at the Salon d'Automne in 1905, he adopted a style rooted in late Neo-Impressionism, with an overlay of Fauvist color intensity, which he maintained until 1908.[14] Late in 1907 and in the spring of 1908, he was frequently in the company of Jan Verkade, a follower of Paul Gauguin and a member of the Nabis, as well as two other Gauguin disciples, Paul Sérusier and Władisław Ślewińsky, then in Munich. Together, they tutored Jawlensky in Gauguin's *cloisonniste* method that recalled the effects of stained glass windows with its broad, flat planes of color, dark outlines of simplified forms and a limited number of bright colors. They also introduced him to Gauguin's theories of Synthetism and the concept of synthesis, which Münter identified as Jawlensky's motto in Murnau. The major formative influences of the artists' communal Murnau style— Synthetism and Fauvism, but also Van Gogh, from whom Jawlensky bought a landscape in 1907[15]—came together in the spring of 1908 but did not find expression until August, in Murnau.

The works show no true transition. A sudden break and a new vocabulary correspond to concepts previously, but insufficiently, carried out, primarily in Münter's prints. Just a few weeks earlier she painted delicate white-on-white impasto studies of blossoming springtime trees in the Tyrol, more fully than ever under the thrall of a decorative late Impressionism. In Murnau, however, she entirely abandoned this method, virtually as soon as she arrived there. She approached the town with initial hesitation, drawing and painting it as she saw it from the window of her room in the Griesbräu inn, much as she and Kandinsky had done in Sèvres and other towns they had visited. Such elevated views, with the implicit framing and the control offered by the rectangular window, was a frequent device of Impressionist painters, such as Camille Pissarro or, in Germany, Max Slevogt. It provided an immediately organized compositional control for its painters while allowing them to keep the distance of a disengaged observer, someone separate and, literally, above the street scenes being depicted, who is capable of chronicling objectively. This distancing clearly could not be maintained once Münter and Kandinsky entered the streets of Murnau to paint, although even here, significantly, they usually portrayed street scenes without the villagers and visitors who inhabited them and who populate the photographs Münter took.[16] When a single woman does appear in *Main Street, Murnau* (Cat. No. 22), she is in the otherwise deserted street not as part of a milieu of traffic and commerce in the town's marketplace, but more as an abstracted representative of Murnau's population; in her simple traditional dress and anonymity, as she carries a bundle of laundry, she is a virtual allegory of women and women's work in Bavarian village society more than an actual presence. It was not the momentary appearance of passersby that Münter was intent on depicting, but the same timeless stillness that emanated from her earlier prints. To use Münter's words, the paintings were to express "the feeling of a content… abstracting… the presentation of an extract," no longer a naturalistic rendition of a scene.[17]

The house facades newly painted by Emanuel von Seidl in their varied colors, with dark shadows to generate additional color nuance, appealed to both Münter and Kandinsky during their initial forays into the town, still staying close to their inn as they depicted the streets immediately outside its doors. The landscape remained blocked off by the constructs of brightly colored or white houses; for *Main Street, Murnau*, Münter turned her back on the Alps to paint, instead, a view facing north. The flat planes of intensely colorful walls, intersecting and buttressed next to each other, linearly arranged in a ready perspectival construction, particularly suited the *cloisoniste* painting methods she now adopted, following Jawlensky's example. For this modernist artifice, nature—fundamental to her Impressionist work —seemed too intrusive, too problematic to render as yet.

A painting dated 27 August 1908, very shortly after Münter arrived in Murnau, and alternately titled *Village Street in Murnau* or—fixing on its

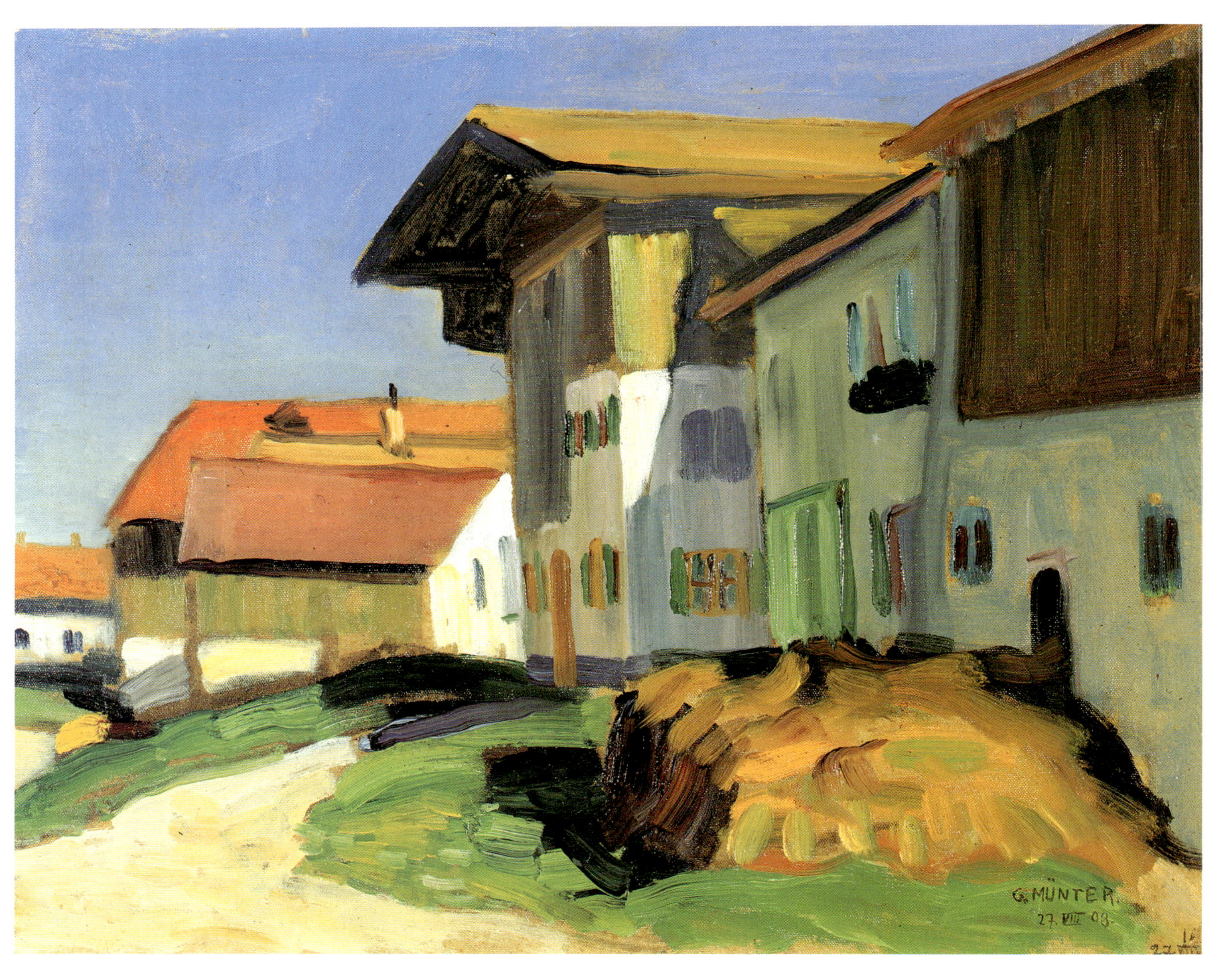

Village Street in Murnau (Manure Pile), 1908 (Cat. No. 20)

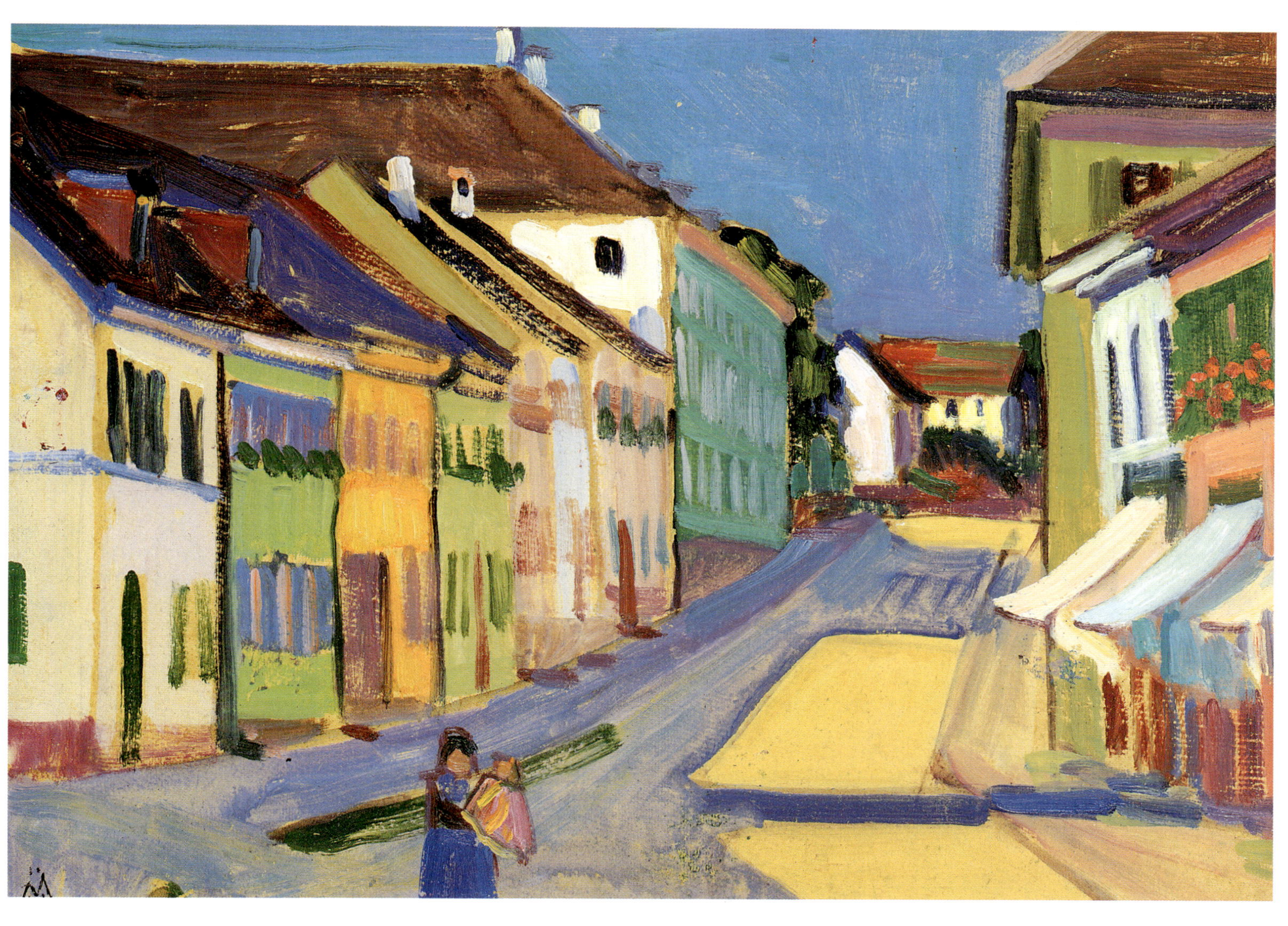

Main Street, Murnau, 1908 (Cat. No. 22)

most significant foreground feature—*Manure Pile* (Cat. No. 20) likewise situates the house and barn complex so as to set it off only against a pale blue sky, rendered without nuance or cloud as a simple, untextured plane. An impastoed paint surface, with clear tracks of her dragging brush, remains in the foreground area, however, as she experimented with how to suppress the tactile, small, divided touches of her Impressionist work. Here, her brushwork is broader, applied in parallel strokes to generate planar patterns that adhere solely to the picture surface, without depth except in the allusions of scale and the color interrelationships evident in the straw mass of the manure pile, the painting's key element. The manure pile is accentuated in the way its rendering breaks in style with the painted surface surrounding it, especially with the very thinly painted facades behind it, where the cardboard's ocher tone comes through. The dichotomy of vocabularies and the pictorial tension within the image thus attract attention, giving necessary testimony to the material means of the paint and strawboard surface of which the image is composed, and detracting from its sense of illusion. While the colors and, to some extent, the brushwork retain a link to her prior Impressionist paintings, as Kandinsky's Murnau paintings of 1908 did even more strongly, here, Münter stresses conceptual and stylistic properties—her accent on the painting's material makeup, on flat color planes, on the juxtaposition of vibrant color complementaries, and on formal or methodological disjunctions within the image— not present in her work previously. In Murnau Münter, Kandinsky and Jawlensky begin to establish the modernist vocabulary of Expressionism, Germany's avant-garde, and, simultaneously, but without contact, evolve from the same artistic prototypes as the artists' group *Brücke* in Dresden. Among the first Expressionists in Germany, Münter was the sole woman.[18]

She did not remain long satisfied with depicting the town alone, its buildings represented from an exaggeratedly low viewpoint so as to stand isolated against the clear blue sky. The indescribable richness of the surrounding landscape soon held her enthralled even more than Seidl's reformed village environment did. Especially as fall began to set in during September—after Kandinsky had left for Munich to move into his new apartment in Ainmillerstrasse—Münter focused on the alpine vistas just outside the village, encouraged by Jawlensky's praise. The view across the Murnau Moors she depicted in broad fields of thin color glowing directly on an absorbent matte strawboard surface, which is visible through the colors (Cat. No. 18). No longer does she use short strokes and dabs of viscous oil paint, memories of Impressionism, but rather thin washes dragged onto the surface with broad brushes and long strokes defined by the contours of objects depicted: the yellow-green meadow in the foreground with its small red-violet mounds of hay, the moors in dark royal pink, and the Wetterstein alpine range in various blue tones. Her landscape was executed with color; she made no preliminary drawing, either in a sketchbook or on the cardboard itself. Münter fashioned the scene with her paintbrush confidently and in one sitting, making no changes. A remarkable, flowing sense of spontaneity and effortlessness not present in her previous painting resulted. "Most of my successful works were painted quickly and without corrections," she noted late in life, "as if by themselves,"[19] but the effortlessness was an illusion she deliberately sought, brought about after five years of learning her craft and its techniques.

Depicted in the painting's broadly simplified and stylized forms is the view across the moors towards the Wetterstein Alps. The landscape panorama is seen late in summer from a hillside meadow, near the "Lourdes grotto" and the small chapel known as the Ramsachkircherl, a site singled out in virtually all guidebooks: "Charm and melancholy simultaneously characterize the broad flat expanse ... when wilting marsh grasses, moss, heather and reeds cover it with a finely tuned play of colors in carmine red, violet and brown tones."[20] Münter selected for the scene colors that essentially correspond to those of nature, but rejected nuances of shade in order to intensify contrasts and the color's subjective effect. "From this time on," she wrote in 1947, "I was no longer concerned with the verifiably 'correct' form of things. And yet I never sought to 'overcome' nature, to defeat or even to deride her. I depicted the world as it appeared to me in its essence, how it moved me. My paintings were said to be unpretentious and introspective."[21]

In an early inventory of her paintings, Münter described painting No. 70, as "View towards the Moors, Approaching Evening, Clouds and Mountains." A second study, her list's No. 65, painted later the same day, originated further down the meadow, roughly in the middle foreground of the previous painting (Cat. No. 19). Identified by her as "Dusk. 2 Barns — Small Lourdes Woods or Moors,"[22] its violet-tinged barns gleam in the shadows of surrounding darker green meadows as the setting sun illuminates them, muted through the mists of the moors. The wisps of fog and mist bleach the pink-orange of the moors and obscure the alpine peaks, cut off by Münter at the painting's upper edge, to emphasize instead the dark rolling masses of the *Kögel*—rocky, hilly islands—that emerge dramatically from the damp flatness of the moors. Again, extensive areas of brown cardboard remain visible as thinned paint is brushed on with broad strokes, now to fill in the gaps between painted lines resembling black scaffolding, which accentuate and define the barns, trees and meadows of the foreground. Throughout, forms are reduced to flat, simplified hieroglyphic renderings or colored signs of the objects they represent.

The simplicity and coloristic harmony of image Münter achieved distinguishes her works from similar paintings executed by Kandinsky and Jawlensky in Murnau. Kandinsky opted for significantly greater complexity, failing to achieve Münter's essentialized but never severe austerity; Jawlensky's works reveal a greater coarseness of color conception and paint application, recalling his previous Neo-Impressionist techniques. As the trio employed virtually a communal style, each maintained an individual voice. Notable, too, is Münter's preference for atmospheric times of day, especially dusk, to lend her landscapes a richly emotive character, whereas the others opted for a less clearly emotional exploration of colors and forms. Münter achieved independence here, often indeed initiating practices the others later adopted, as she sought to produce expressive visual synopses of the Murnau landscape. But all three gave shape to a painting mode no other artists in Munich matched. In the radicality of their Expressionist modernism they were alone.

During his brief Munich visit in 1908, Władisław Ślewińsky wrote to a fellow follower of Gauguin: "We are in Munich now and will remain for some time. The atmosphere is little encouraging, here there are only paint smearers and beer. The paint smearers are horrible, but the beer is excellent. The artistic niveau is so horribly low that one has absolutely no desire to have an exhibition."[23] Since the demise of the Phalanx in 1905, there was no organization that represented or supported Munich's radical artists. The Munich Secession regularly rejected entries submitted by Jawlensky, arguably the most progressive painter in Munich before Münter and Kandinsky returned. Long absent, they also now had no venue to display their newest works. In January 1909, the New Artists' Association Munich was founded, and issued a manifesto that announced: "We proceed from the thought that the artist gathers experiences in an inner world in addition to the impressions that he receives from the external world, from nature; and the search for artistic forms which should give expression to the mutual interaction of all these experiences—for forms that must be freed of all that is accidental in order to bring only the necessary to strong expression—in short, the striving for artistic *Synthesis*, this appears to us to be a solution which is uniting ever more artists at this very moment."[24]

Kandinsky was the author. He centered the program's ideas around the concept of synthesis so frequently employed by Jawlensky the previous summer, and ultimately derived from Paul Gauguin. Beyond Jawlensky, the concept now used to define the new art developed by Münter, Kandinsky and Jawlensky in Murnau was a vital one in art criticism and aesthetics at the time. Although the concept varied widely in meaning as it was used by Symbolist, *Jugendstil* and other painters and writers between 1890 and 1910, as Münter and Kandinsky employed it, it referred to a fusion of color and line, of the recalled visual object and its abstracted form,"... the collection of the Impressionist multiplicity of natural appearance into a great, simple presentation."[25] The accidentals of nature were subjectively extracted from their forms in order to reveal an abstracted essential entity. Color, the most overt visual characteristic of an object, thus lost the nuance and refinement it had in Münter's earlier Impressionist paintings, for example, and was presented in broad, simple forms, unmodulated and precisely

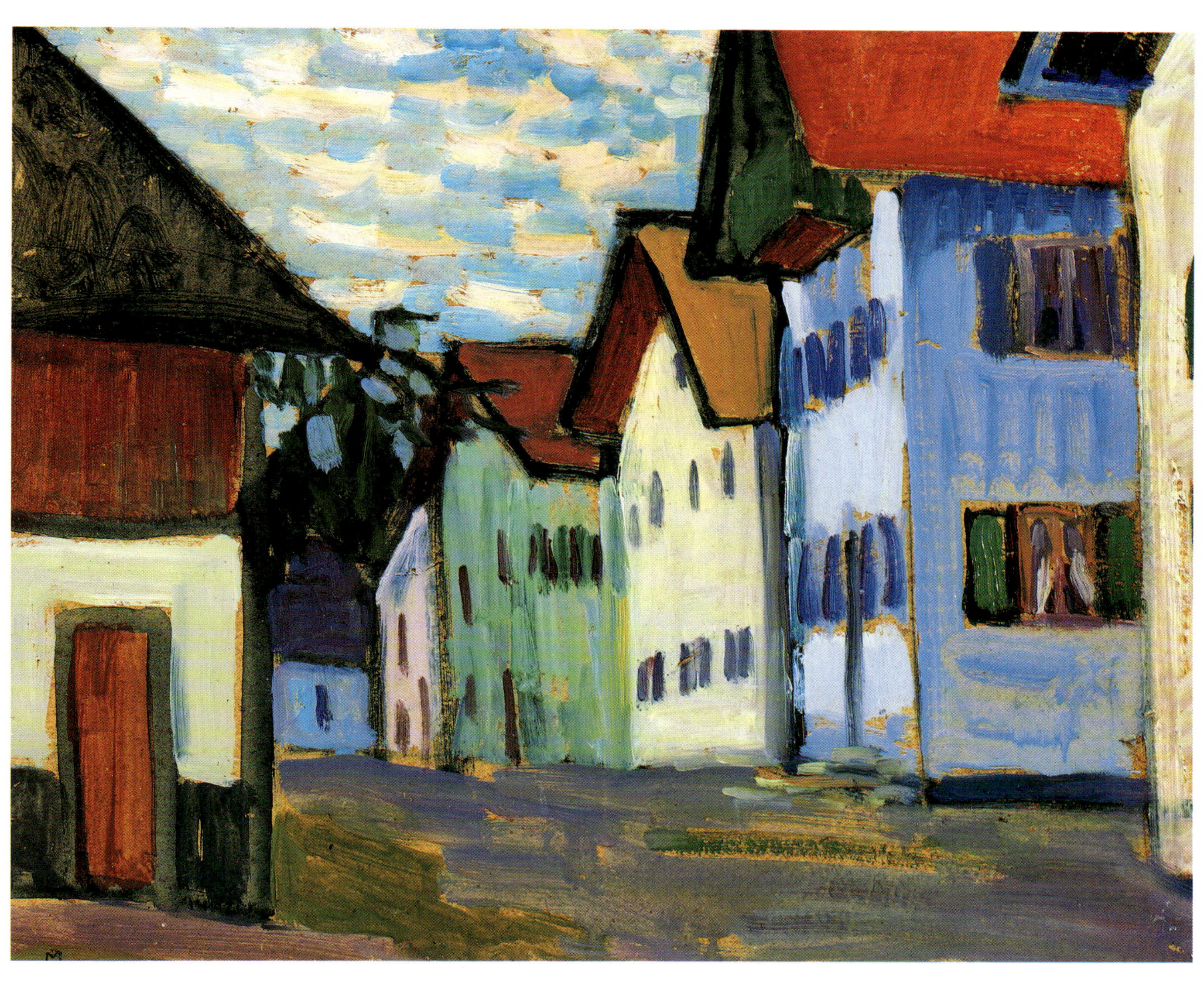

Small Street in Murnau, 1908 (Cat. No. 21)

defined. It was color—red, blue, green, yellow—not as physically seen with multiple variations, but as "spiritually experienced," according to Kandinsky: the color concept associated with the word was given material form. Similarly, line functioned to simplify and abstract the forms of nature, to transform them into the "spiritual beings" or "extracts" of which Münter spoke. The program formulated a new aesthetic, fundamentally Expressionist, to justify the painterly experimentation the artists together had entered into in Murnau during the few weeks they were together. The new artists' organization now provided the means to propagate it and to proclain their doctrine of Expressionist modernism.

Still Lifes and Interiors

Returned to her room at the Pension Stella in Munich, during the last months of 1908 and the initial ones of 1909, as the New Artists' Association Munich was being founded, Münter sought to apply her new stylistic vocabulary to depictions of her urban environment—not the city as such, however, which many other Expressionist artists rendered, but portraits and still lifes. Her attention focused on people and objects as they appeared to her, from within the confines of her personal milieu, defined and limited by her social background, her profession, her sex and her marital status. Her activity and contacts within the city of Munich were restricted according to the norms of propriety imposed on middle-class women; many of the public spaces and events open to men were closed to her and other women unless they were escorted by a man. Because Kandinsky expressly disapproved, she no longer attended with any frequency the plays, operas, balls and artists' festivals she had regularly enjoyed earlier in her life. Since her respectability and suitability for reception in people's homes was severely compromised by her "immoral" relationship with Kandinsky, she had virtually no social contacts outside Munich's very small group of progressive artists and writers, their companions, and a few members of the Eastern European emigré community. Her world had become extremely circumscribed. From it, Münter gleaned the motifs of her art.

Unlike Marianne Werefkin or Kandinsky, she did not attempt to generate a grand metaphysical reality in symbolic compositions to counteract the containment of everyday life. She concentrated instead on the mundane and the ordinary. A small painting on cardboard, most likely from the late fall or early winter of 1908/09, *Return from Shopping* (Cat. No. 27),[1] focuses modestly on several neatly-wrapped packages resting on a woman's lap. Clothed in a dark dress intended for street wear, the woman herself is seen only as a torso segment with fragments of her arms and white-gloved hands. She remains only partially seen, unidentified and anonymous as she sits in a streetcar on her way home, set against a background and enframing the objects she bought and now carries. Two elements distinguish her somewhat, however: the potted plant with red flowers that she cradles gently in her hands and a small white purse, dangling from her hands, with a bead-work design that echoes in yellow the red flowers above. The handcrafted purse, similar in design to those Münter and Kandinsky made together,[2] and the pristine white gloves, offer clues as to her social status as they suggest both a recognition of decorum and a sense of fashion. They are attributes of a middle-class woman, not a servant or a working-class woman; the small purse with its personalized design may be a sign of vanity, something out of the ordinary that attracts the attention of others and marks its carrier as unique. That she has shopped alone and carries her purchases herself, moreover, most likely identifies her as neither married nor notably wealthy, since no servant accompanies her, carrying flowers or packages. The woman revealed in this way is someone much like Münter herself. Her identity in a public setting is totally reduced, however, to the objects she carries, to the still life she has tastefully arranged on her lap.

With its thinned paint, flat color application and outlined forms, *Return from Shopping* draws on the stylistic repertoire Münter developed in Murnau. The surface-affirming vocabulary is broken, however, by the tubular allusion to the arms, lending visible tension and formal irreconcilability to the image as dual orders of organization and visual reference are juxtaposed, without transition. The simple, flat decorativeness of *Jugendstil* or of Münter's prints is thereby avoided by means of visual disjuncture, establishing a principle Münter continued to apply frequently in her work thereafter. She affirms the modernist shift from naturalistic illusionism to a self-affirming pictorial language that insists on the ideational quality of the image and its function as the record of a memory or an idea, not the external visual world. The arms and the purse pose a frontal screen that encloses plant and packages, shielding and protecting them from being viewed in their entirety by the observer.

The still-life reality Münter extracted from her milieu and fixed in an ideational pictorial presentation can, in a sense, serve as a synopsis of contemporary attitudes towards women and their functions in a male-dominated society. The still life ranges from the decorative prettiness of the purse to the protection of new, blossoming life. All is presented, moreover, in a manner that denies the woman both personality and individuality as the frame cuts off everything but the central torso, where her reproductive organs and breasts are located. It is fundamental to Münter's vision, however, that precisely this sexually charged torso is rendered invisible. It is relegated to function as a dark background, so that packages, purse and flower constitute the painting's unusual visual focus.

Münter liked to compare her painting to a singing bird.[3] She extends the analogy in observing that her"... pictures are all moments of life—I mean instantaneous visual experiences, generally noted very rapidly and spontaneously."[4] Insofar as this analogy of the instinctive, impetuous production of beautiful song by a bird without thought or preconception is true, the programmatic content apparent in *Return from Shopping* runs counter to her insistence that she does not "tell stories." Indeed, the various levels of reading seem to be denied by the small size of the painting, its gentle coloration, its charm and the intimacy of its presentation. However, even if Münter's insistence on the passivity of her gaze and its "natural" presentation is accepted, hers was the gaze of a woman necessarily aware of her status. As an artist and as the unmarried companion of a married man, she

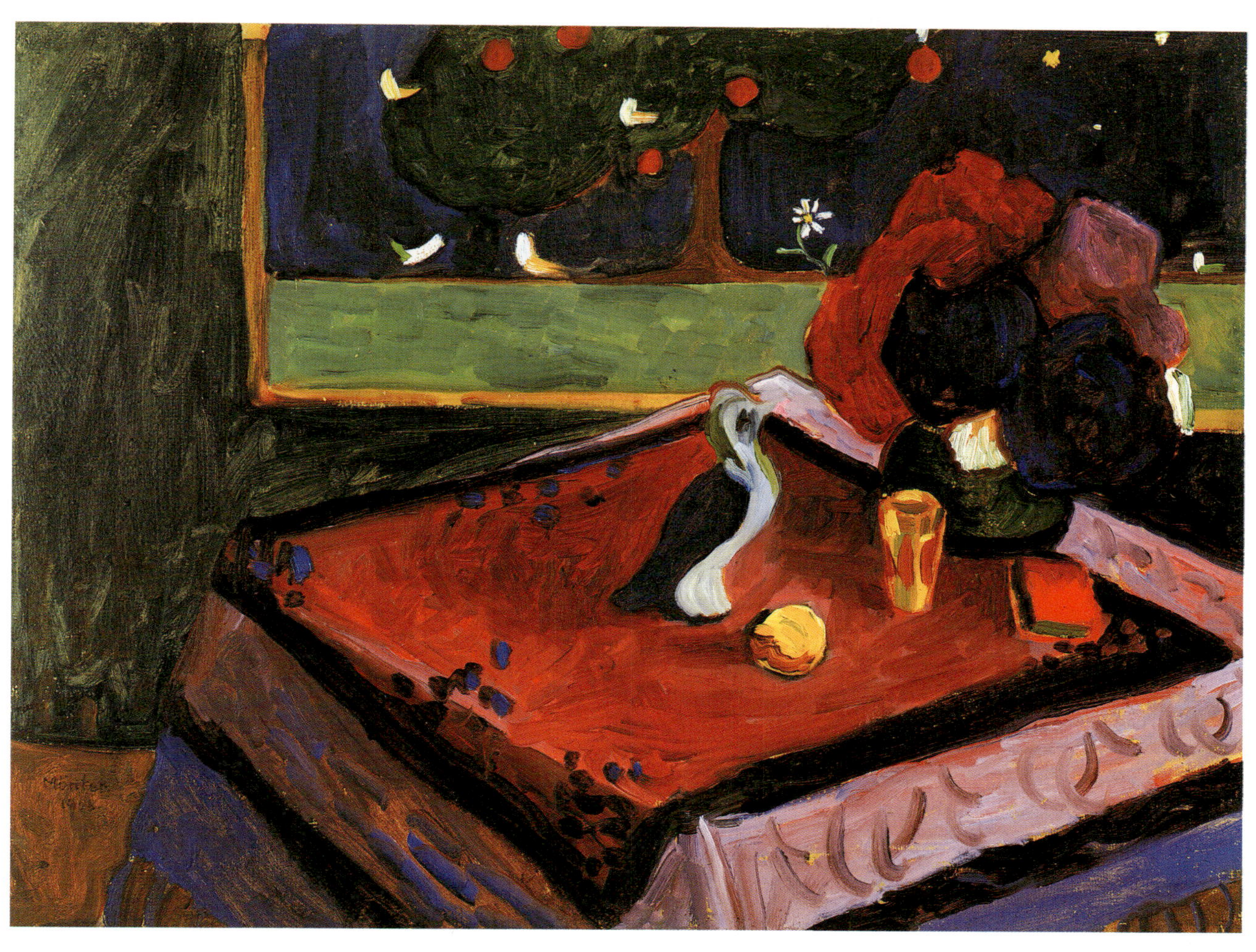

Interior (Still Life), 1908 (Cat. No. 16)

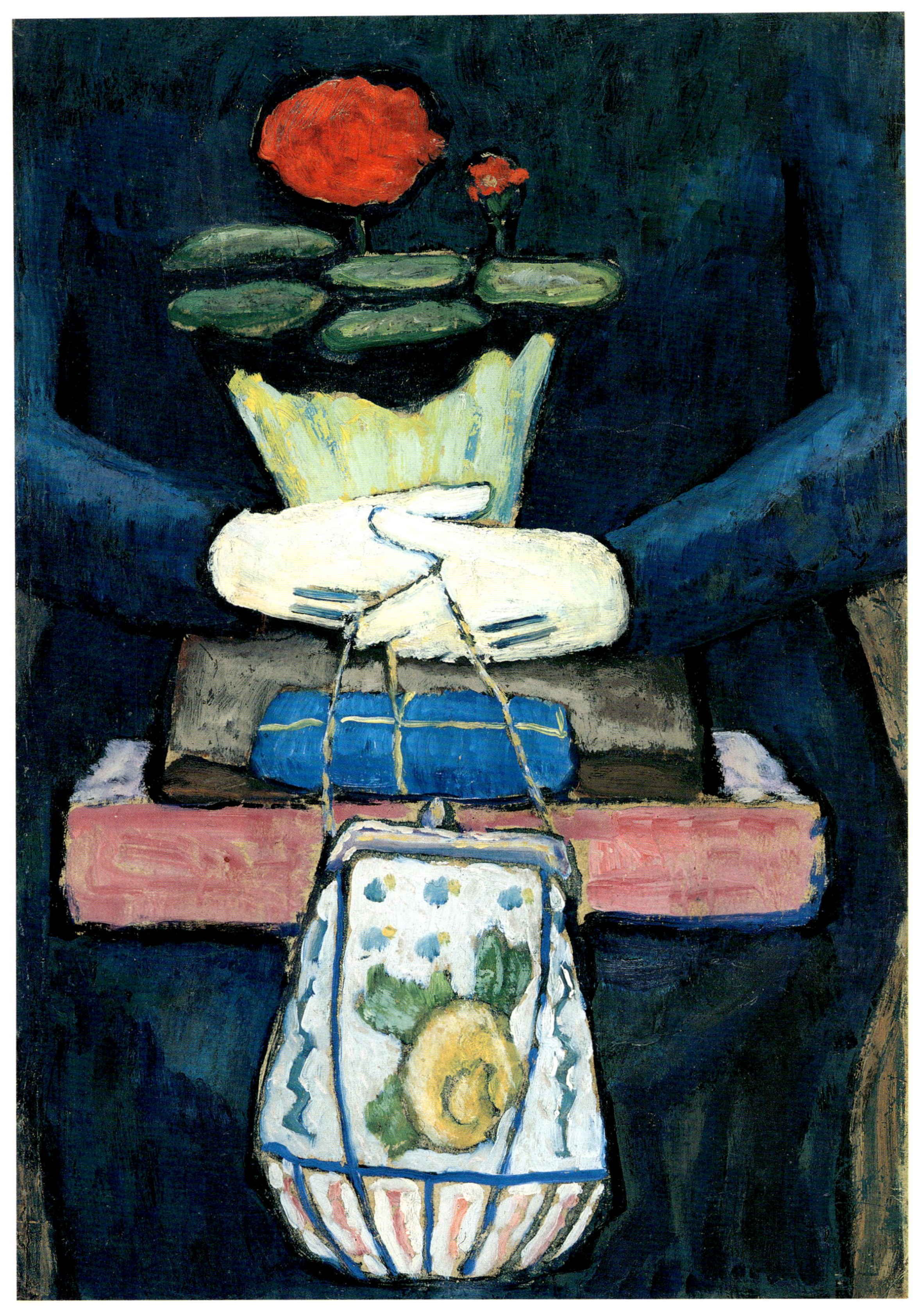

Return from Shopping (In the Streetcar), 1908/09 (Cat. No. 27)

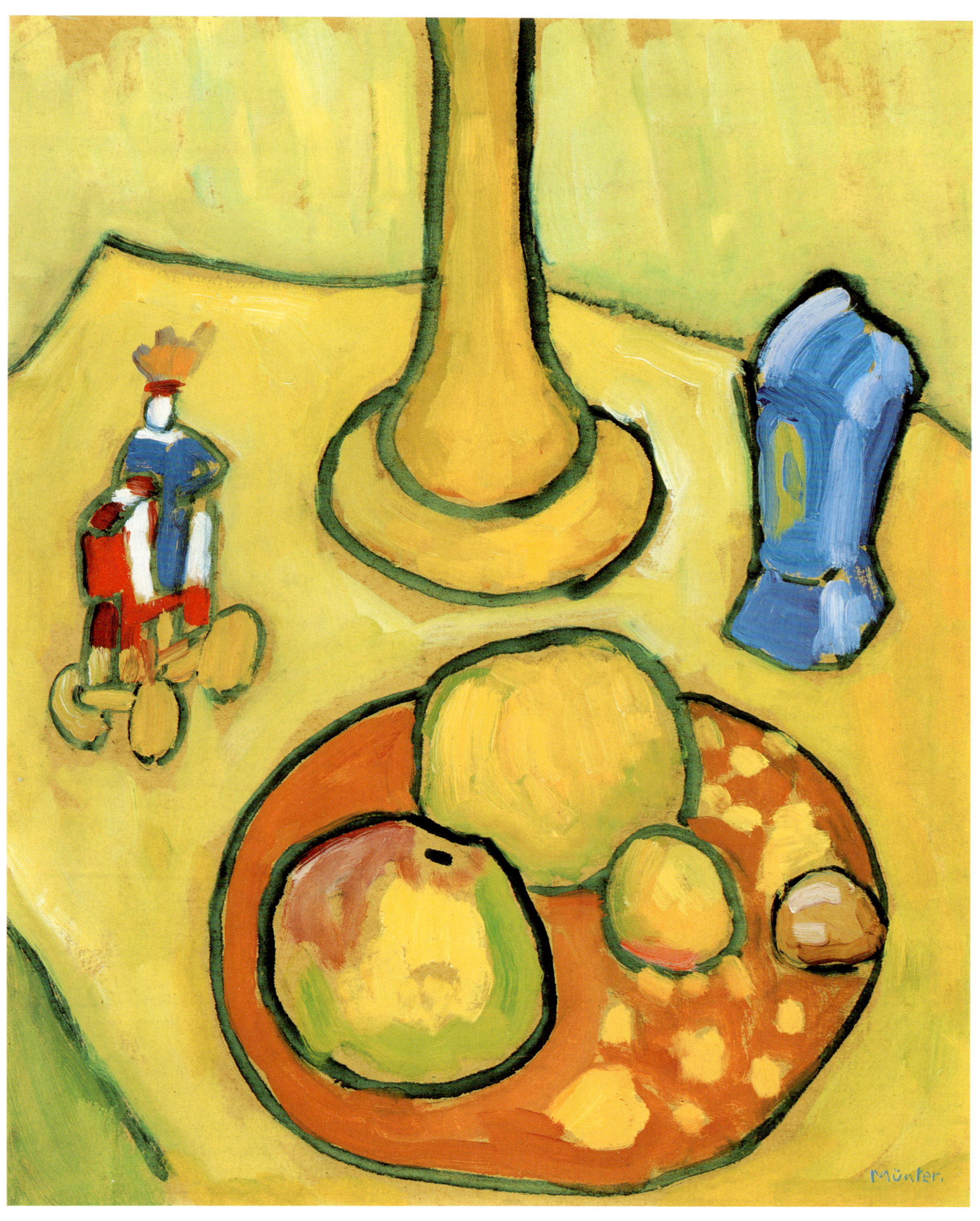

Still Life, Yellow, 1909 (Cat. No. 30)

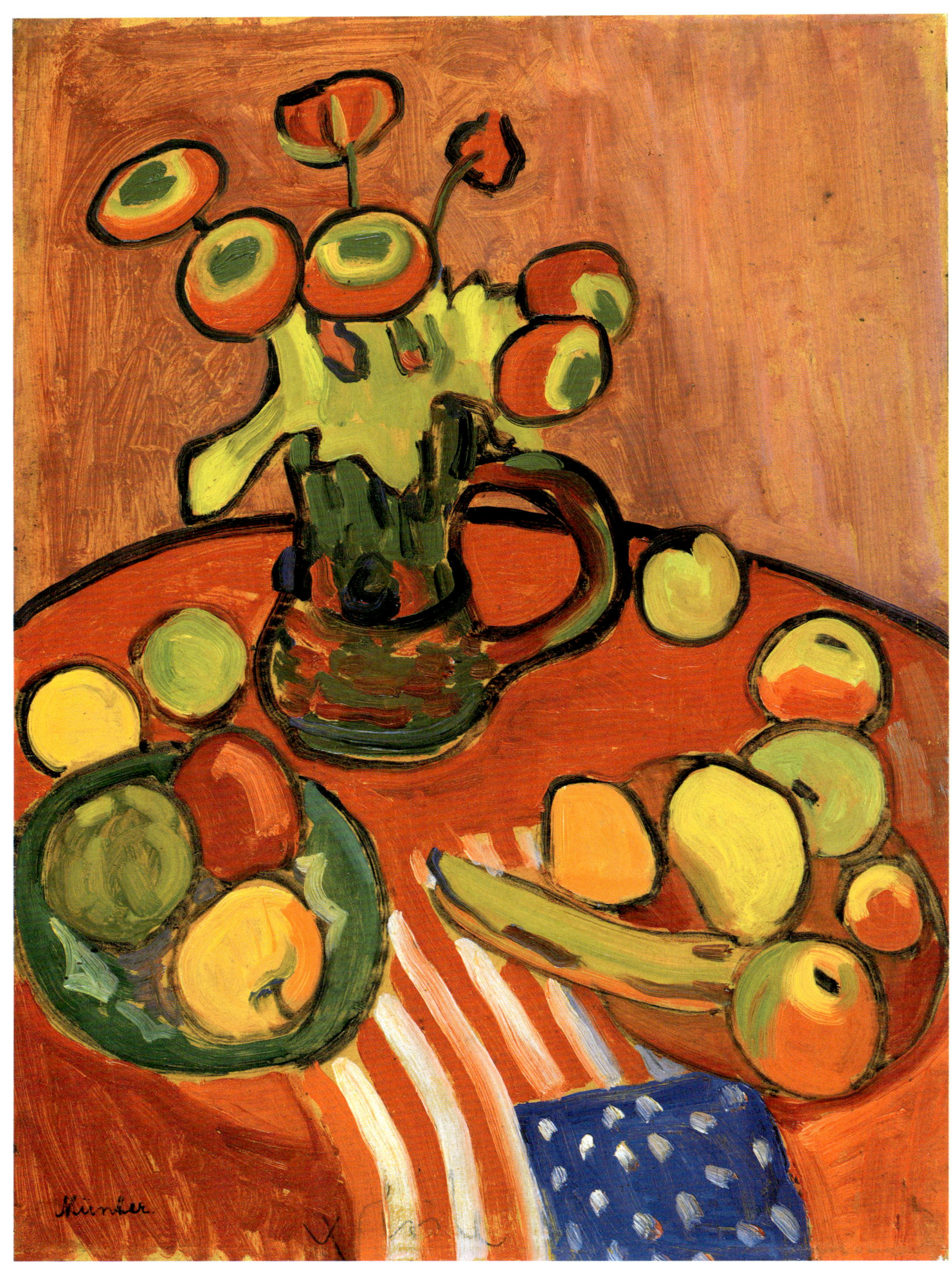

Still Life, Red, 1909 (Cat. No. 31)

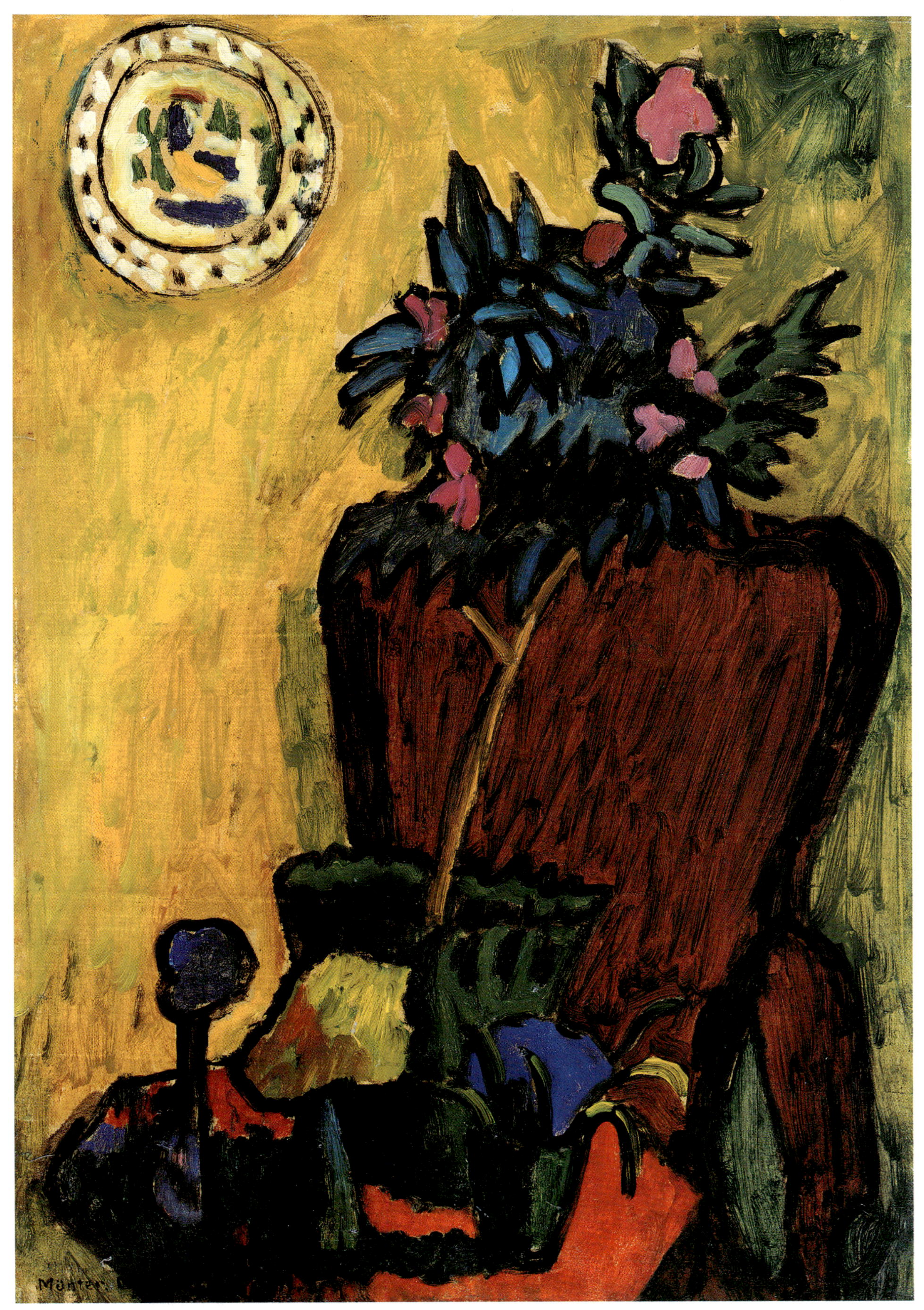

Still Life with Armchair, 1909 (Cat. No. 32)

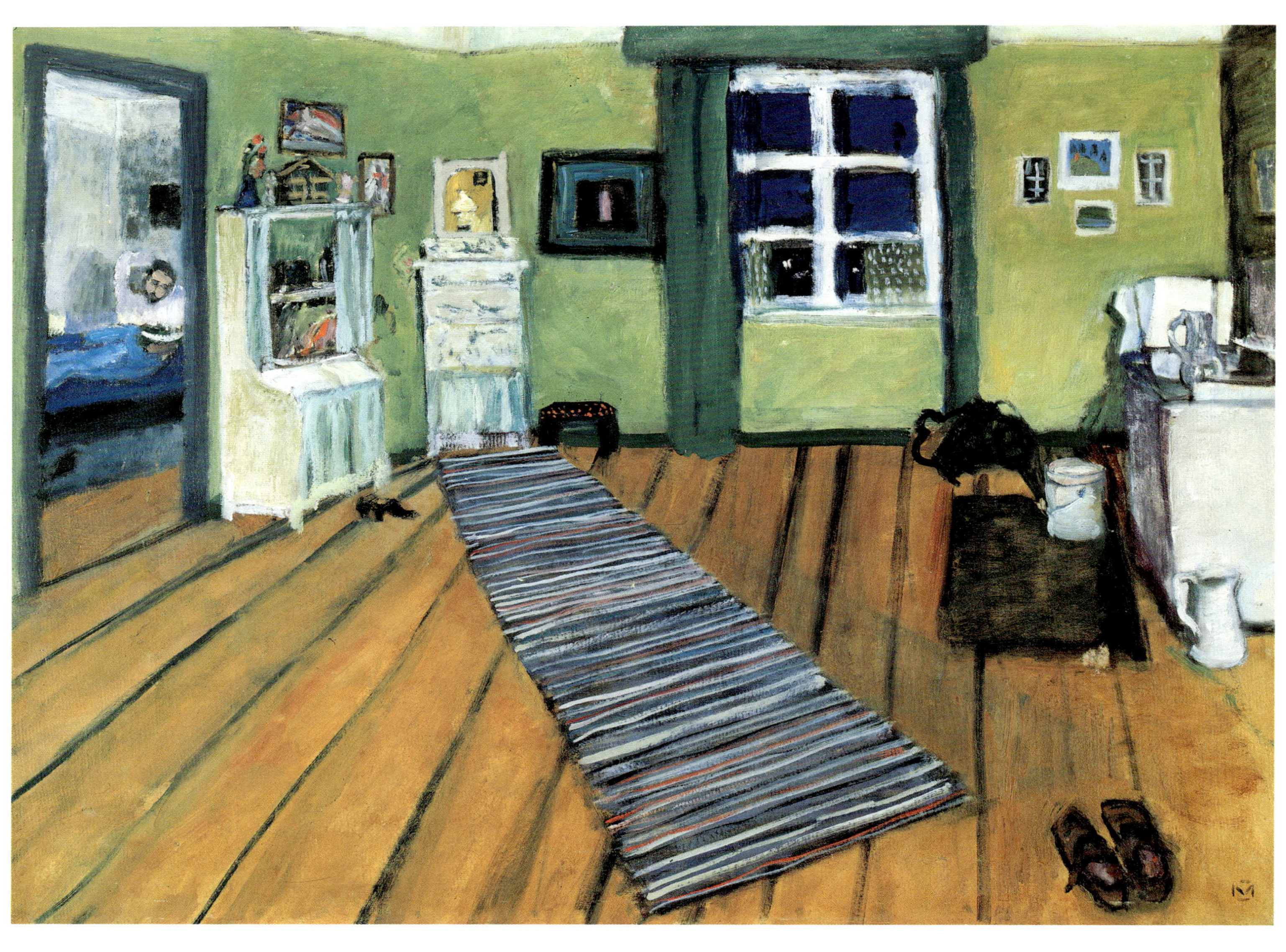

Interior (Still Life, Bedroom), 1909 (Cat. No. 33)

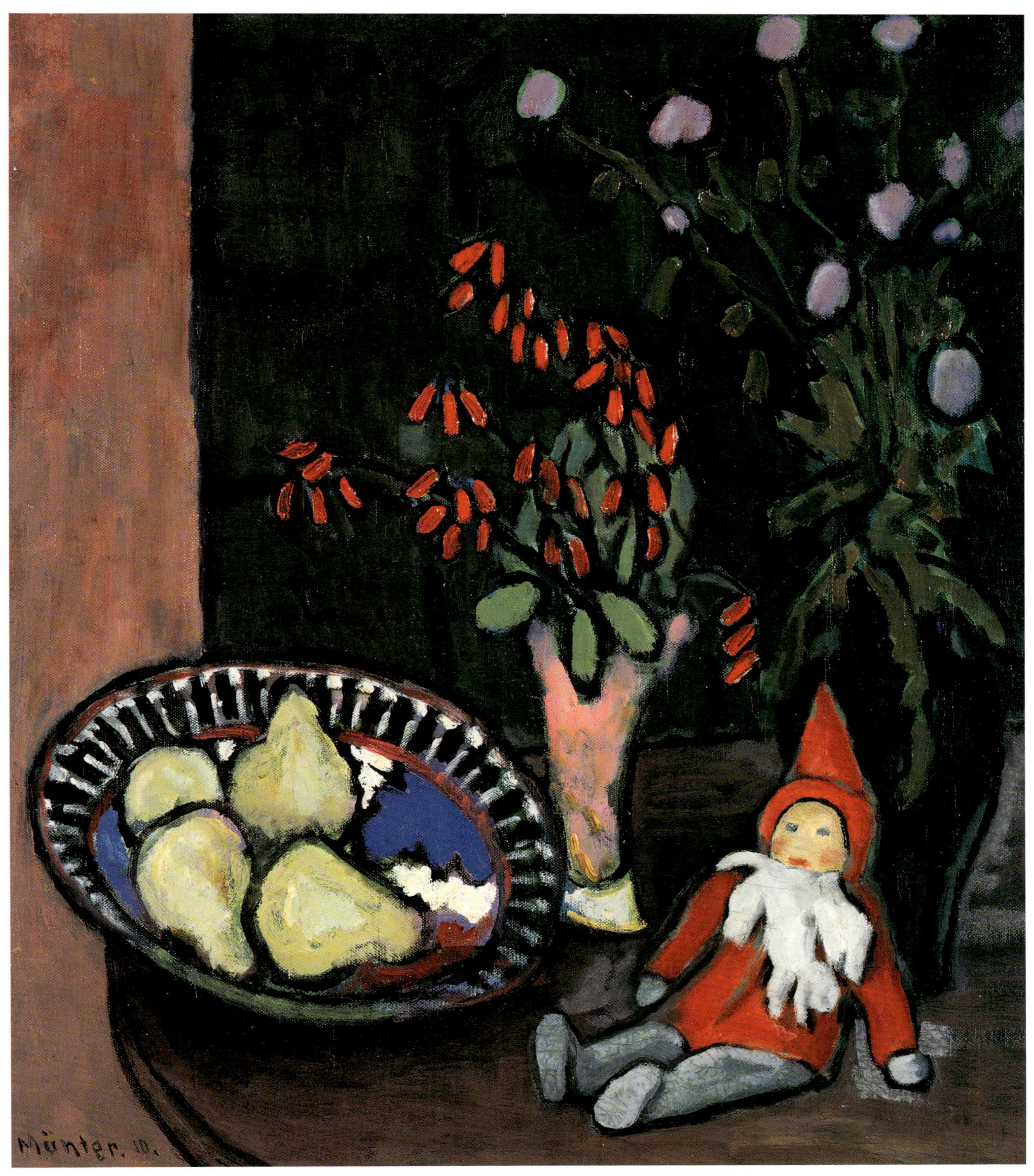

Still Life with Elf, 1910 (Cat. No. 43)

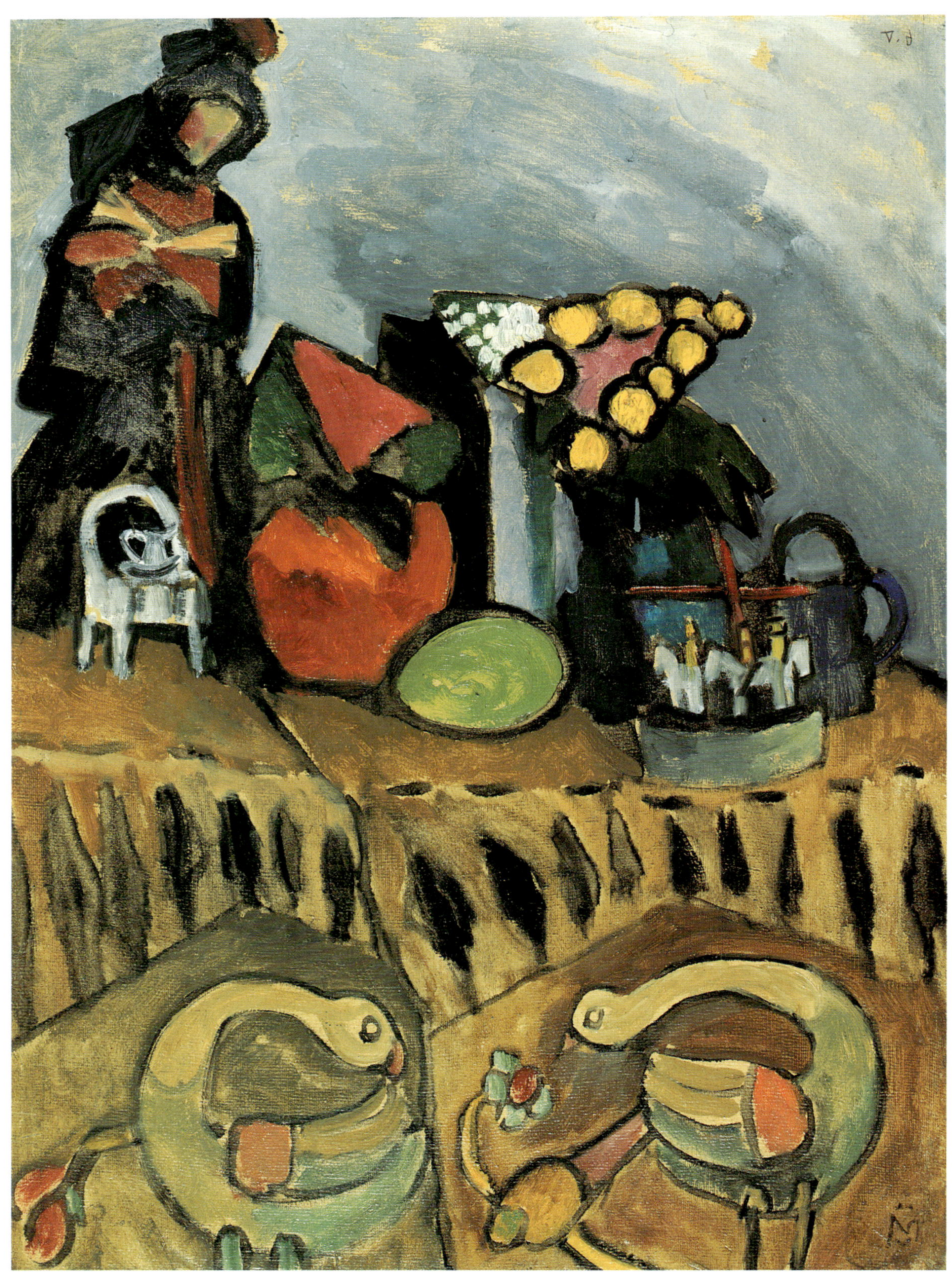

Still Life with Russian Tablecloth, 1910 (Cat. No. 42)

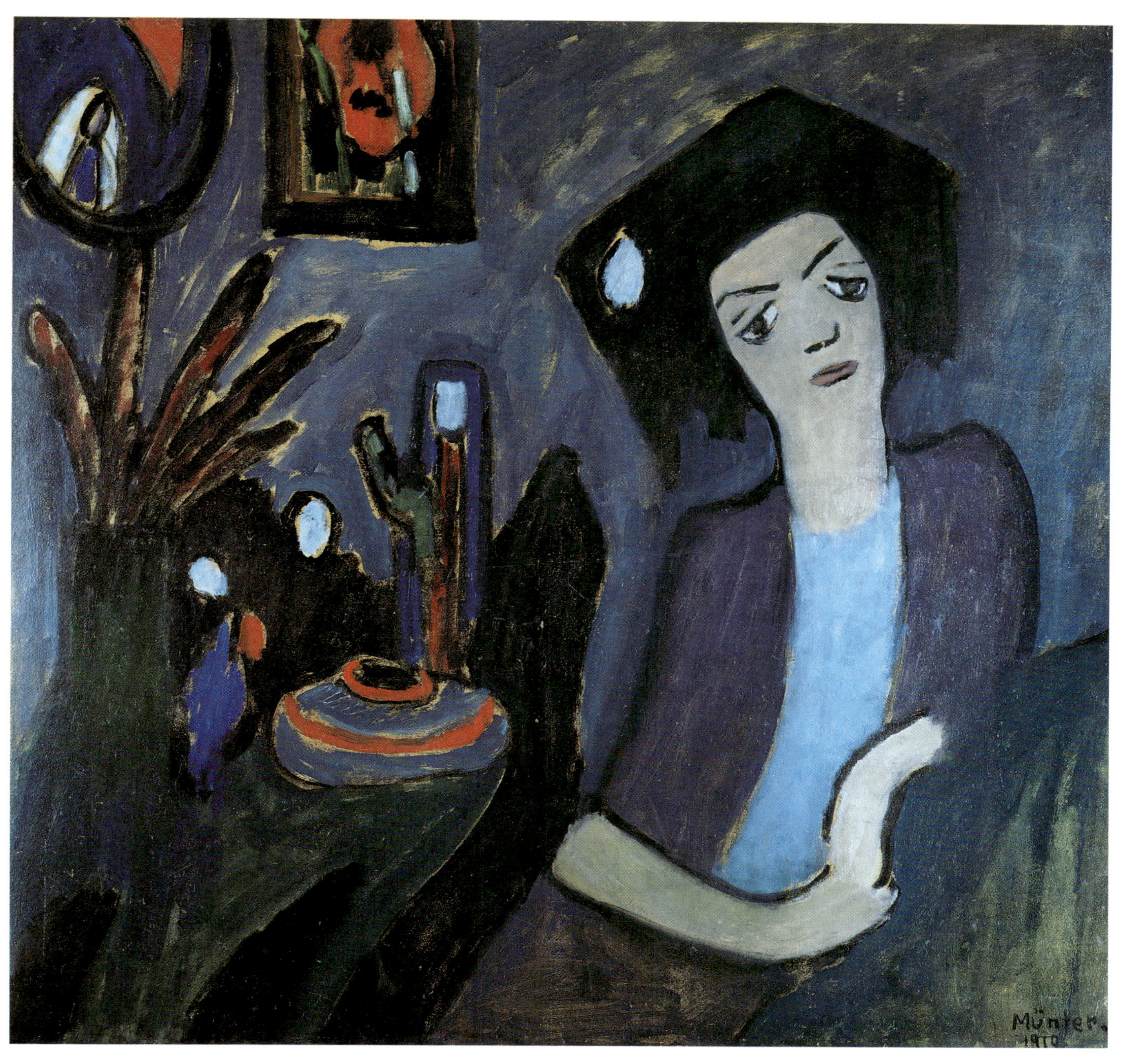

Still Life with Figure II (Mrs. Simonovich), 1910 (Cat. No. 44)

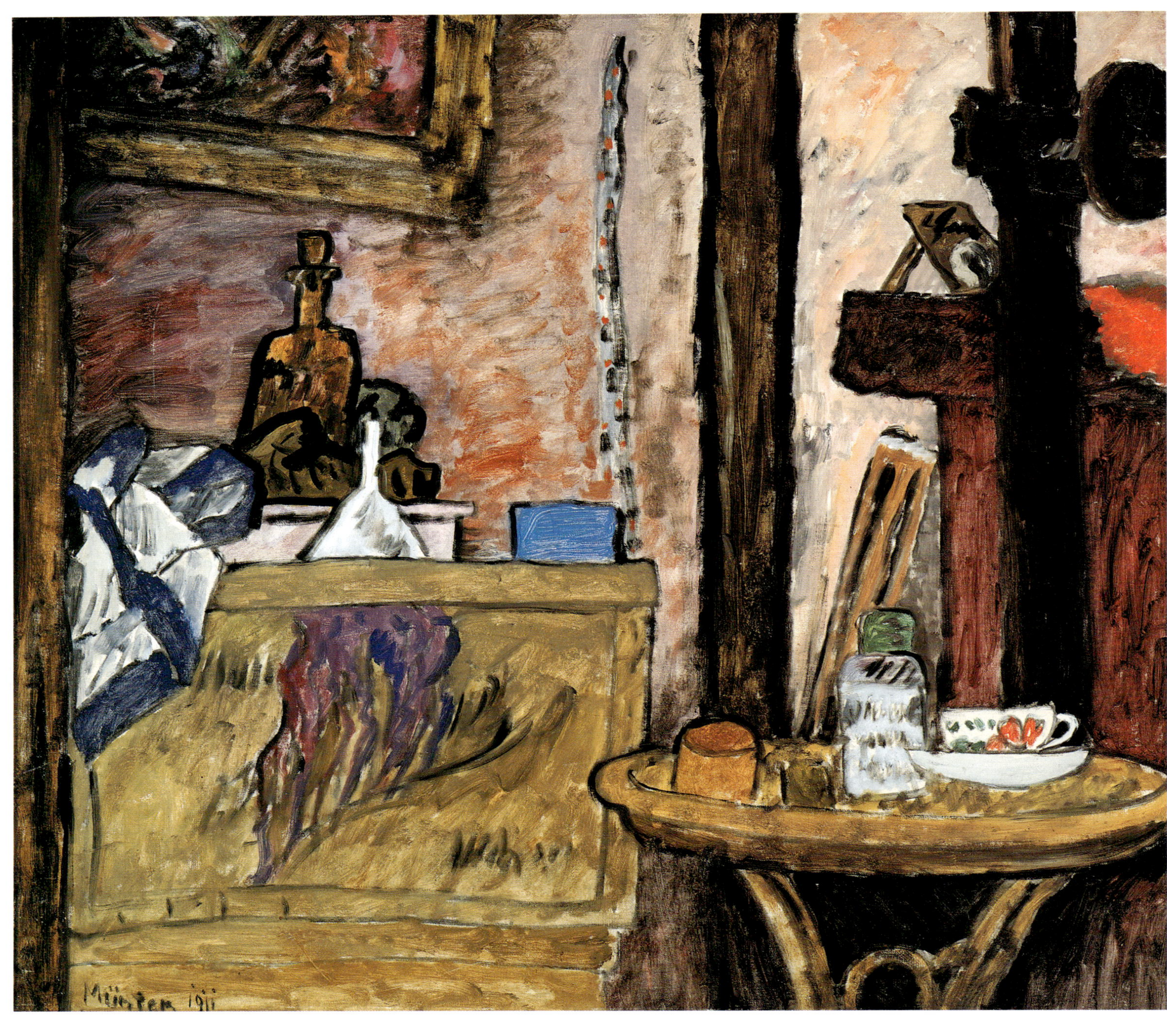

Still Life, Pink, 1911 (Cat. No. 53)

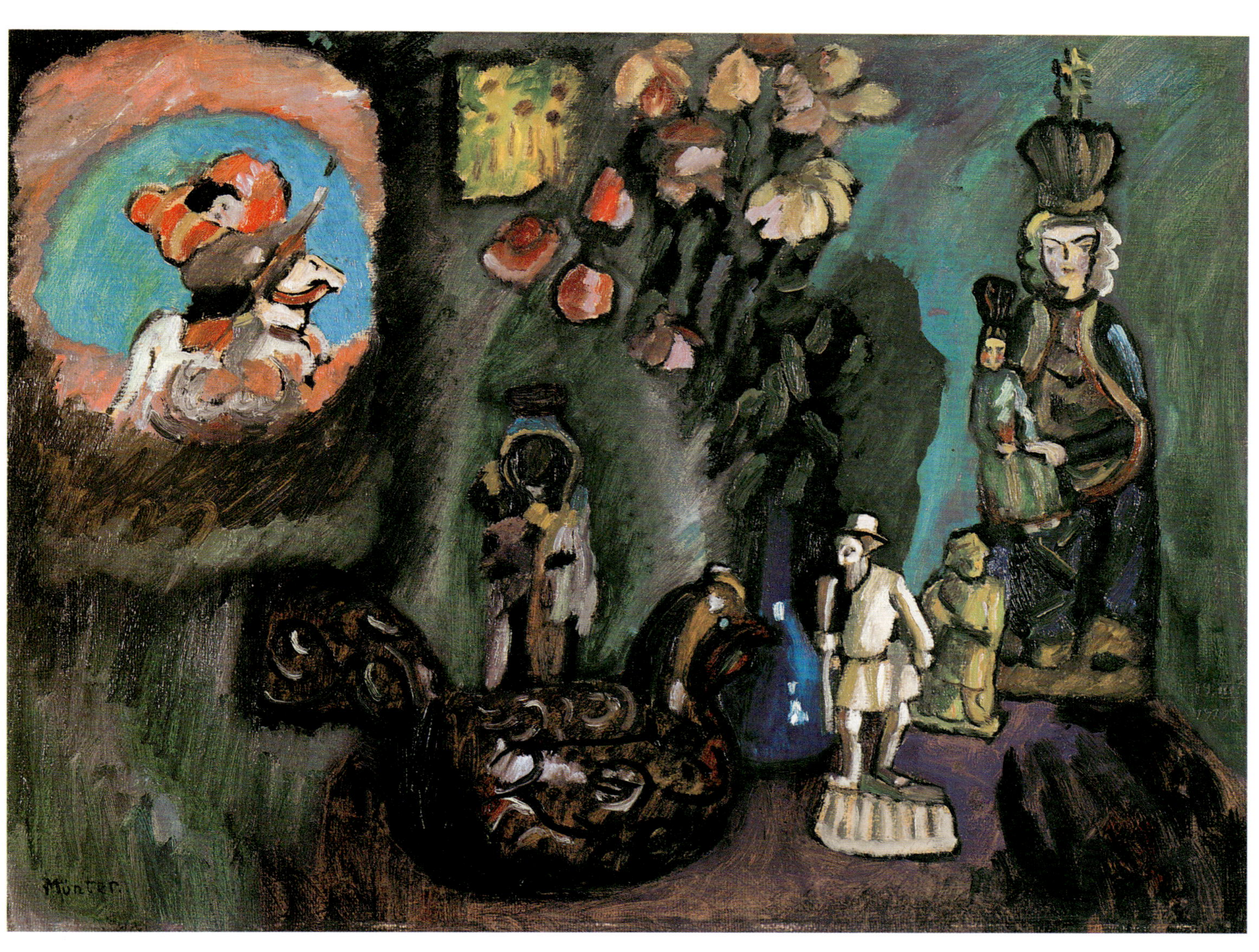

Still Life with Saint George, 1911 (Cat. No. 54)

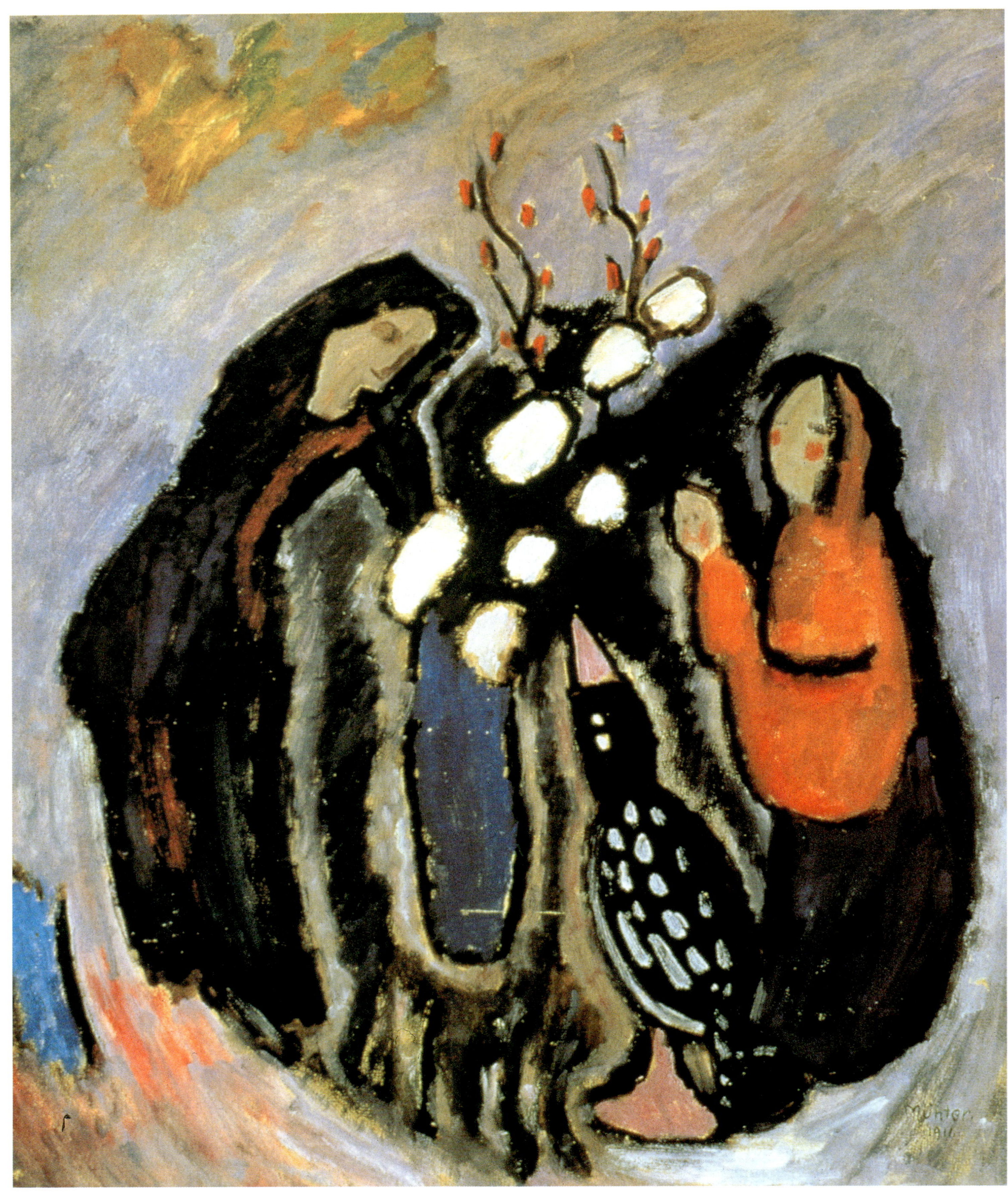

Still Life in Circle, 1911 (Cat. No. 52)

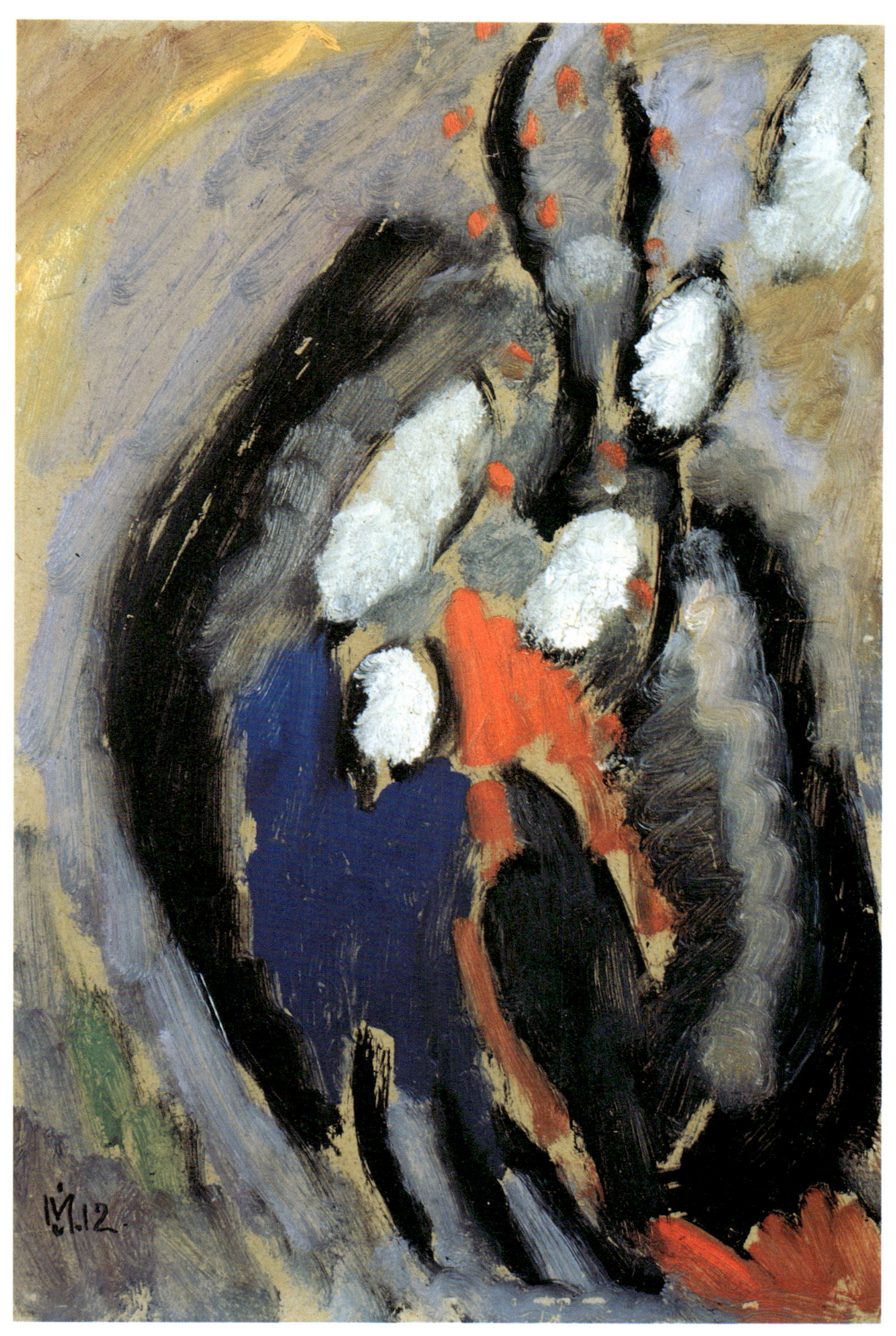

Study with White Spots, 1912 (Cat. No. 62)

consciously rejected many social preconceptions, mores and moral precepts.

Women in streetcars, buses or trains, subject to the gazes of whoever sat opposite them, have frequently been depicted in both high art and popular imagery since the mid-nineteenth century. Generally depicted by male artists, the beauty of these women was usually accentuated or, alternatively, they were caricatured in matronly plainness. Münter eliminated all such references. The manner in which the woman is depicted as she sits in the streetcar with her packages and purse testifies to Münter's sympathy for and understanding of her peer. Münter's vision and focus, defined through her sex, encompassed a different reality than what her male contemporaries presented. Her vision necessarily echoed the limits imposed on her sex, but also reflected her own interests.

It was Kandinsky, Münter recalled, who taught her to paint small segments and fragments of the scenes she saw.[5] Although she was referring to landscapes and the reduction of expansive vistas to an amalgamation of segments, she applied this technique to her still-life images as well, as *Return from Shopping* clearly demonstrates. She depicted the milieu around her in terms of its fragments, isolated and dissociated from their surroundings, with new signification gained in their very separation and their enhanced juxtapositions. The lino- and woodcuts from the "Toys" series of 1908 (Cat. No. 14) anticipated this process, but Münter radicalized it in her paintings after her first summer spent in Murnau. She manipulated not only juxtapositions but also the very manner of viewing objects. Often their precise identity is rendered uncertain by means of drastic simplification and the arbitrary use of the picture's edges to cut off portions of an object that would clarify what it is.

In *Still Life, Yellow* (Cat. No. 30), the base of a lamp appears behind a platter of fruit and nuts set on a table. Its darkly outlined form is filled in with one of the various shades of yellow that are a theme of the painting, while the base is cut off at the upper edge of the picture, just where one would expect the lamp shade to appear. As a result, the lamp base cannot serve as a viable reference. Just enough of its form is presented to enable the viewer to identify it as perhaps a vase or a stand, which infuses uncertainty and equivocation into the reading of the still life. This semiotic ambiguity emphasizes the lamp base as a formal note in the harmonious composition. Münter uses the questioned identity of the lamp base to draw attention to it, lending it significant weight in the viewer's visual perception despite the simplicity of its rendering—no more than two dark lines curving back on themselves—and the golden neutrality of its color.

A small wooden toy, an intensely blue vase and a vibrantly red platter with apples and nuts complete the inventory of the objects portrayed in this still life. Each isolated and set against the yellow-green of the table and the surrounding background, the objects do not combine to form a harmonious arrangement as is common to still-life painting. Unlike the artists of traditional still lifes—in which various comestibles or flowers are grouped together, displaying a certain degree of coherence—Münter, in this painting, accords greater significance to each pictorial element by depicting disparate objects that exhibit no signs of affinity or kinship. The viewer's gaze jumps abruptly from one contained area of color to another within the large yellow-green field of the painting so that only the separate realities of the platter, the toy, the vase and the lamp base are readily identifiable. Similarly, the flatness of the representation and the absence of shadows, as well as the heavy outlines delineating each object, lift the image out of the realm of naturalistic illusionism, placing it in a realm of signs or hieroglyphs, each distinct from the other and categorically separate.

Münter provides no uniting principle or category to serve as a link between the still-life objects or to explain why they are seen together. As in *Return from Shopping*, however, there is a certain logic in the arbitrariness of the juxtapositions. Arranged on a table near a lamp, whose light may serve to justify the overwhelming yellow of the image, the objects' placement is the result of common happenstance. Apples and walnuts, an empty vase and a child's Christmas toy, even the need for artificial light, together imply that it is winter, but otherwise they represent a relatively ordinary collection of objects commonly placed on a table—a collection in which the toy alone appears out of place. It provides the major sense of disjuncture that requires explanation, just as its form and the blue-red-white-gold color combination make it visually the most complex object in the painting despite its small size. Moreover, as a representation of a human figure, the plaything casts the relativity of scale in the table display into doubt, further threatening its internal logic, continuing to push the ordinary towards the extraordinary.

Münter's still lifes assault the commonality of objects. They grant significance to the mundane, and exalt their reality from the commonplace to poetic prominence. She continued the historical practice of rhopography, "...the depiction of those things which lack importance, the unassuming base of life that 'importance' constantly overlooks,"[6] whose goal lay precisely in granting visual appeal to the overlooked, but broke with its logical unity, as she accented modernist, Expressionist disjunction and fragmentation instead. However, even as in her painting vocabulary she pioneered Expressionism, her commitment to the still life was not shared by other artists associated with the movement. Only Jawlensky and August Macke, both admirers of Münter's work, painted a significant number of still lifes; others avoided them.[7] Münter's sex is important, not because it somehow gave her a predisposition to still lifes, but because the still life was little valued by other Expressionist artists, almost all of whom were male.

In the all-male domain of the German art academies, still life retained its traditional academic rank as the least important of the genres of painting

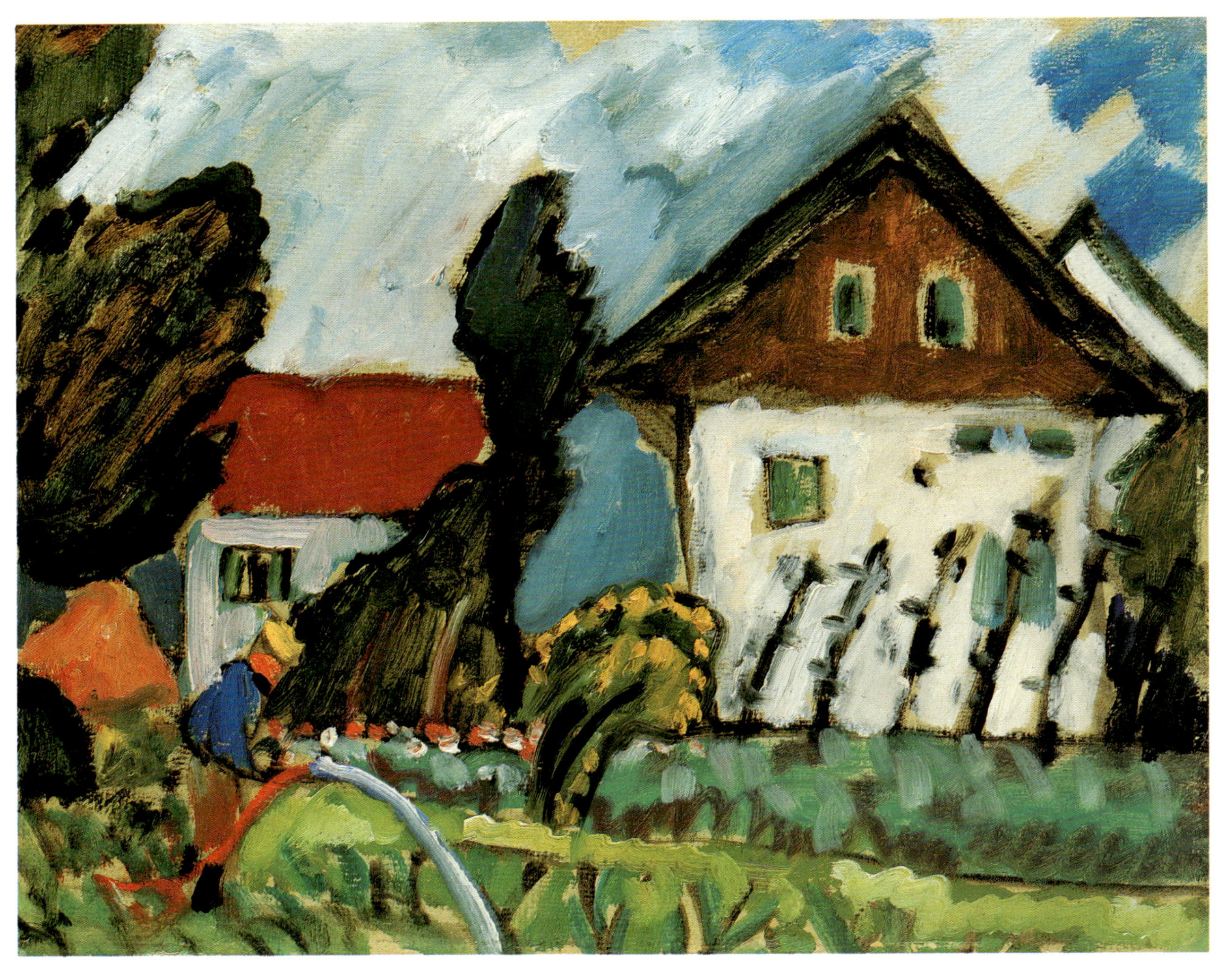

Country Homes (Kandinsky in the Garden), 1912 (Cat. No. 64)

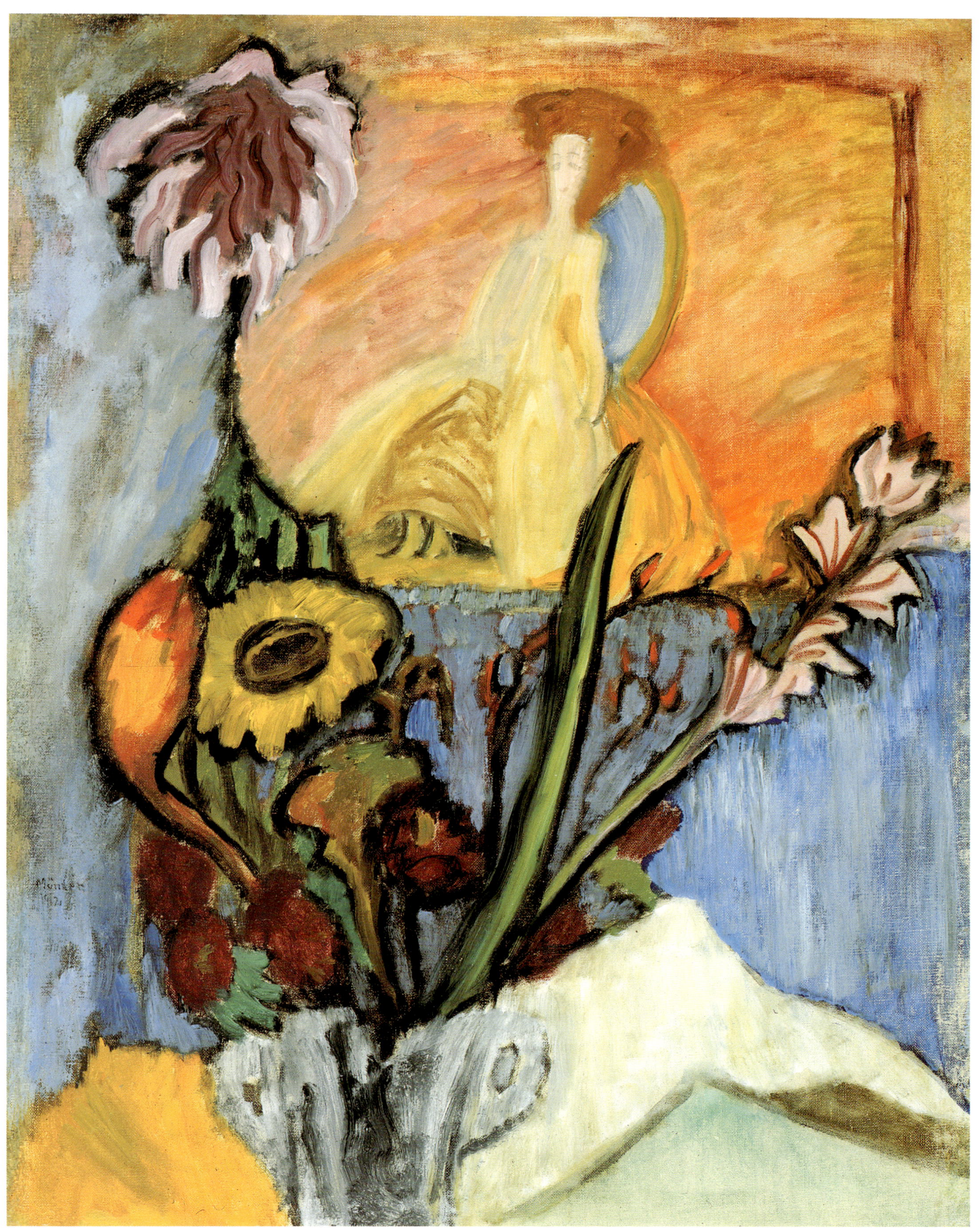

Still Life with Queen, 1912 (Cat. No. 65)

and found few practitioners. In a system where figure painting was supreme, still-life painting was relegated to those students who were unsuccessful. It did, however, have a sizable following at the schools of applied arts, where women were allowed to matriculate; similarly, at the various private art schools established notably for women at the end of the nineteenth century still life was taught. The still life, therefore, was widely viewed as a woman's genre, practiced by the "tribe" of female dilettantes so popularly decried and ridiculed by progressive and conservative artists and critics alike. Münter's consistent presentation of still-life paintings in the fora of public exhibitions from 1909 onwards placed her in danger of being dismissed as an amateur artist by confirming common preconceptions regarding the sex of still-life painters. But it was also a bold move in an attempt to counter precisely such dismissals of still lifes as insignificant "women's work." Her still lifes were in direct competition with the ambitious art of progressive male artists. Possibly inspired by the great role still life played in the contemporary French avant-garde, in which the leading Fauve and the early Cubist painters consistently employed still-life motifs, Münter's rhopographic images were not separated, isolated or diminished, but rather demanded recognition as being equal to her male counterparts' overtly ambitious, non-still-life exhibition entries.

In her campaign to accord the still life the same status as that of other paintings, Münter's practice of distorting her mundane subject matter by means of fragmentation and disjunctive juxtaposition was a tactic to garner recognition. She combined this technique with the use of intense color harmonies in which she drenched the still-life image with a single, rich, dominant color, as in *Still Life, Yellow*. With it and three other still lifes, in a total of ten paintings, she premiered at the first exhibition of the New Artists' Association Munich in December 1909, the exhibition that inaugurated avant-garde Expressionism in Munich. Encouraged by Kandinsky, Münter defined her art precisely by accentuating still life, employing its motifs to foster the innovations of Expressionist modernism, endowing still life with a radicalism antithetical to preconceptions of the genre as "women's work."

Similarly, for the Salon d'Automne in October 1909, where she exhibited two paintings, she selected a still life to represent her; likewise, for the layout devoted to her work in the periodical *Tendances Nouvelles*, she chose another of her monochrome paintings, *Still Life, Red* (Cat. No. 31).[8] Again, the inventory of objects depicted, all with dark outlines and highly stylized, flat ideational representations, is readily discernable: a round table covered with a red tablecloth and a background of red-violet; a glass pitcher holding red zinnias with a single banana and apples arranged around it; in the foreground, a small American flag. Disrupting what would otherwise be a standard European still-life motif of flowers and fruit is the prominent flag, which appears as if enframed between the fruit-filled green and red platters, accented in its central placement to achieve prominence. With its red and white stripes, and its blue field with white, in its rectangular forms and in its color combinations the little flag breaks with the character of the rest of the painting, where organic and rounded forms dominate in various shades of red and the corresponding green and green-yellow color complementaries. A conceptual and a coloristic dissonance imbues the image owing to the presence of the flag.

Münter's practice of giving her still lifes titles according to their dominant color is indicative of an aesthetic in which formal or abstract values prevail over motifs and subject matter. In this she confirmed the beliefs concisely stated by Kandinsky in the founding manifesto of the New Artists' Association Munich,[9] and reiterated by him in a brochure printed on the occasion of the Association's second exhibition in September 1910:

> Cold calculation, patches leaping at random, mathematically exact construction (clearly apparent or concealed), silent, screaming drawing, meticulous working out, fanfares of colors, their violin pianissimo, great, calm, heavy, disjunctive surfaces.
> Is this not form?
> Is this not the *means*?[10]

With his enthusiastic catalogue of contrasting formal attributes, Kandinsky identifies form as the fundamental means of art and rejects thereby subject matter as a major criterion. Accordingly, "Red" was considered an aptly descriptive subtitle for Münter's still life, and the flag's presence could be suppressed or subsumed within this coloristic domination. She adopted the practice, initially applied by James McNeill Whistler and emulated by numerous artists at the end of the nineteenth century, of painting moodily nuanced "nocturnes" and other monochromatic images. Around 1910, other than Münter, the most noted practitioner of such "color harmonies," using intensely expressive colors, was Henri Matisse, although it is uncertain whether she knew of this aspect of his work then. "I am sure you are aware," she wrote to Kandinsky while he was in Moscow in 1910, "that I never think how does so-and-so do it or how did I see it in this or that picture. I had to try various techniques myself...."[11] She was trying to assure the ever professionally and personally jealous Kandinsky that, during his absence, she had not begun emulating Jawlensky's painting or even that of Picasso, but her avowal of a lack of concern for the art of others and of her need to experiment independently correspond to her working habits at the time. She absorbed influences from Van Gogh, Gauguin, Matisse and Munch, but less through direct emulation than by obtaining similar effects to those recalled from their paintings through her own means.

In 1909, the monochromatic redness, the severe simplification and the conspicuous stylization of forms in *Still Life, Red*, all of which broke with

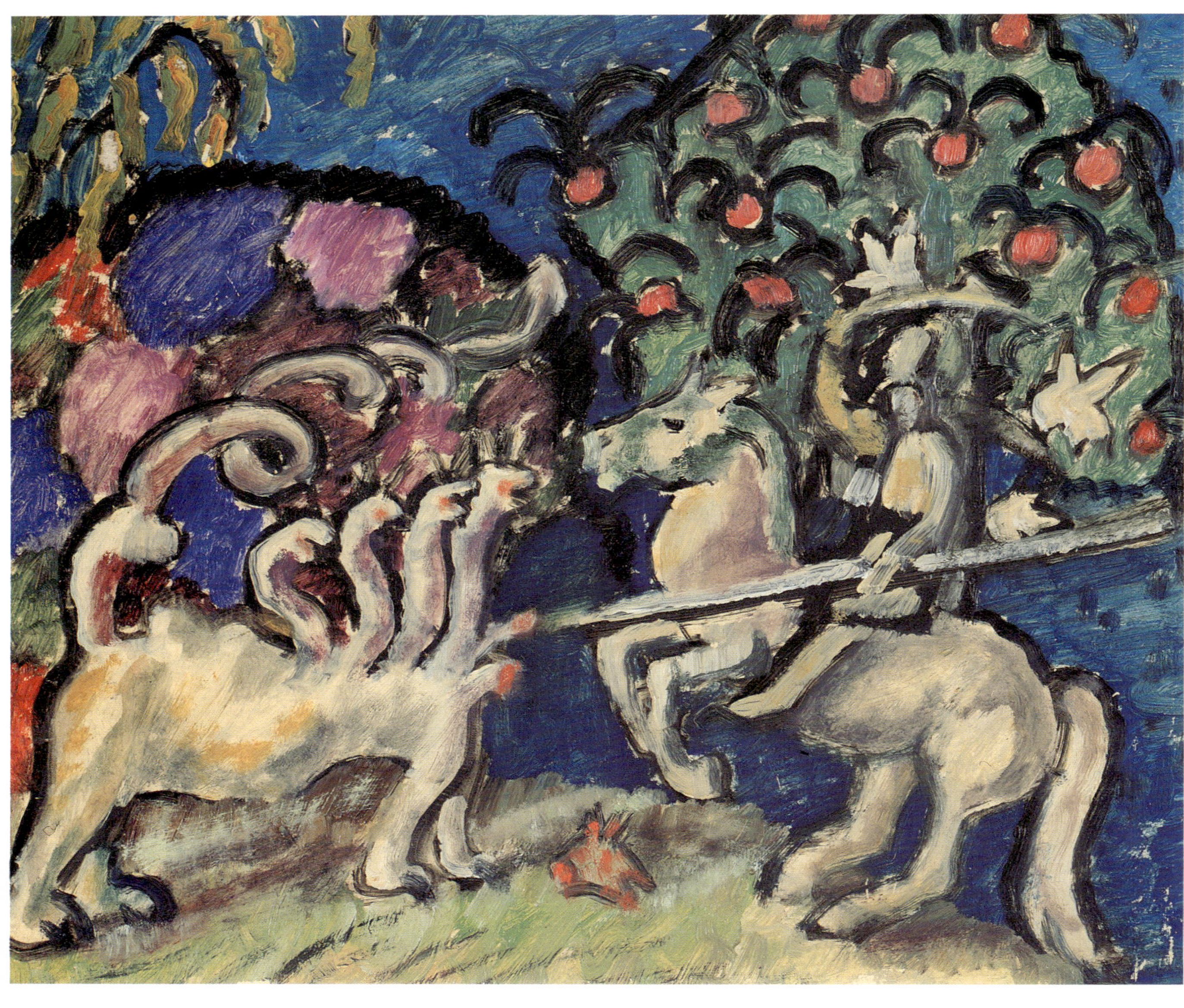

Dragon Fight, 1913 (Cat. No. 68)

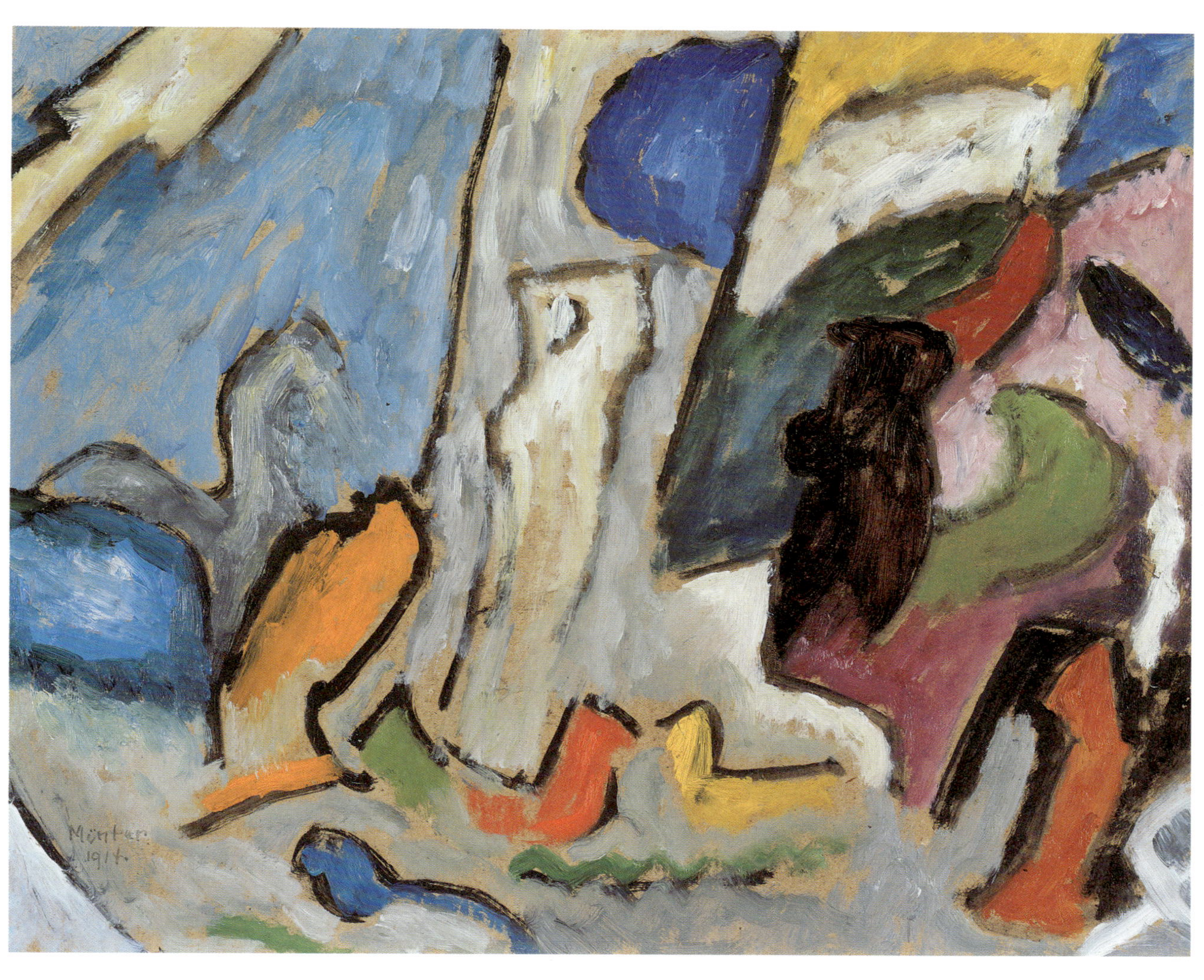

Still Life Abstract (Abstraction), 1914 (Cat. No. 70)

established as well as more progressive *Jugendstil* and Impressionist norms, would have attracted an exhibition visitor's attention. Within the still-life vocabulary, the American flag, likewise, would have stood out as incongruous in the German or French settings where Münter displayed her work. The note of incongruity, of being out of place, is removed only once one knows of Münter's personal links with the United States and recognizes the flag as a souvenir of her earlier lengthy trip there. Then the still life's disruptive juxtapositions become resolved in a recognition of Münter's milieu, her interests and her past. But this is privileged information, so to speak, which we today share, but which the exhibition visitors who were Münter's contemporaries and whom her art addressed did not know. To them, the flag was necessarily an odd intrusion, its presence inexplicable except perhaps as an exotic reference to the world of Teddy Roosevelt or of Karl May's popular adventure novels of Indian life, resonating with European conceptions of an only half-civilized America, and reasserting the "wildness" of Münter's Expressionist style.

Münter arranged her home and surroundings into still-life compositions. "Still lifes are tempted forth from every corner," she wrote to Kandinsky. "With all the flowers it is *so* wonderful here."[12] Particularly a small table with objects on it—"the table near my armchair with many Madonnas and flowers"[13]—continually intrigued her. In *Still Life with Armchair* (Cat. No. 32), the table covered in red merges with the seat of the wine-red chair as Münter collapses the space between them into a synthetic flatness by means of thin paint brushed onto cardboard and bordered in meandering dark lines. On the table, a blossoming azalea and other smaller flowers and vases serve as substitutes for a human presence in the chair. The background wall glows in complementary yellow-orange and green shadows, while it displays an ornate ceramic plate as if it were a sun shining in a brilliant sunset. Even as they remain readily recognizable, the surface-adherent forms and shapes take on semi-independent existences, moving in and out of discernible identities according to the degree of their stylization, as they interact with each other in their shadowy, moody surroundings.

Such paintings represent virtual inventories of her possessions and of the interior environments she created. For her audience, Münter's comfortable and "wonderful" surroundings become picture puzzles, dream landscapes whose "banality is to be deciphered," as Walter Benjamin put it,[14] since their prosaic quality has already been transmuted into synthetic color harmonies by Münter. Her gaze frequently took in not only corners and segments of rooms, but the interior beyond them as well. *Sill Life, Pink* (Cat. No. 53) depicts her studio in 1911, drenches it in pink and somber wine-red tonalities, and allows its objects—stovepipes, easels, tables, paintings, cups, bottles, a samovar and a tablecloth—to intermingle in a depersonalized atmosphere of brooding unreality. A large painting on canvas, a medium Münter used only for ambitious "syntheses" while she painted "studies" and "notes" on cardboard,[15] it was included as a key image in the first Blue Rider Exhibition that opened in December 1911. Along with a work by Franz Marc, it flanked Kandinsky's monumental *Composition V*, the painting whose rejection by the New Artists' Association Munich exhibition jury precipitated his, Münter's and Marc's resignation from the organization. The three paintings joined together in a virtual triptych that functioned as a visual manifesto of the Blue Rider's Expressionist aesthetic.[16] Next to Kandinsky's grand apocalyptic composition and its mystical message of abstraction, Münter's studio scene provided a vision of the mundane lifted into a sphere of emotive signification. In a twilight atmosphere, her shadowed, silhouetted forms loom enigmatically, and are only vaguely decipherable as fragmented objects dematerialized or transformed into painted ciphers of an artist's reality, the workspace in which the painting was conceived.

With its programmatic ambition, *Still Life, Pink* is unusual in Münter's work as it manifests her interpretation of the Blue Rider's artistic credo, for which Kandinsky supplied most of the theoretical formulations in his writings of 1910–12, notably his book *Concerning the Spiritual in Art* and the essay "On the Question of Form" in *The Blaue Reiter Almanac.* Münter seldom wrote significantly about her work at this time, but when she did briefly, as in her letters to Kandinsky, she applied formulations held in common with him. Concern with authenticity, with inner truth or necessity, with contemplative inwardness and synthesis is constantly reiterated. With regard to a still-life arrangement painted in Murnau and composed of a table, a lamp and a chair, she wrote to Kandinsky: "Not bad at all—there's something of myself in it. [I] believe it's one of my good, inward ones. At least more inward than externally oriented! Because the external [objects] are really not significant at all."[17] The world of ordinary reality is transformed as she renders it to contain or emanate her own personality and inner vision. A freely drawn, seemingly hastily rendered, linear scaffolding and thinly brushed coloration with its readily discernible ductus of brushstrokes makes visible in *Still Life, Pink* the process of her work on the canvas, thereby lending testimony to her painterly activity and its interpretive function, rejecting all notions of naturalistic illusionism. Testimony to the artist's activity, the artist's personality and personal reality and to the artist's inner vision becomes primary. With black outlines and flattened forms in an antinaturalistic illumination and space, the objects in Münter's studio form a synthetic material reality as a painting that should reverberate in the viewer's soul, as Kandinsky wrote later:

> The vibration in the soul of the artist must ... find a material form, a means of expression, which is capable of being picked up by the receiver. This material form is the ... external element of the work of art. The work of art is the inseparable, indispensable, unavoidable combination

> of the internal and the external element, i.e. of content and form.... Form is the material expression of abstract content.[18]

In effect, Münter's programmatic painting of her studio depicts the site where the quasi-mystical transubstantiation from material to artistic reality takes place, the mundane locale of artistic activity, where objects are arranged as if on altars, awaiting their sacrificial interaction with an artist, a virtual priest.

Münter began her series of still-life interiors in 1908 (Cat. No. 16). Many of these paintings possess the brooding colorism, wine reds and yellows glowing amid deep blues and greens and muted violets, that characterizes *Still Life, Pink* and lends the images a sense of the mysterious and the mystical, an almost sacerdotal content. *Interior (Still Life, Bedroom)* of 1909 (Cat. No. 33) differs as it instead offers a study in bright illumination, of pale yellow greens, whites and yellow-ocher, that contrasts with the darkness apparent through the window. A private rather than a public image, without overt programmatic content—and apparently not exhibited by Münter—it depicts Münter's bedroom at the summer house she bought in Murnau at Kandinsky's urging in 1909. A comfortable openness pervades the scene owing to the intense illumination which, notably, casts no shadows as it delineates precisely the various objects in the room. Dressers, a washstand, pitchers, a water bucket, towels, a rag rug, pictures on the wall, a rucksack, sandals and shoes—all are itemized, while Kandinsky, visible in the adjoining room through an open door, reclines in bed and reads. With its simple peasant furnishings, some of which Münter and Kandinsky painted with decorative patterns and scenes, its extensive surrounding garden and its location in Murnau, the house functioned as a refuge from Munich's urban milieu. "The sole love to which Kandinsky remained true," it also provided a site for Münter and Kandinsky to be together in harmony—conceived to be a place devoid of the frequent strife that marked their relationship and the otherwise necessary professional distractions of exhibitions and artists' organizations. In a remarkable mixture of the traditional and the modern, the "peasant market town" of Murnau, newly refurbished, served as an environmental frame and could be panoramically viewed from the house in Kottmüllerallee, a summer *Jugendstil* villa constructed in modified forms of the indigenous domestic architecture of southern Bavaria, using local materials and accenting the relationship between dwelling and landscape. As they wore simple clothing based on Bavarian folk costumes, Münter and Kandinsky entered into a bourgeois masquerade in which their domestic space and private life of a perceived peasant-like simplicity acted therapeutically to alleviate the travail of urban everyday life.[19] In the brightly illuminated work, whose precursors include the bedroom paintings of Adolf Menzel and Vincent van Gogh, Münter portrays a private realm devoid of conflict, as the interior space "...disguises itself [and], like an enticing creature, dons the costumes of its moods."[20] It was Münter's painted dream in which the house, particularly its nucleus of bedrooms, served as a physical testimony to the artists' "marriage of conscience," in which they "work on [their] own a lot & yet [are] together—going for walks and so forth!"[21]

Still Life, Pink and *Interior (Still Life, Bedroom)*, each conceptually different, demonstrate the stylistic scope to which Münter had recourse during the years she spent in Murnau and Munich before 1914, and which ranged from expressive color harmonies to relatively objective renderings of a scene—a variety that disturbed her as she failed to settle on a single stylistic approach. In a letter written to Kandinsky in 1910, she asked: "... how am I going to find 'form' ... anyway[?] What is appropriate? What not? Should one paint, as I do, in a variety of ways? These are really nothing but experiments."[22] Moreover, in her still lifes, she continued to approach the realm of abstraction in which the depicted objects and their individual identity became subsumed in the effect of colors and brushstroke renderings. In *Still Life with Russian Tablecloth* (Cat. No. 42), the massive figuration of the tablecloth decoration already tends to overwhelm the still-life arrangement. As was her practice before, here, she juxtaposes realities in such a fashion as to cast doubt on the various orders to which the elements belong. The process, with different means, likewise takes place in *Still Life with Queen* (Cat. No. 65), as she incorporates a puppet of a queen presented to her and Kandinsky by the Russian dancer, Alexander Sacharoff, into a complex still life of flowers. With all colors—yellow, red, orange, blue, green and even black—mixed with white, the painting takes on an unusual tone of lightness for Münter's work. But more importantly, she worked these colors into a type of catalogue of brushstroke effects, employing different types of paint application in the foreground and background, whose division is interrupted by the pink flower that extends upwards, from the bouquet below to the enframed area of the queen above. The effect, however, melds the two spatial areas as the disparity in scale between flowers and figure distinguishes them in an inverse relationship of scale, where the human figure seems diminished next to the flowers below. "The still life by Münter shows that a dissimilar and uneven translation of objects in one and the same painting not only are not harmful, but when used properly will achieve a strong, complicated inner resonance," Kandinsky noted. "The accord that externally has a disharmonious effect in this case is the origin of the inner harmonious effect."[23]

This effect of doubled confusion occurs in part because artifact and human become interchangeable in Münter's still lifes, as she disrupts expected continuities of scale by substituting a world of figurines with the world of everyday experience. *Still Life in Circle* (Cat. No. 52) thus places a Madonna, a figurine from a manger scene, a small vase with pussy willows and a painted wooden bird in a new reality, enveloped in a circular ambience of violet, blue, pink and green that hints at a landscape arrangement. The folk figurines she and Kandinsky collected, part of the aestheticized interior milieu they manufactured for themselves, become the image's reality, but as in other works by her, it is a reality whose identification involves the privilege of historical research. To the contemporary viewer, the figurines read instead as actuality, as women next to an incongruously large bird and a vaguely inscribed tree-like formation, all submitted to the Expressionist distortions of Münter's painterly hand. This is a conceptual radicalism that readily vies with the abstraction towards which Kandinsky was simultaneously striving, offering an alternative, fundamentally surreal solution to the problems he formulated. Both artists suggested a vision not bound by the rules of ocular logic, but where Kandinsky projected a monumental abstraction of apocalyptic visions, Münter provided visionary poetry of the prosaic, the diminutive and the private, gleaned from the environment she inhabited and to which she was confined.

Portraits

In an implicit criticism of Vassily Kandinsky's concept of the "spiritual in art" and his emphasis on abstraction, but also of the early 1950s celebration of non-representational art to the exclusion of all else in Western Europe, Gabriele Münter wrote in 1952:

> The task of representing the human being is so great that I never felt myself tempted to go beyond it, for example to dissolve the human appearance, to submit it to willful reconstructions and to replace it with non-objective imagery. One may believe that in this manner the spiritual in itself is grasped, that in a certain sense the aura of the human is depicted, [or that] an analogue, a symbol is created. But the bodily appearance of the human being, specifically the face, is already a symbol. Because personality is rooted in the spiritual and is active from within the non-visible. For this non-visible, which is what matters, the visible body is the natural symbol.[1]

Broadly humanist values pervade this statement as Münter confirms her faith in the transcendence of the human and the individual, especially as manifested in the primacy of individual human visual experience as the source for artistic imagery. She likewise reaffirms the conviction long promulgated in Western European thought that the human body functions as an external sign of a person's spiritual essence. Dissatisfied with the conventional teachings of established Christianity, earlier in her life she had sought to communicate directly with this spiritual side, psyche or soul of individuals as she explored the teachings of theosophy and, especially during her years in Scandinavia, regularly participated in spiritualist séances. Art was another means for her to approach the spiritual in an individual, especially as the portrait interpreted physiognomy subjectively to make visible the invisible core of the person depicted. Raised to this level, portraits necessarily demand the attention of a true artist, not only of amateurs or those who paint portraits on commission to flatter the egos of their sitters:

> The portrait in our time has to do with the individual. To each their own! It is too insignificant a project, no more than simplistic copying? In photographs we can recognize how superficial, indeed, how frequently false appearance can be. The appropriate symbol must first be discovered from varied perspectives, from the momentary accidental expression. Then the laws of the image wait to take the objective up in

themselves and to give it form. And, in addition, the individual artist injects more or less conscious desires into the pictorial form. Thus, portrait making expands into being one of the greatest problems.... The painting of portraits is the boldest and the most difficult, the most spiritual, the most extreme task of the artist.[2]

Münter took pleasure in rendering likenesses. In her memoirs, she repeatedly refers to portrait drawing as her first endeavor as a child to approach art. She relished in telling the story of being fourteen years old, drawing portraits of guests at a summer spa, and how "... the adults found my likenesses to be so accurate that they enjoyed stealing them from me," or how, half a century after her journey to America, she sent portrait sketches made during it "...to the children of the people since then deceased as gifts of thanks for the nourishing packages sent to me during the difficult time after the war, and they were all delighted at how accurately life appeared before them in these pictures."

Particularly in portrait drawings, she consistently tested her observational ability and sought refuge from the doubts that plagued her with respect to her painted work. When she needed money during her stay in Scandinavia and during the 1920s and 1930s, she turned to her facility in painting portraits, though she often found herself toiling over a commission, not satisfied with her efforts. "There are cases," she wrote, "when the task of bringing what is presented, the commission, into harmony with artistic demands, with one's subjective convictions, is irresolvable.... I often got stuck in the forecourts of art." Nevertheless, she also filled numerous sketchbooks, from cover to cover, page after page, with quickly rendered portrait sketches of family members, friends and acquaintances, of people observed in cafés, at concerts and on trains.[3] The sketchbook "... was my friend, and the drawing [was] the record of my visual experiences. Especially then, it was people that interested me most in the world."[4]

As was standard academic practice, Münter's early formal training as an artist consisted in executing portrait drawings; when she graduated to painting, under Kandinsky's tutelage in 1902–03, she immediately employed oils to paint portrait images of him and of her family. Learning and mastering a technique, according to habits instilled in her, compelled her to experiment in portraiture. As part of her exploitation of the linocut medium between 1906 and 1908—initially formulating *Jugendstil*-inspired motifs possessing a synthetic quality—Münter experimented with portraits, in which the tension between the demands of stylistic reformulation and external likeness was most pronounced (Cat. Nos. 3–5). Facial features, here, were rendered in a shorthand of basic descriptive marks, with the recognizable forms of eyes, a nose or lips often suggested rather than depicted. In her portrait of Kandinsky (Cat. No. 3), he consists largely of broad, black and reserved planes ordered around the characterizing configuration of his face; complex

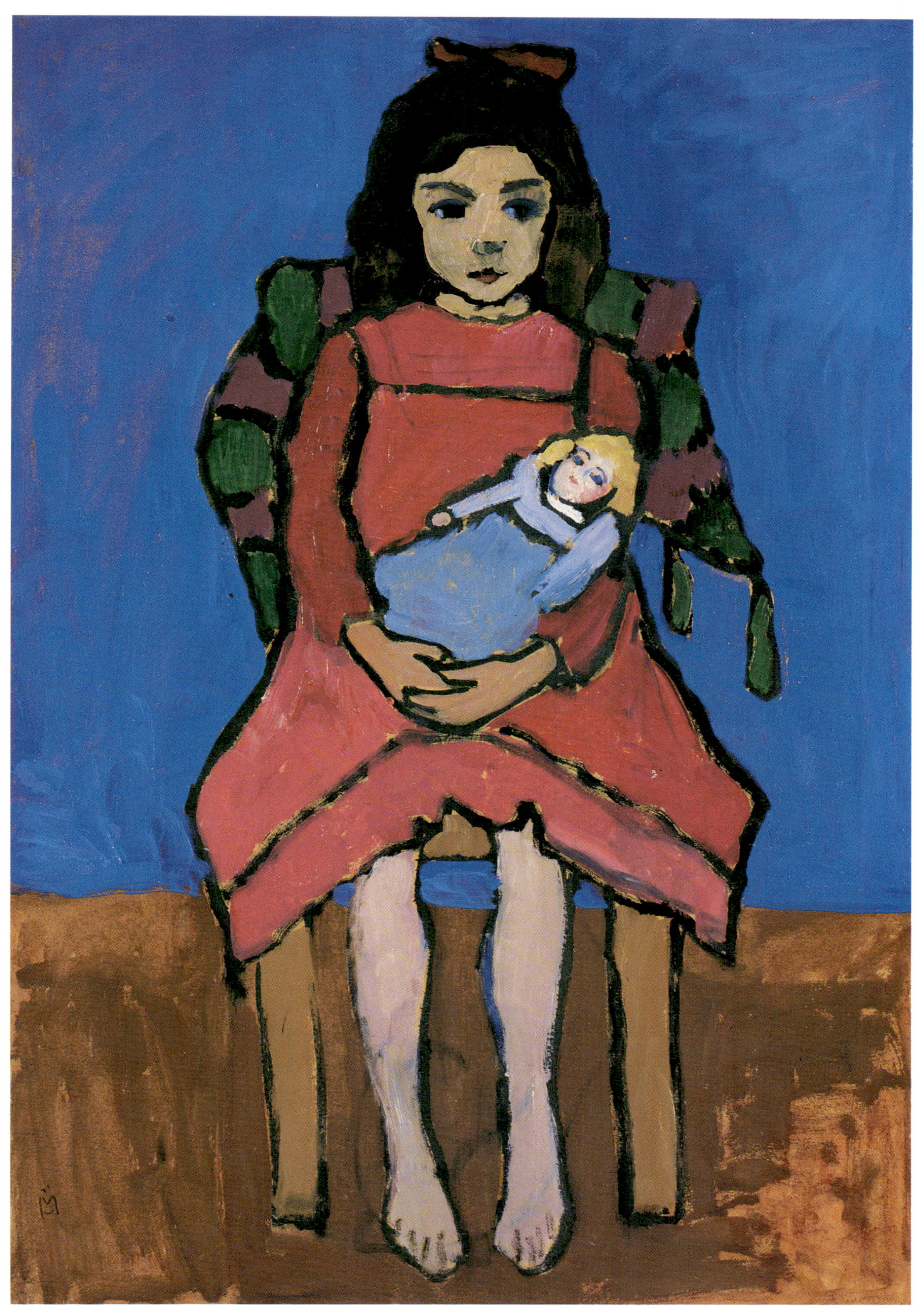

Girl with Doll, 1908/09 (Cat. No. 28)

patterns of shadow, decipherable only in the context they themselves shape, take on just enough referential order to become ciphers of eyes and a beard, seen against broad bands of color, outlined in black, that imply a synthetically conceived landscape. Reductivity is extreme in such a print, and yet the features of Münter's teacher-lover-mentor are, remarkably, immediately recognizable, demanding little effort of the viewer. In these linocut portraits of 1906, Münter established the principles that she proceeded to apply in her painted portraits, transferring the effects of one medium to another, when she resumed portraiture in Murnau.

Surrounded by a virtual theme park of Bavarian peasantry, Münter began her portraits in Murnau with depictions of people staying at the Griesbräu inn, like herself. Women posed in traditional folk costumes and the daughter of the innkeeper sat as model in her simple, unadorned skirt and blouse as Münter reverted to the type and character studies of peasant and working women, which she had been required to do at the Ladies' Academy. Returned to Munich after the first epochal Murnau trip, she turned her attention once more to her immediate surroundings. Her friends, as they came to visit her, were now the central motif of her portraiture, and in the ensuing five years she painted a veritable catalogue of the Munich artistic avant-garde. But it was a personally shaped catalogue, not an inclusive one, determined by who entered Münter's and Kandinsky's homes. Women—the wives and companions, mothers and daughters of the male artists and their admirers—dominate the inventory of Münter's Munich portraits.

In her new manner of portraiture and during the winter of 1908–09, Münter depicted a young Polish woman standing, her head turned slightly, her eyes downcast (Cat. No. 34).[5] Münter painted on canvas on a relatively large scale, unlike her more frequent smaller images on cardboard, indicating her ambitions for the work, and distinguishing it as a developed "synthesis" rather than a sketch or a study according to the terms she applied to her paintings. In the portrait she concentrated her current artistic aims. The image is kept extremely simple, with broad areas of glowing ultramarine blue and aqua used to define the plain background, against which the woman's jacket in wine red is seen, as it in turn enframes a yellow-green blouse with a pink necktie and a moss-green skirt. The face, in an unmodulated flesh color, is isolated by means of the small but intense white area of the blouse collar and a shock of golden brown hair on which rests a yellow-green hat with a wine red hatband. Differing brushstrokes and paint consistency generate a shifting surface effect, accenting both the flatness and the synthetic antinaturalism of the image, a quality further enhanced and stressed by means of the deep black lines drawn around all forms and used to delineate sparely the woman's facial features.

The influence of Jawlensky and, through him, Henri Matisse, has been postulated for this and other Münter paintings from the winter of 1908–09,[6] and indeed the kinship is undeniable. However, rather than simply emulating the two male artists and becoming a twice-removed, female Fauve epigone, Münter saw in their example confirmations of her own synthetic stylistic experiments in lino- and woodcuts. To a large extent, the *Portrait of a Young Woman* is the translation into paint—with painting's more intense coloration and grander scale—of the effects she achieved in her print portraits, and the ties to other artists' prototypes are secondary.

In particular, however, the portraits from the winter of 1908–09 raise another issue regarding influence and emulation in Münter's art; their celebration of the contour with heavy black outlines, broad flat color areas and the absence of shading three-dimensionality matches the practice of Bavarian *Hinterglasmalerei*, or reverse-glass painting. Murnau remained a center for the practice of this folk art, in which images, most often of religious motifs, are painted on the reverse of a pane of glass, to be viewed through the glass. Heinrich Rambold, one of the major artists to employ the technique at the beginning of the century, was active in Murnau, and a collection of over one thousand Bavarian, Swabian and Bohemian reverse-glass paintings—today housed in the Heimatmuseum of Oberammergau—was at that time publicly accessible.[7] Münter later recalled:

> Kandinsky and I were in the Tyrol (I believe it was spring 1907) and there saw wonderfully painted votive panels (*Marterln*) and such things—old folk art. But it seems to me that we first learned of reverse-glass paintings here in Murnau. It must have been Jawlensky who first made us aware of Rambold and the Krötz collection. We were all enchanted by these works. Rambold showed me that, and how, it could be done—and in Murnau I was the first, as far as I know, in the entire circle [of Munich artists] who took panes of glass and made some [glass paintings] myself. At first copies, but then various ones of my own.... I was fascinated by the technique and how easy it was and constantly told Kandinsky about it in order to inspire him to take it up as well.[8]

Münter's first copies of Rambold's paintings date from the winter of 1908–09.[9] Unlike Fauve painting, in Rambold's *Hinterglasmalerei*, the artist first inscribed the contours of an image onto what would become the back of the painting; these lines remained visible when viewed from the other side of the glass pane. The fields defined by the drawing were filled in with color, contrary to Matisse's technique of applying color first, adding contours and details later. This was a technique of painting in which drawing played a key role, permitting Münter to exploit what she perceived as her greatest strength as an artist; colors interacted in intense planar fields, allowing her to employ the theories of expressive color Kandinsky had taught her. "Whoever looks carefully at my paintings finds the draftsperson in them," she later wrote. "Despite all colorism, a firmly drawn scaffolding

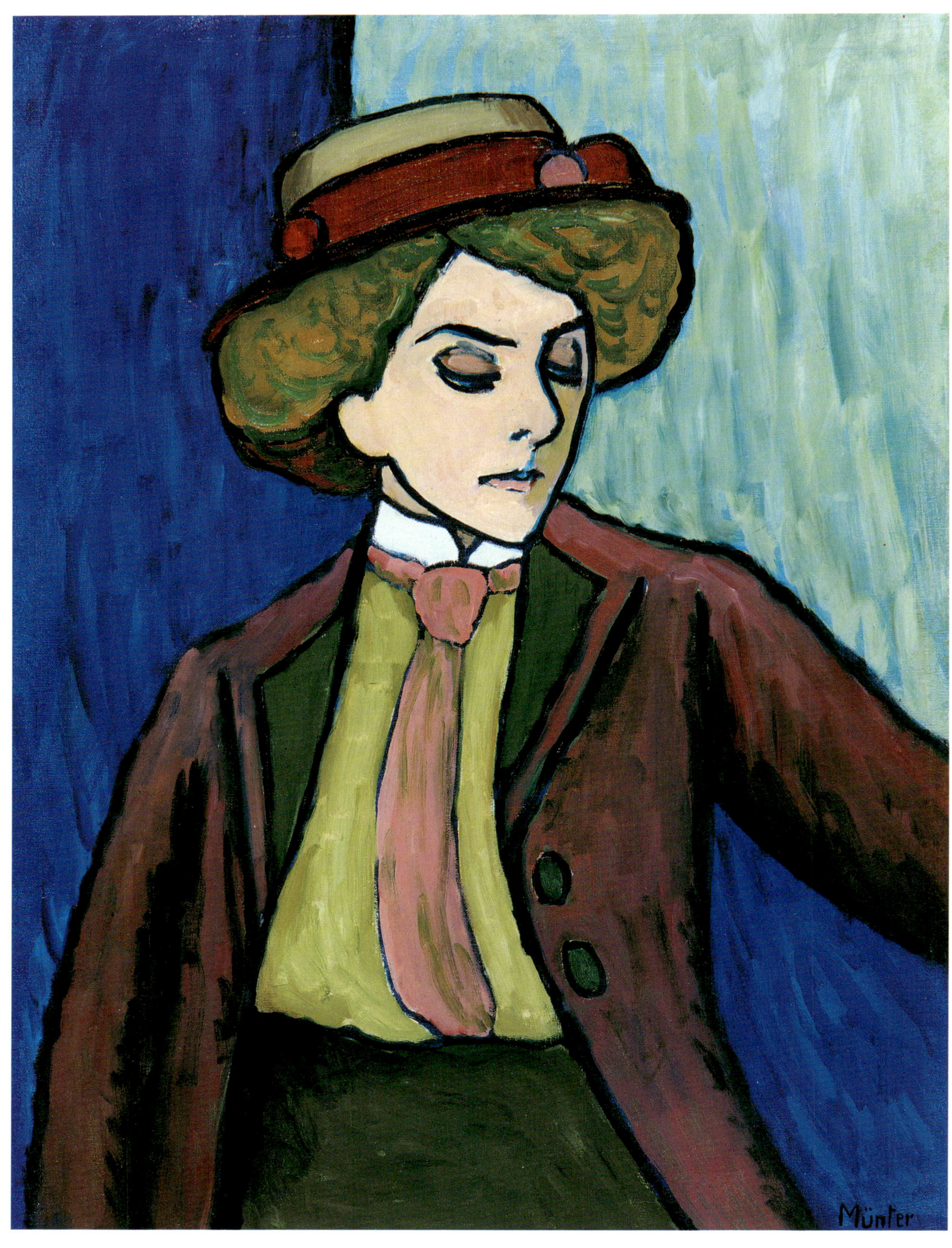

Portrait of a Young Woman (Young Polish Woman), 1909 (Cat. No. 34)

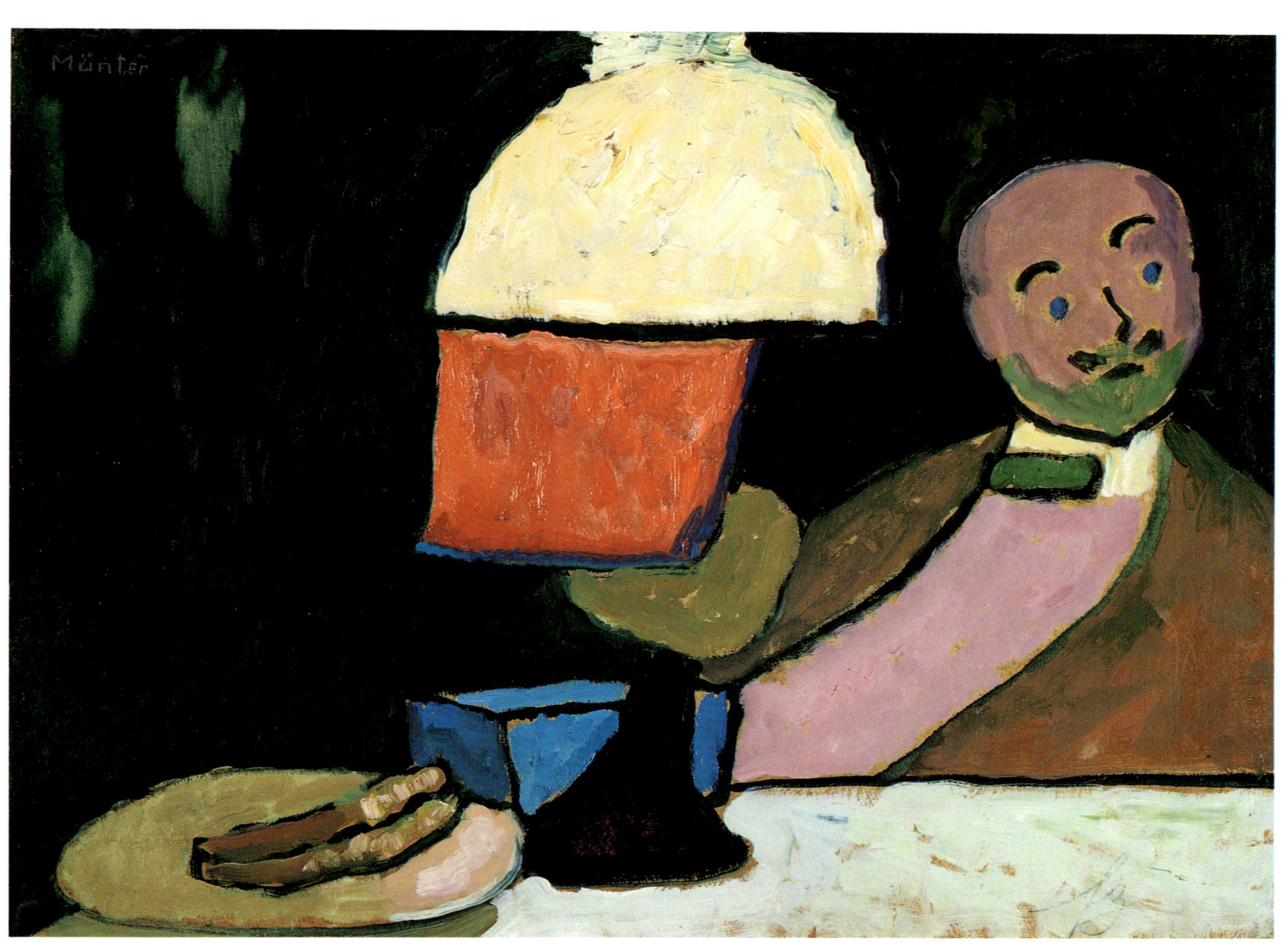

Listening (Portrait of Jawlensky), 1909 (Cat. No. 35)

is present. Normally, I draw my paintings on cardboard or canvas with a black brush before I turn to color."[10] In the confluence of influences Münter experienced in Murnau, the Bavarian reverse-glass paintings she discovered and began to collect provided her with technical and stylistic prototypes that she readily adapted to the modernity she sought in her paintings.

Girl with Doll (Cat. No. 28), another work from the winter of 1908–09, clearly demonstrates Münter's new process and was one of the works she featured in her collective exhibition at Herwarth Walden's Expressionist "Der Sturm" Gallery in Berlin.[11] Without the aid of a preliminary drawing, she freely painted the contours of the girl seated on a chair onto the cardboard, exactly situating the figure along the central vertical axis. The figure appears drawn with an extraordinary sense of certainty and precision, almost as if it were the result of one extended brushstroke, without hesitation, alteration or correction. Applied in thin paint in totally flat but delicately nuanced tones, contrasting colors fill the forms identified by the black contours; all impasto effects are avoided, brushstrokes are accented and cardboard is visible through the pigment or is left bare in spots. Enveloped in an ambience of glowing ultramarine blue—a color favored by Münter during these winter months—the ground of which is a muted burnt umber color, the young girl appears frontally posed, her face framed by a shock of deep brown hair, and her carmine red dress formed into a bell-like configuration of frontal stability from which dangle her thin legs between the echoing legs of the chair. Simplicity of composition and rendering, iconic frontality, limited color usage in planar configurations and enhanced black contours are the characterizing features of the painting that recall the art of reverse-glass painting, but other factors point to a more nuanced conception than the essentially formulaic practices of *Hinterglasmalerei.*

Münter's girl appears to be in the center of the composition but, owing to the moderately incongruous configuration of the various pictorial elements, she is spared the stiff rigor such placement often engenders. The head is turned slightly, shoulders vary in height, the legs seem out of line with the torso, the hands are shifted left of center and the doll in pale blues, yellow and a single strong white tone introduces a diagonal that finally destroys all sense of stiffness and immobility—even as it is rendered in a characterizing posture that contrasts with that of the girl's, precisely in its lifeless rigidity. The subtle lessons of *Jugendstil* and printmaking more than the discovery of *Hinterglasmalerei* shaped these refinements necessary for the gentle naturalness and childhood innocence the portrait appears to transmit, so antithetical in effect to the dominant sexuality projected by most Expressionist representations of young girls.[12]

Child in White (Cat. No. 46), which takes up the motif of a young girl again, was also exhibited by Münter at her "Der Sturm" collective exhibition, where it was displayed with the title *Head of a Girl (White Blouse).*[13]

The distinction seems relatively insignificant, but Münter's title emphasizes the portrait as being of the girl, the reference to her sex lost in the term "child." It was, moreover, one of several paintings identified as depicting a young girl that she included in her exhibition, with the bracketed "white blouse" added only as an aid in distinguishing between the four otherwise identically titled works. Serial unity and cohesion are made overt through the simple, yet defining titles. The variation on the theme "head of a girl" was primary, conceived as a formal motif and not as a specific portrait likeness. Posed against a dark ground, the head is rendered in an impasto technique to a greater extent than other paintings by Münter at the time, a technique perhaps modeled on Kandinsky's contemporary practice and shared with the three other "Heads of Girls" in the Sturm exhibition, all painted late in 1909 or early in 1910.[14] Together, they demonstrate an experiment in technique, but also a variation on the German academic practice of portrait depiction, which favored bust-length portraits. Münter thereby updated and modernized, but also continued, the lessons she was taught at the Ladies' Academy, where children, too, were often favored as models. The paintings simultaneously proclaimed an independent maturity and cast that independence and terminated study into doubt as, in technique, they were modeled on Kandinsky and not on Münter's discovery of reverse-glass painting. Broad simplification and the flattening of forms in her portraits once again are linked to heavy black contours, painted over the colored form as was Kandinsky's practice, and with almost coarsely drawn facial features to offer a resemblance bordering on the caricatural. With their large, wide eyes, the traditional "windows to the soul," the children's portraits recall the encaustic mummy portraits of Greco-Roman Egypt that also fascinated other Expressionist artists as "primitive" prototypes of a spiritually-oriented depiction of the human face, an effort to present what Münter called an "extract."[15] In their variation on a theme, the portraits become demonstrations of Münter's painterly abilities, especially as they demonstrate technical variety in the selection on display at the exhibition. But they are also studies that accent incompleteness and rapidity of rendition, stylistic metaphors for the artist's presence and emotional involvement with the subject, while they portray each child, contrary to convention, as an alert and conscious presence, as an individual who gazes back at the viewer with steadfast certainty.[16]

The series of young girls' portraits is fundamentally an exercise in typological portraiture. One of Münter's best-known portraits, the portrait of Jawlensky (Cat. No. 35), with its extremely caricatural appearance, might similarly function as a portrait of type more than of Jawlensky, the individual. Münter insisted it shows Jawlensky "...with an expression of puzzled astonishment on his chubby face, listening to Kandinsky's new theories of art."[17] She titled the painting *Listening*, and it is indeed a listener she portrays, someone without a personality or distinguishing characteristics,

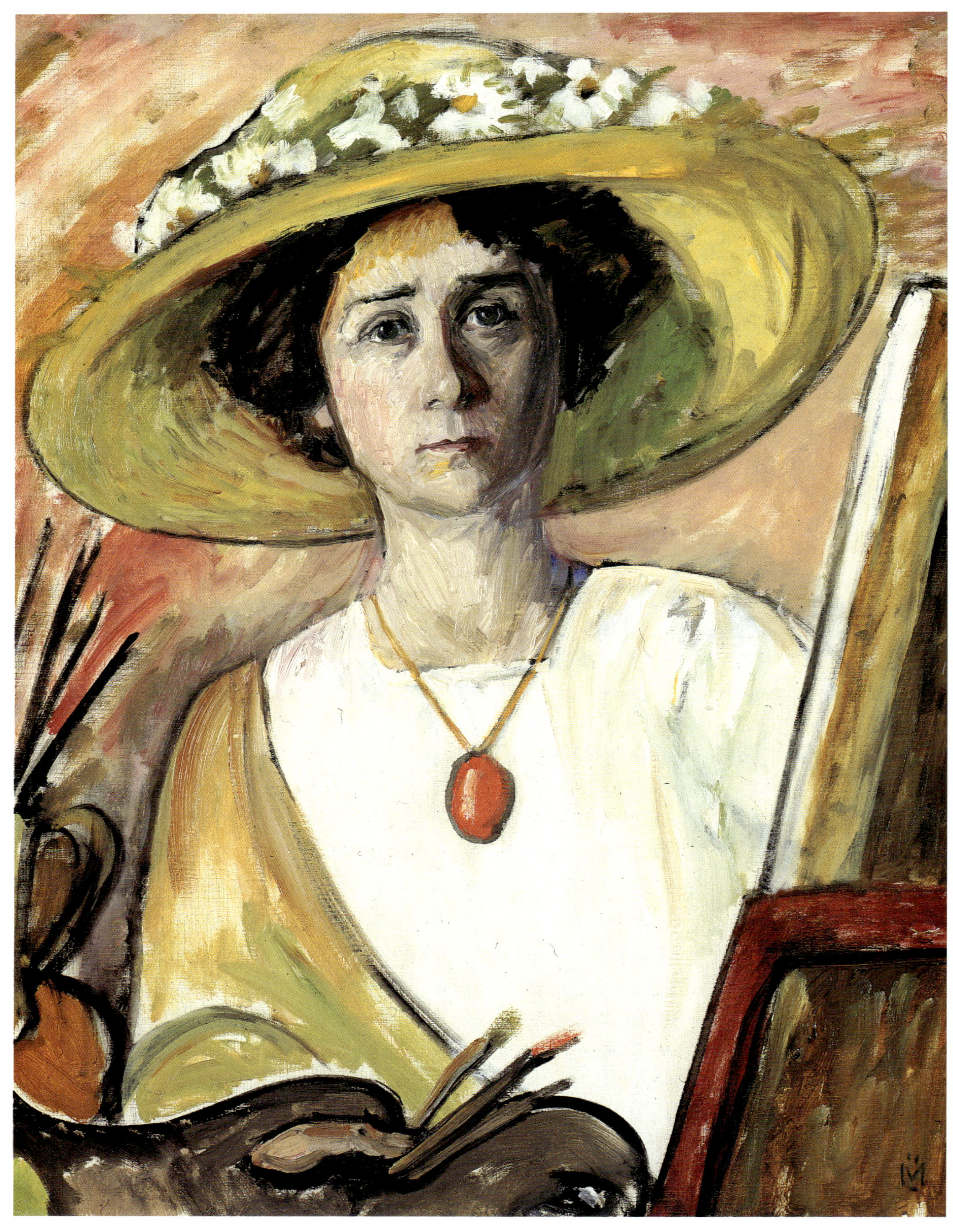

Self-Portrait in Front of an Easel, ca. 1909 (Cat. No. 36)

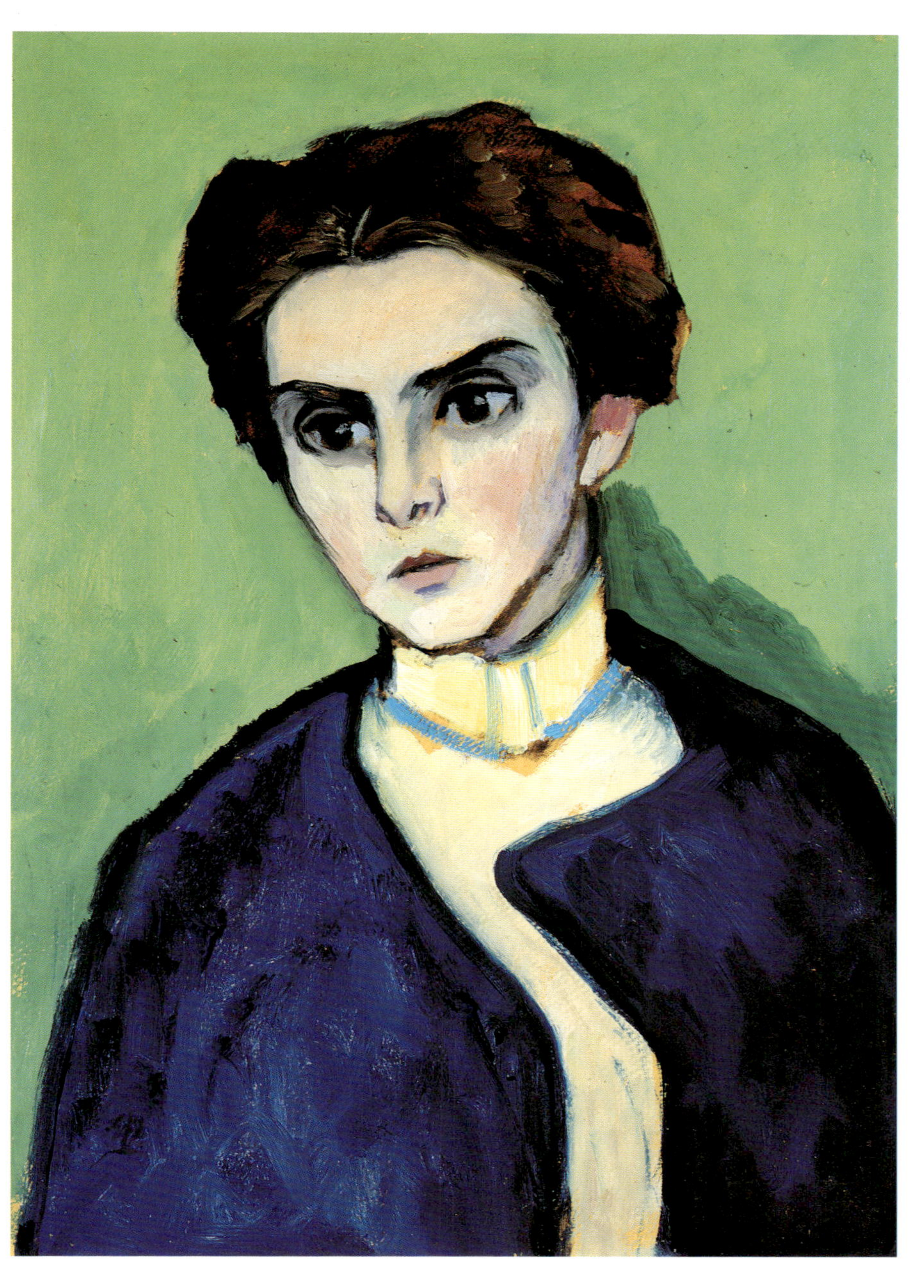

Portrait of Olga Hartmann, 1910 (Cat. No. 45)

except his expression of astonished listening. She transformed physiognomic features into shorthand, cartooned signs, while accenting his action, his open-mouthed amazement as he leans to one side, almost threatening to fall out of the painting itself, boorishly straining to hear better what is said or whispered nearby. The exaggerated comedy of *Listening* emerges repeatedly in Münter's work as an almost slapstick diversion, not infrequently with a mocking or caustic undertone. More often, however, she manifested an empathetic approach, especially in her portrayals of women, her most frequent subjects.

The diversity in concept and appearance of Münter's portraits painted during the prewar years in Munich and Murnau stretches from the caricatured buffoonery of the Jawlensky portrait to a quiet naturalism with only limited stylization or overt interpretation, as in the portrait of Kandinsky's mother, Lydia Kojevnikoff, painted when she visited her son, his first wife and his "fiancée" in the spring of 1913 in Munich and Murnau (Cat. No. 69). A beneficent, neutral gaze characterizes the image of her, as it does the several portraits of Olga Archádina von Hartmann, also a painter and the wife of the Russian composer Thomas von Hartmann. Befriended by Münter and Kandinsky, von Hartmann began collaborating with Kandinsky in 1909 on a musical setting for the play entitled *The Yellow Sound*, published in *The Blaue Reiter Almanac* in 1912. The two pairs of artists regularly visited one another, as when Münter and Kandinsky went to the Hartmann home in Kochel, near Murnau, in February 1909; the men worked together on Kandinsky's play, the women painted together in the snow. Münter portrays Olga von Hartmann (Cat. No. 45) almost in the manner of her children's portraits, but with a less assertive stylization, the drawing of Olga's features more muted, with none of the mocking characterizations of the Jawlensky portrait.[18] The young woman's face with its large, dark eyes instead appears softly pensive and melancholy above the blue cloak and the high-necked white blouse she wears, while the background is bathed in an unmodulated soft yellow-green. Introspection and contemplative sadness seem to overpower the portrait of Olga von Hartmann, who Münter singled out in her 1911 diary notes for her friendship.

Olga von Hartmann's portrait shares its hint of sadness with Münter's first painted self-portrait (Cat. No. 36), where she too gazes through eyes that seem tear-filled, keeping her lips tightly closed. Beneath the wide brim of her flowered sun hat, Münter's face imposes its three-dimensional appearance on the overall flatness of the painting. One side deeply shadowed, the face's serious mien disrupts the painting's coloristic cohesion; its melancholic expression denies the subjective cheerfulness of the surrounding bright pinks, yellows, greens and whites. The situation in which Münter portrays herself—at an easel, palette and brushes in hand, working on a painting—is a frequently depicted one in the history of self-portraiture by such diverse artists as Rembrandt, Elisabeth-Louise Vigée-Lebrun, Vincent van Gogh and Arnold Böcklin. Her broad-rimmed straw hat may represent a particular homage to Van Gogh and a desire to associate her work with this most prototypical of Expressionism's precursors, but Münter above all situates herself here proudly in the company of professional artists; she employs the large self-portrait as an announcement of her own artistic maturity and of her art's competition with that of the past and the present. The self-doubt that appears to be expressed in the conflicting components of the face and its surroundings may be an indication of the anxiety she felt in entering this historical competition and submitting her works for public exhibition.[19] Alternatively, as with the Olga von Hartmann portrait, Münter may be articulating something of her personal life in 1909—the promise and success of her art, the newly purchased house in Murnau and its embodiment of optimism about the future, but also Kandinsky's continuing reluctance to obtain his divorce and the resultant compromise of her own social and moral situation—as she sharply juxtaposes vocabularies of hopefulness and sadness in a private self-portrait that she did not include in her exhibitions until 1960.

The privacy of her self-portrait is unusual, however, and contrasts sharply with Münter's effort to make an ambitious artistic statement in her portraits. She worked extensively on *Still Life with Figure II* (Cat. No. 44) in sketches and in two paintings on canvas during 1910–11 that fused the genres of still life and portrait into a new, collaged entity in a manner previously practiced by Degas, Gauguin and Munch.[20] A willed competition takes place in the painting, therefore, with artists particularly admired, collected and emulated at the time Münter painted it; like the self-portrait, it is a statement of artistic maturity, but for public, not private, consumption. Depicted is a visitor to Münter's and Kandinsky's Munich apartment, Mrs. Simonovich, whom both artists in their letters identified as beautiful, charming and extraordinarily attractive to the men in Munich's artistic milieu, but say nothing else about her, and she today remains unknown. She appears coequal with, or almost overshadowed by—as if being pushed out off the picture—a still-life arrangement of flowers, figurines and vases on a small table and a selection of Bavarian reverse-glass paintings on the wall. Like them, Mrs. Simonovich becomes an artifact, an element to be manipulated within the economy of Münter's painting and artistic vision; she becomes transformed into a marginalized formal element, her personality suppressed within the totality of a compositional and coloristic constellation defined by and defining the artist. Repeatedly in exhibitions before 1914, Münter and Kandinsky gave the painting pride of place in exhibitions, as it presented a dramatic personal statement by an artist employing signs of visual reality in the "greater realism" of its image.[21] It showed Münter both liberated from her status as Kandinsky's student and confirming the Expressionist aesthetic theories he developed.

A similar combination of artistic ambition and personal statement char-

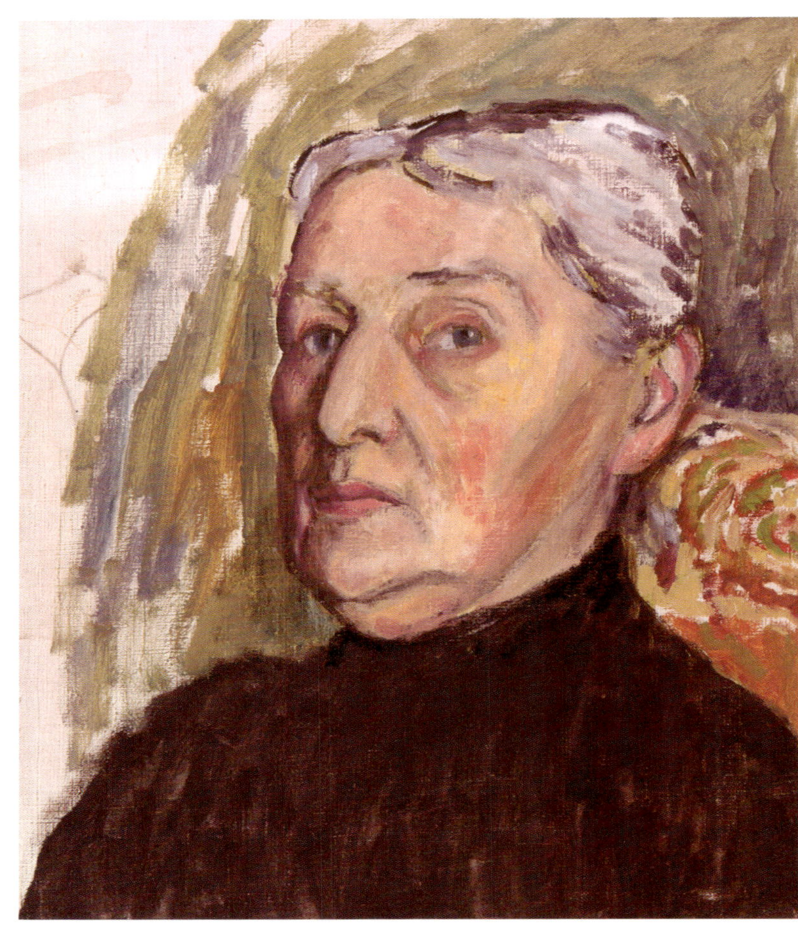

Portrait of Kandinsky's Mother, 1913 (Cat. No. 69)

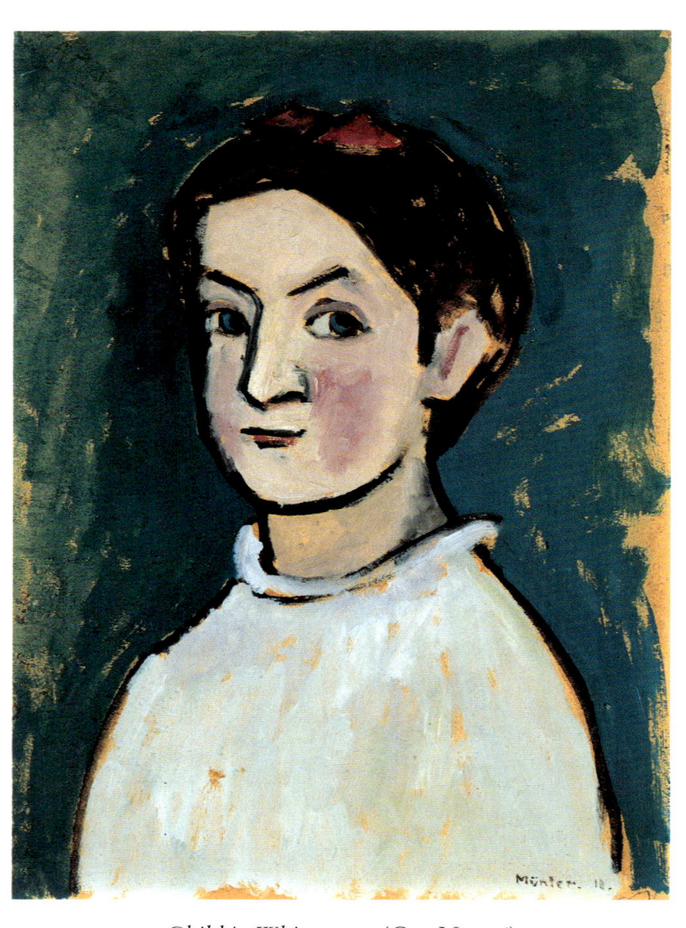

Child in White, 1910 (Cat. No. 46)

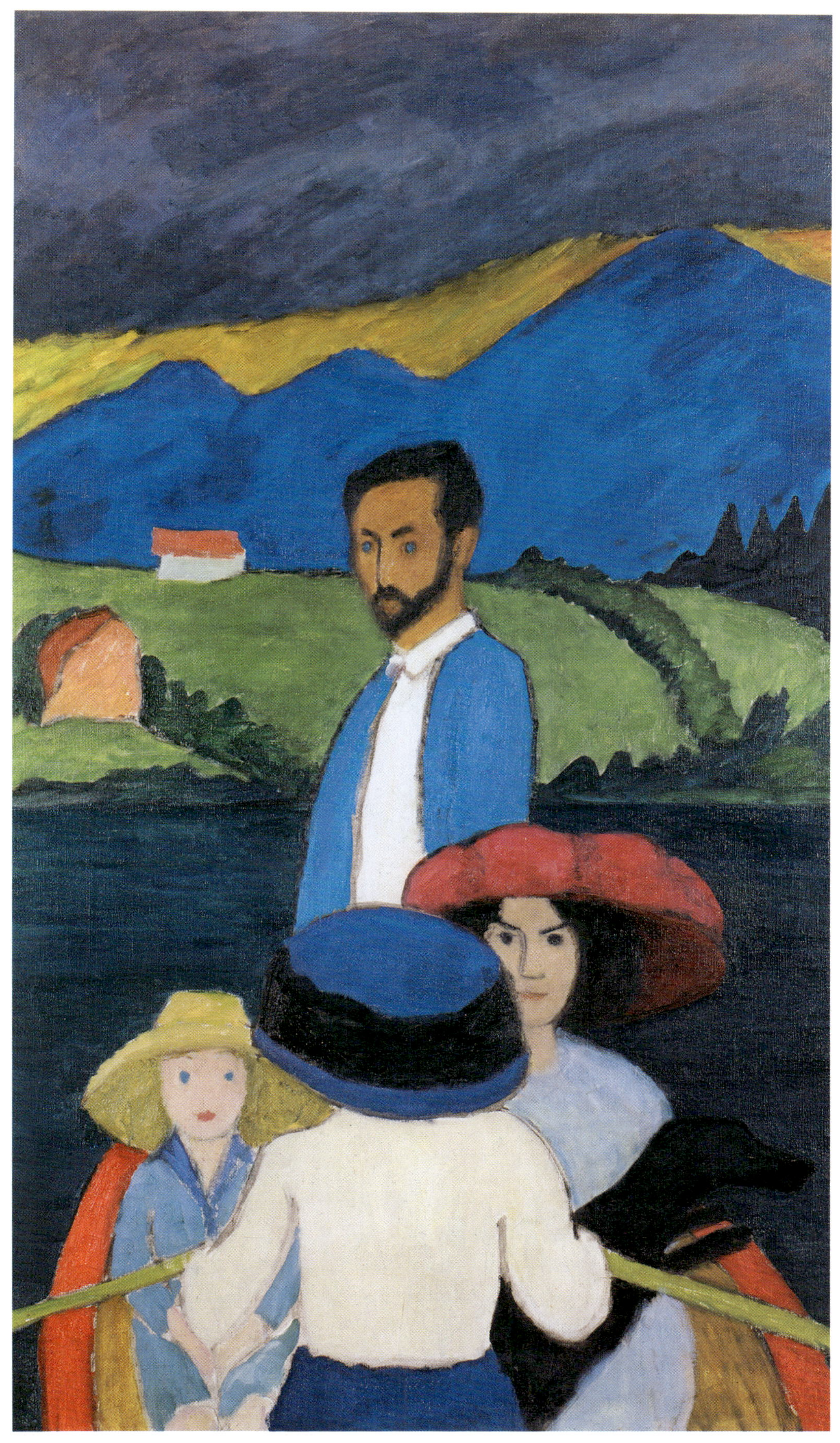

Boating, 1910 (Cat. No. 47)

acterizes *Boating* (Cat. No. 47), possibly Münter's best-known painting, executed on canvas and one of her few multi-figured portraits, both marking her aspirations for the work. Again, she worked the painting through phases of pencil sketches and painted variations before settling on the final, large composition that shows Kandinsky, Werefkin, Andreas Jawlensky and Münter herself in a boat on Staffelsee. A pencil sketch, dated 31 July 1910, recording an outing with Jawlensky, was the first notation for the painting, but it excludes Kandinsky. It is Kandinsky, however, who dominates the final vertical composition, as he stands towering over the two women and the child in the boat.[22] Thematically, the painting has its roots in such German Romantic themes as crossing lakes and seas—metaphors for life's grand transitions—and wedding parties, but also urban dwellers entering the revelation of nature's glories. As Kandinsky gazes with wide blue eyes, and Werefkin and the boy echo his gaze, such a metaphysical scene of entry is implied as Münter again transforms an anecdotal incident into a pictorially synthetic presentation. That Münter in this scene is rowing, thereby providing the labor that makes the experience possible, is both an analysis of her role within the artists' group and a reformulation of her actual role in the making of the painting, which her creative efforts produced.[23] Her vocabulary of thinned paint, flattened forms and accented contours, and of deeply emotive color harmonies—variations of blue cut into by yellow, red and green—conveys in this painting one of its most cohesive statements as coequality of figure and landscape is established, much as the Simonovich portrait gives equal expression to figure and still life. The group of figures and the landscape each dominate half of the composition, with Kandinsky acting as mediator between the two realities, between human and nature, within the context of the third reality of art, the painting itself. It was a grand synthetic pronouncement Münter sought to achieve through this work as she exhibited it repeatedly in Munich, Berlin, Paris, Zurich, Stockholm and Copenhagen until 1919, when Kandinsky broke the personal bond between them, which was inconspicuously expressed in this painting in the way her form leads directly into his, the two of them linked in a single configuration.

Landscapes

Chapter 5

"You have probably understood that I have always been mainly a *plein air* painter," Gabriele Münter told Edouard Roditi during her interview with him in 1958, when she found herself painting less and less, "although I have also painted portraits and still-life compositions."[1] Landscapes were her favored motif. She often painted still lifes, especially late in life, to keep artistically active. "Still life is [like] the piano—landscape = the orchestra," she wrote in her diary in December 1941.[2] Towards portraits, she had mixed feelings. "The portrait is a matter of luck," she told herself, "and is always problematic. But I'm intrigued by it nonetheless."[3] She enjoyed making portrait sketches, and regarded portrait painting as challenging, provided that she could control the production; however, in painting them on commission during the first three decades of this century, she grew to resent them. Johannes Eichner, her companion, tried to convince her in the 1930s that portrait painting was business. But it was precisely this commercial aspect she found so repulsive.[4] Only to the landscape did she turn with joy, no matter what the circumstances of her life were. In it, she found release.

Münter developed her interest in landscapes during her American journey. In drawings, watercolors and photographs she gave pictorial expression to the Mississippi River and its shores, and to the woods and fields of Arkansas and Texas, whose distinct difference from the German countryside awoke in her a new sensibility for the distinguishing characteristics of local landscapes. This she retained after returning to Germany in 1900, refining it at the Munich Ladies' Academy and the Phalanx School. It was the countryside that figured so prominently in her first oil paintings at Kallmünz and it was in landscape motifs that she integrated radical innovations into her works executed in Murnau. Landscapes also prevailed in her selection of paintings—thirty-five out of eighty-four works—for her premiere exhibition in 1913 at Berlin's "Der Sturm," Herwarth Walden's influential gallery that played a significant role in defining the German Expressionist avant-garde. Her most important artistic aspirations are concentrated in her landscapes.

The precedence landscape took as a genre of progressive painting was far from unique to her. Especially after Impressionism, landscape was internationally the perpetual site of modernist experimentation and innovation. Moreover, since Romanticism and earlier, many German artists have imbued their depictions of nature and the countryside with a sense of the religious, the idyllic, the sublime and the emotive, often stressing mystical associations. Nature was a refuge, a place to which to escape from modern

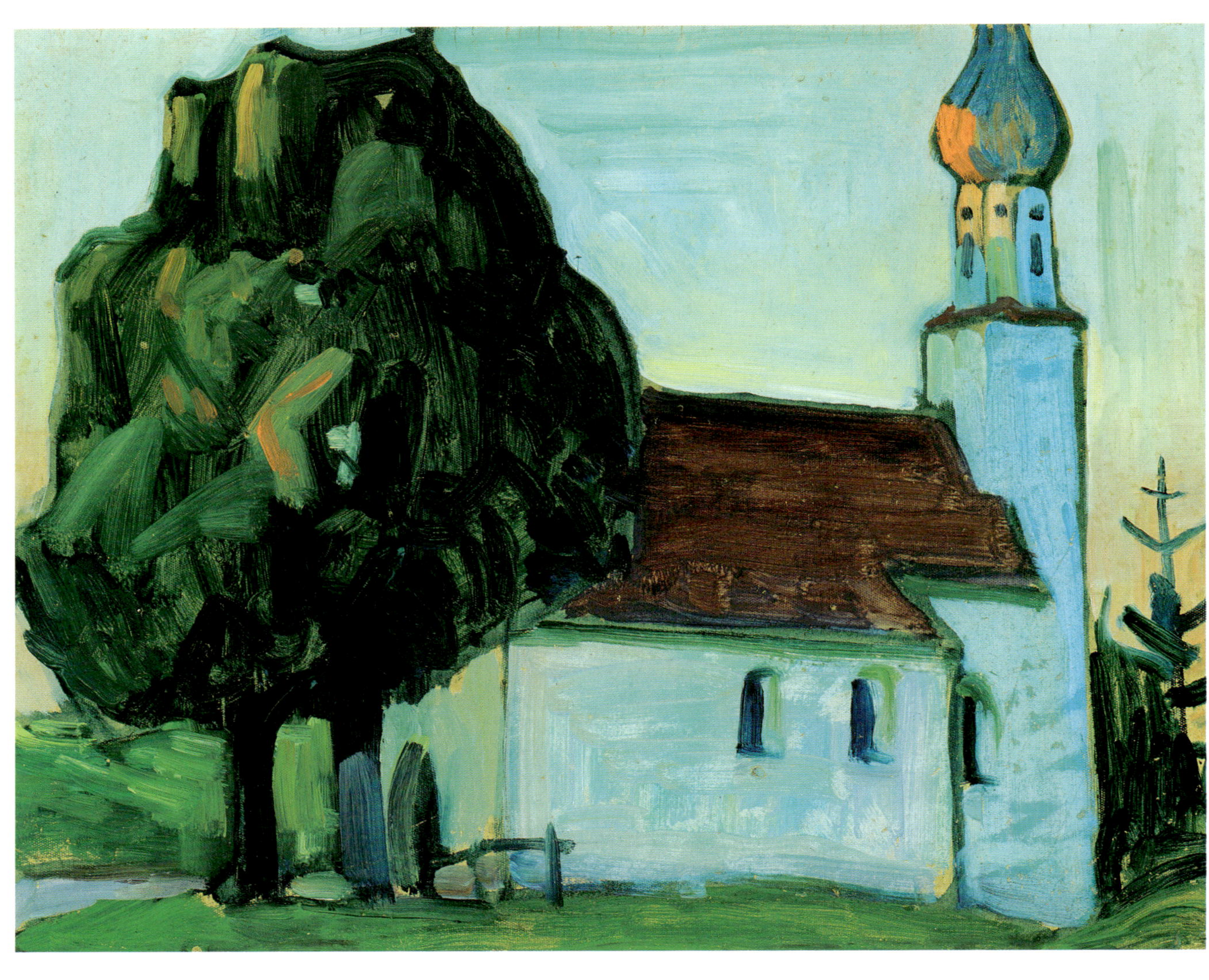

The Village Church, 1908 (Cat. No. 17)

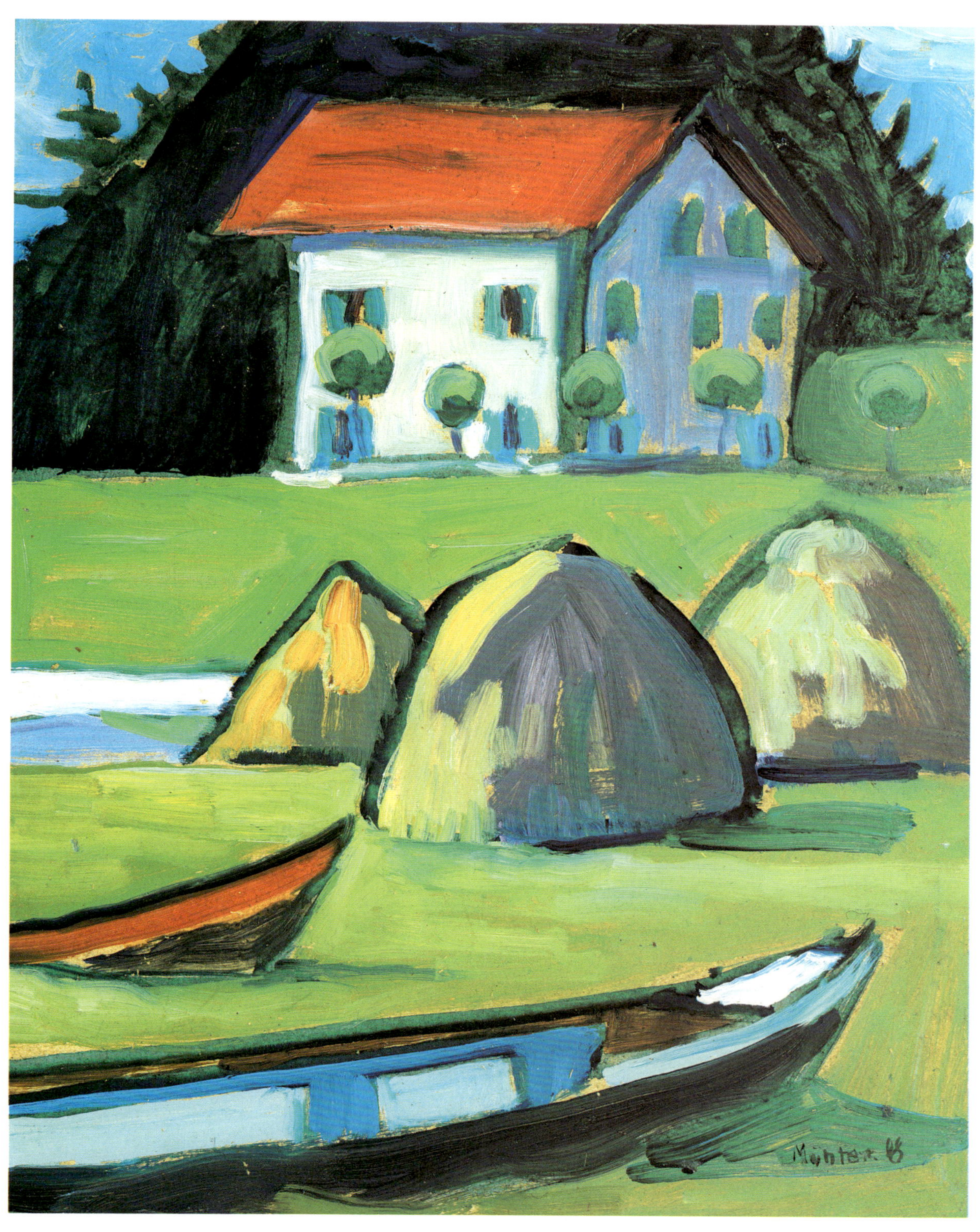

Fisherman's House, 1908 (Cat. No. 23)

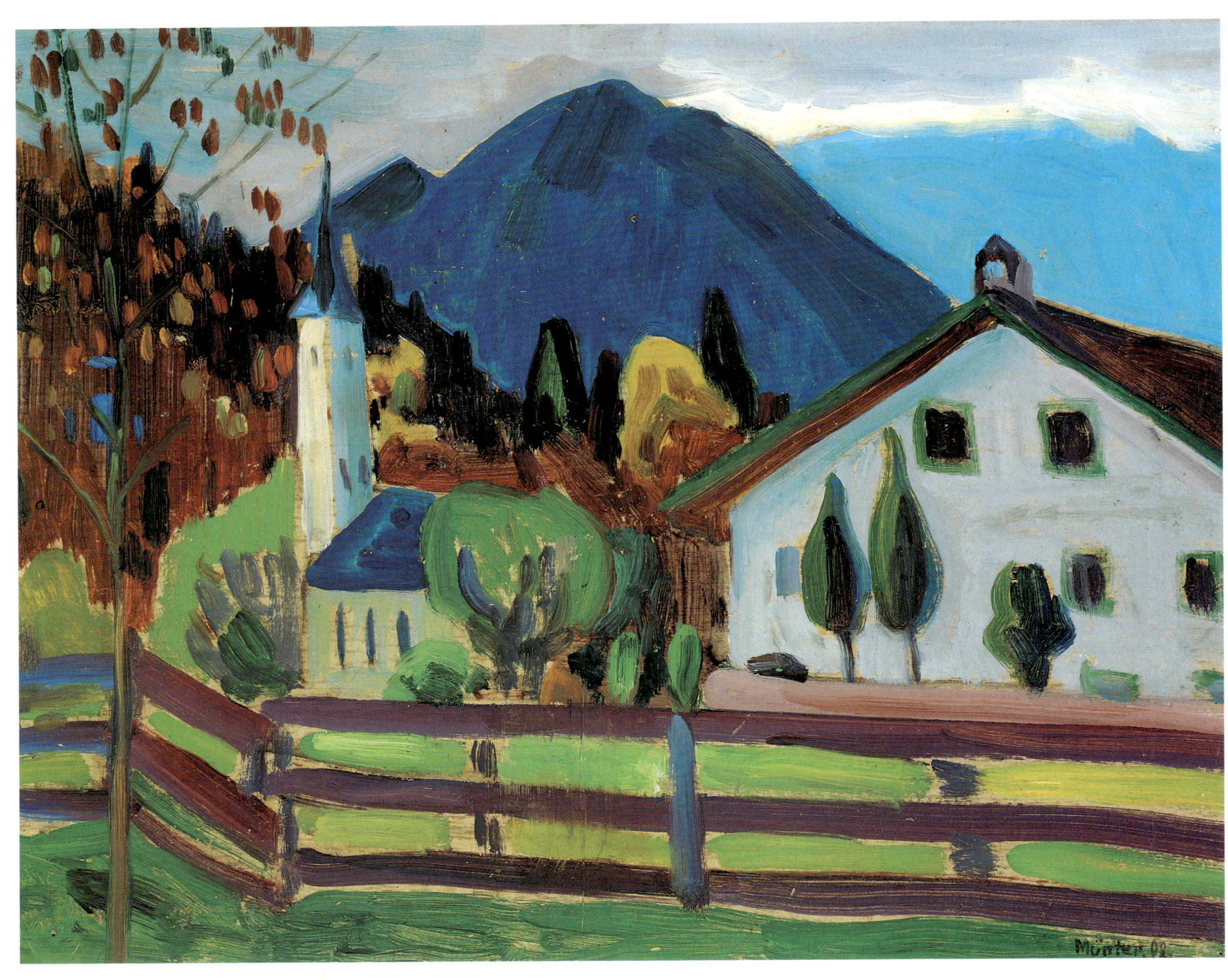

Oberau, 1908 (Cat. No. 24)

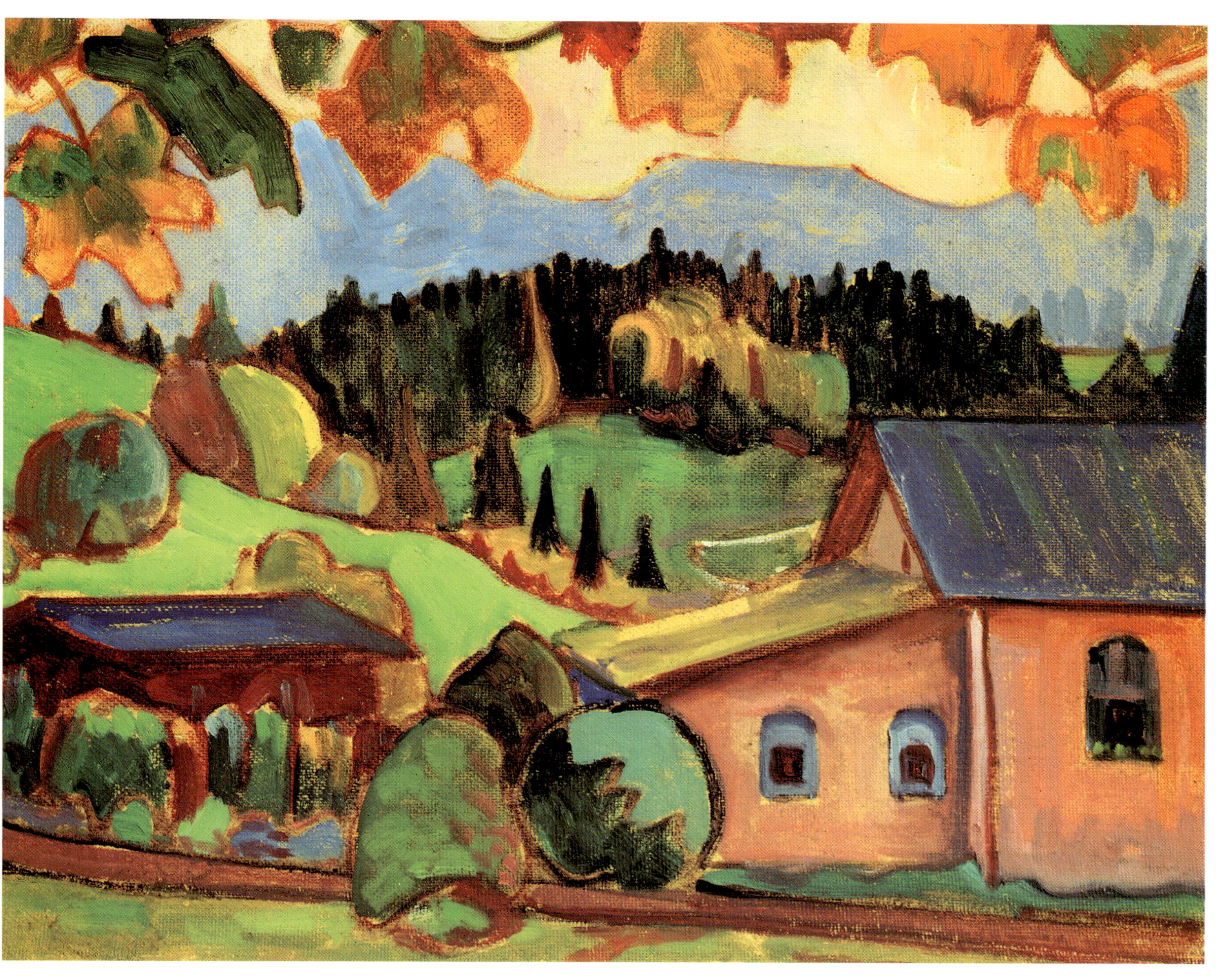

Factory, 1908 (Cat. No. 25)

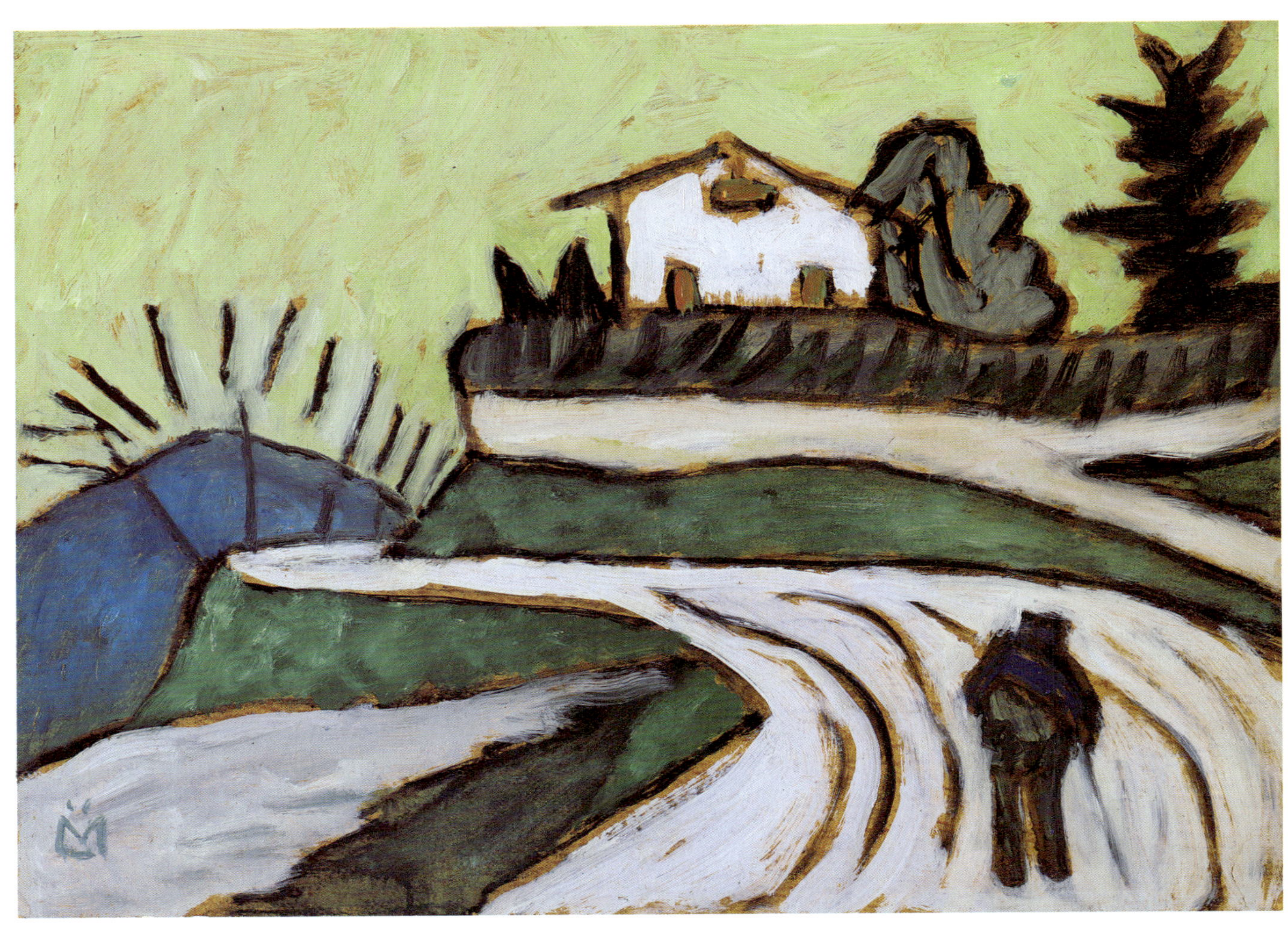

Country Road in Winter, 1909 (Cat. No. 38)

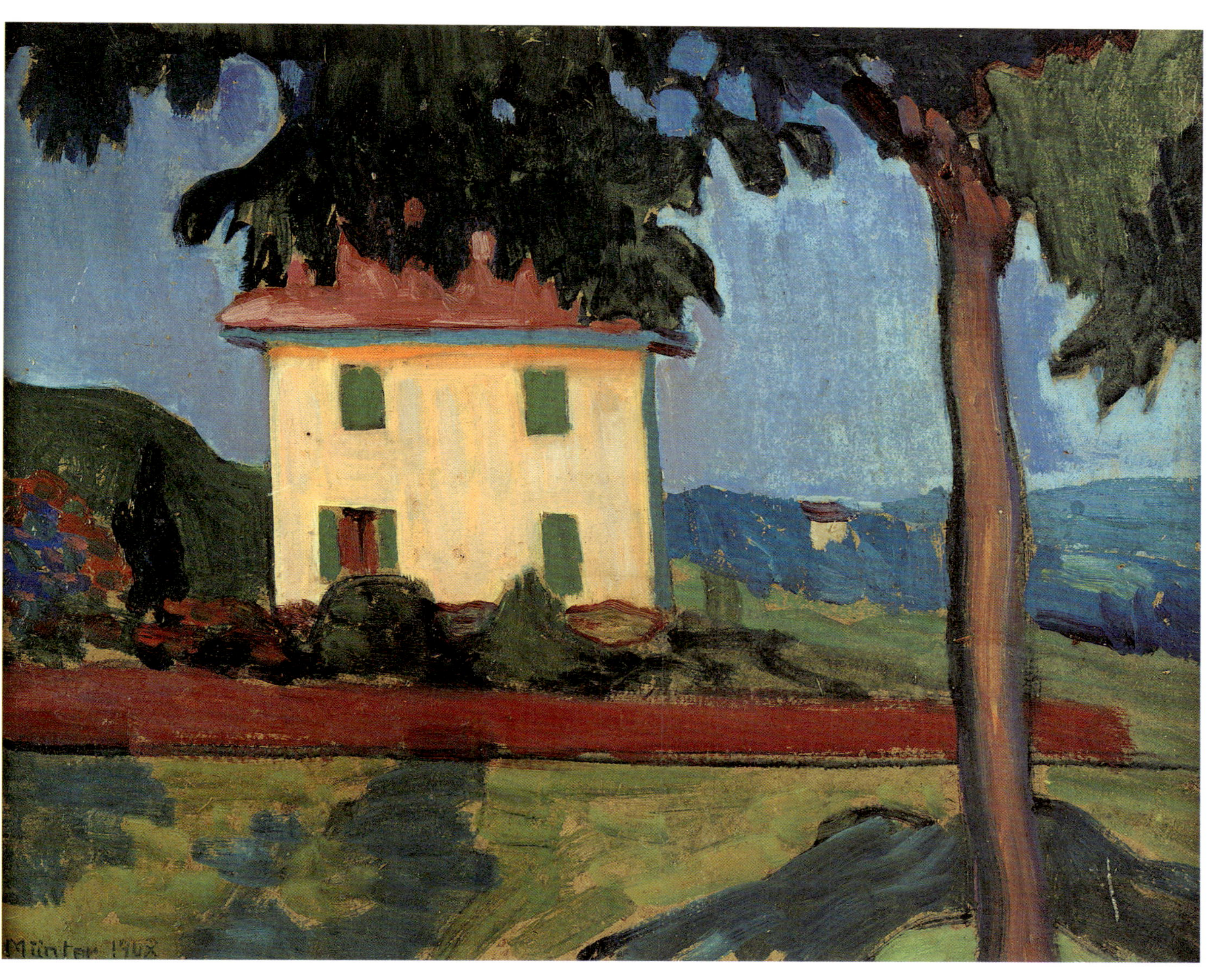

The Pink House (Country Home near Murnau), 1908 (Cat. No. 26)

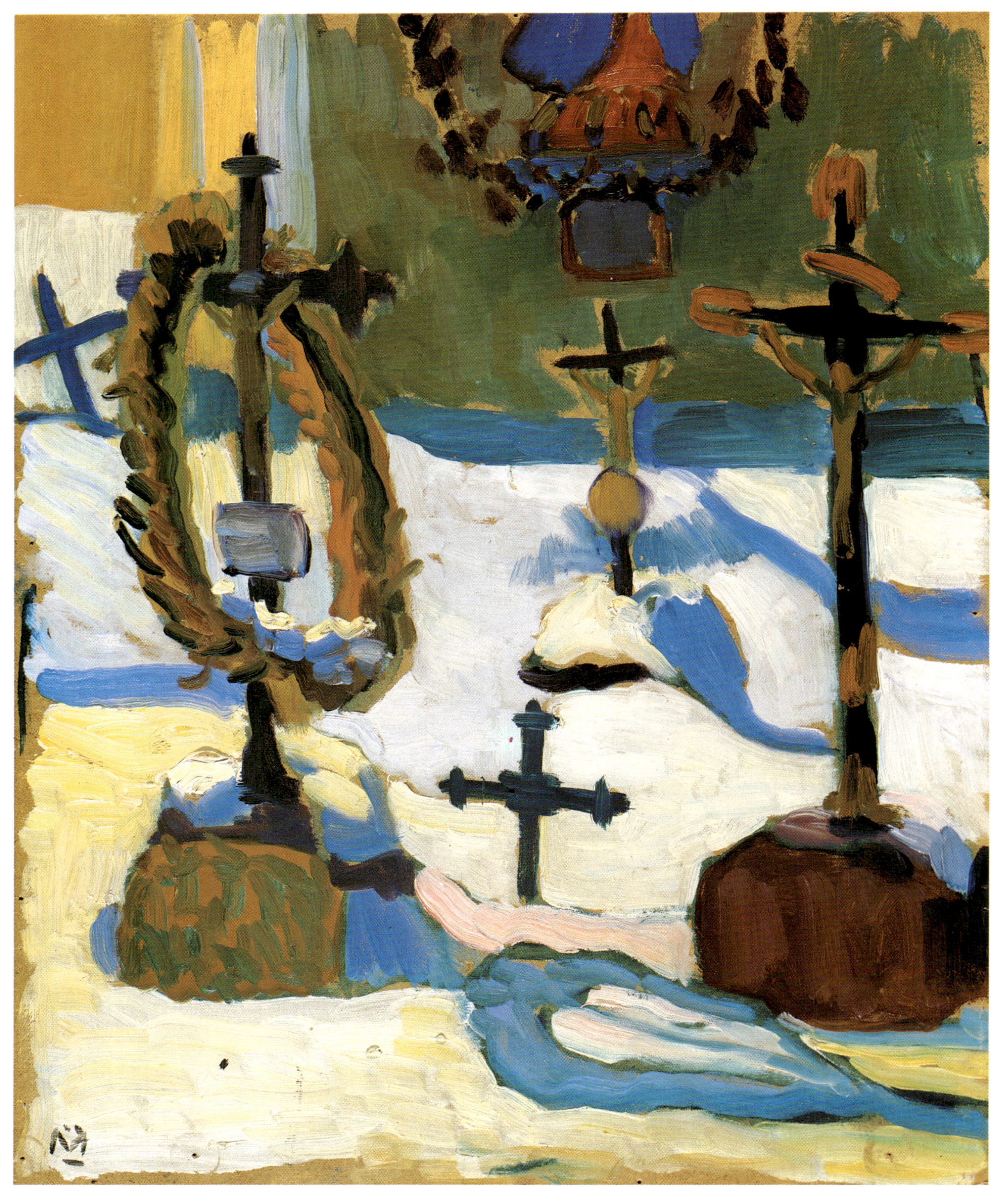

Grave Crosses in Kochel, 1909 (Cat. No. 29)

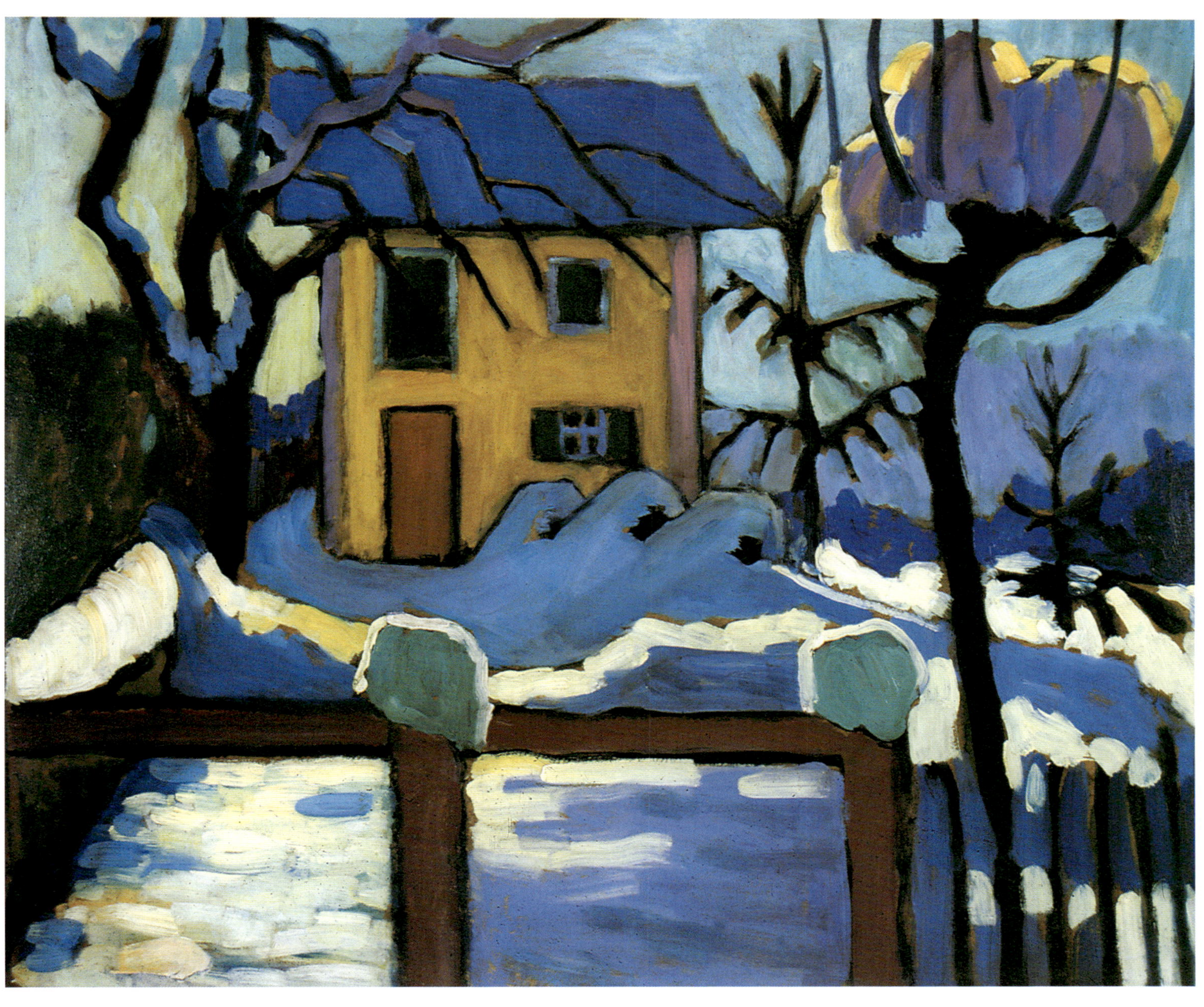

House in Winter, 1909 (Cat. No. 39)

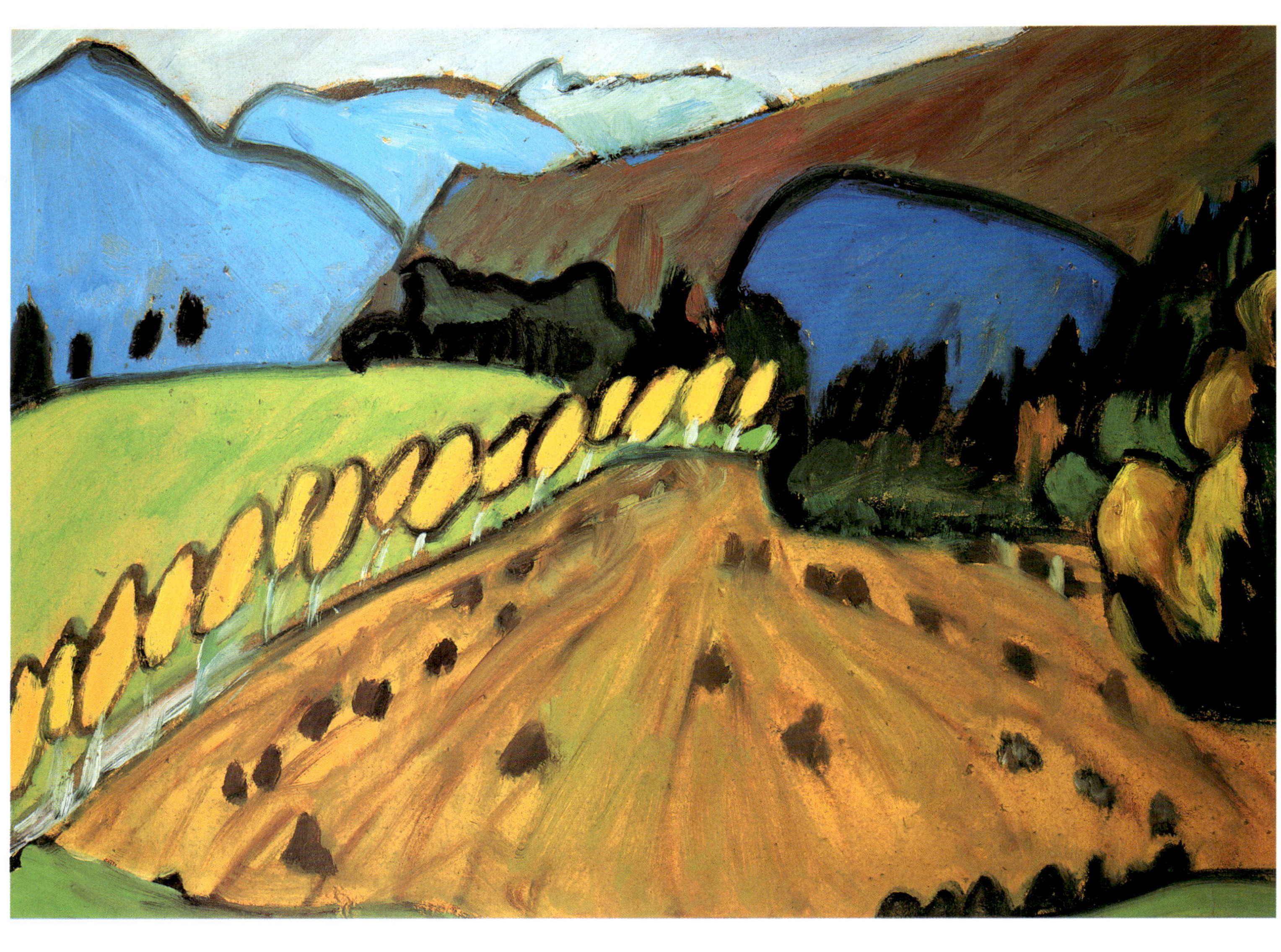

Fall Landscape, Study (Yellow Trees), 1909 (Cat. No. 40)

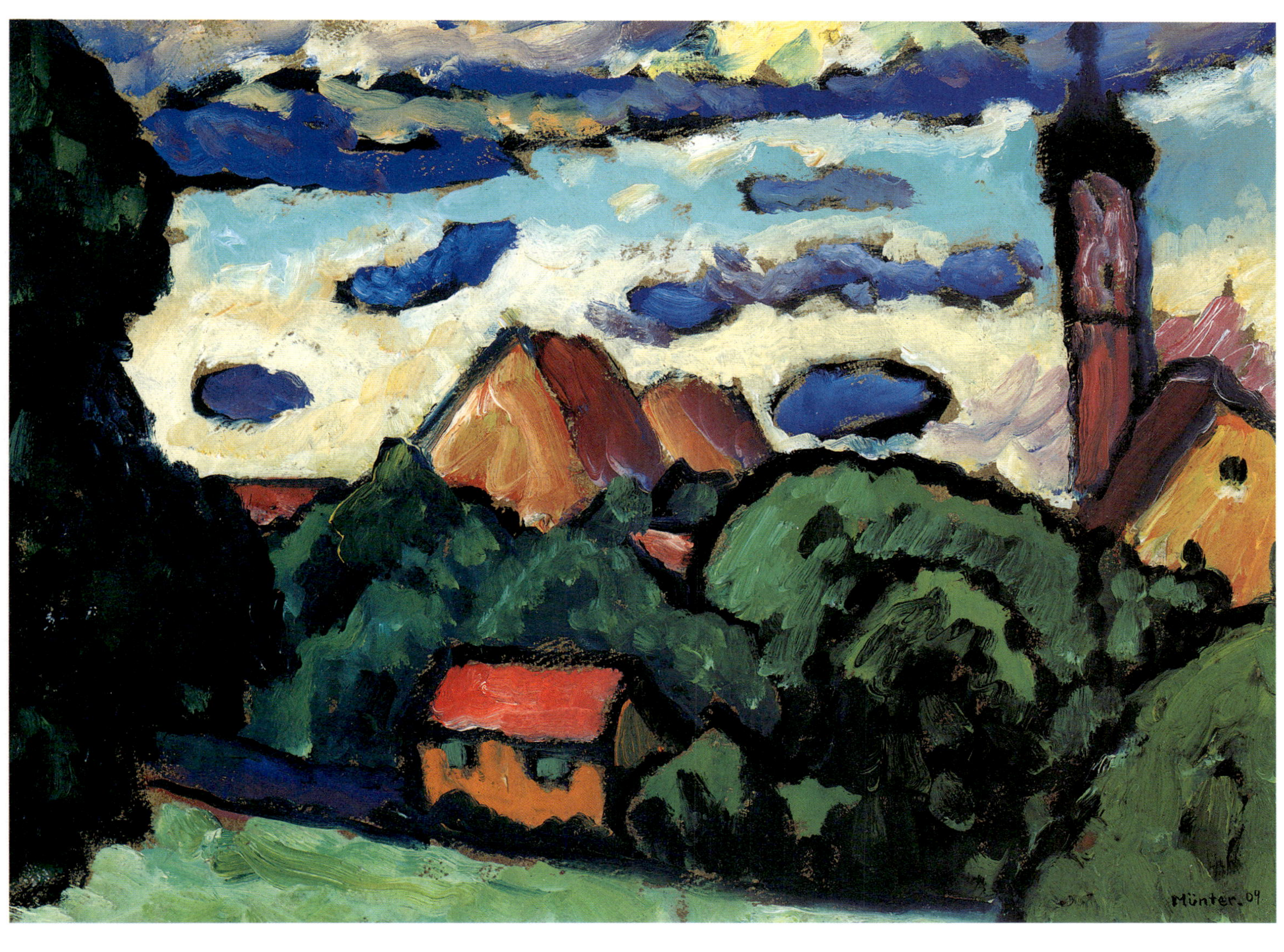

Landscape with Church, 1909 (Cat. No. 41)

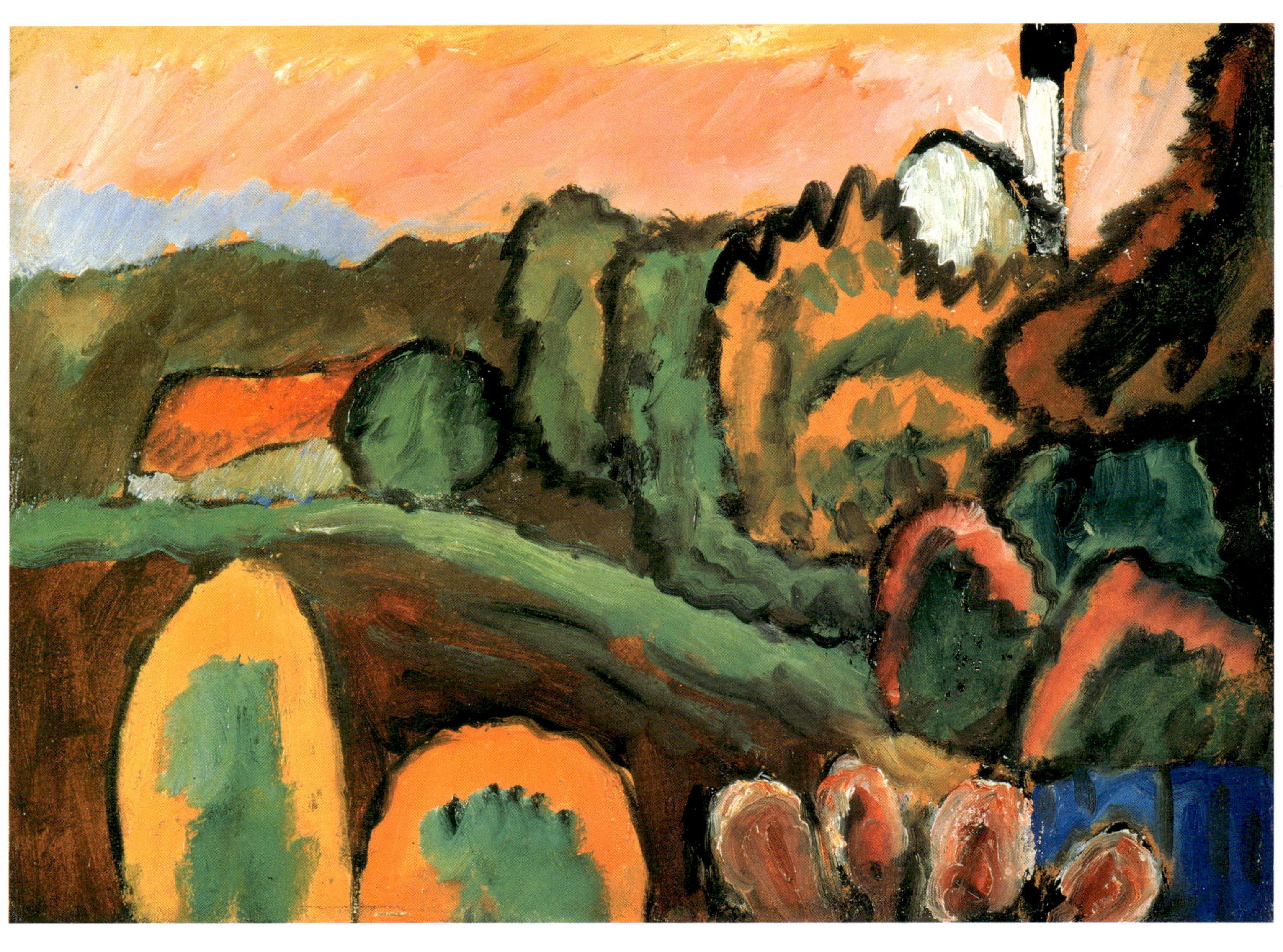

Landscape with Church, 1910 (Cat. No. 49)

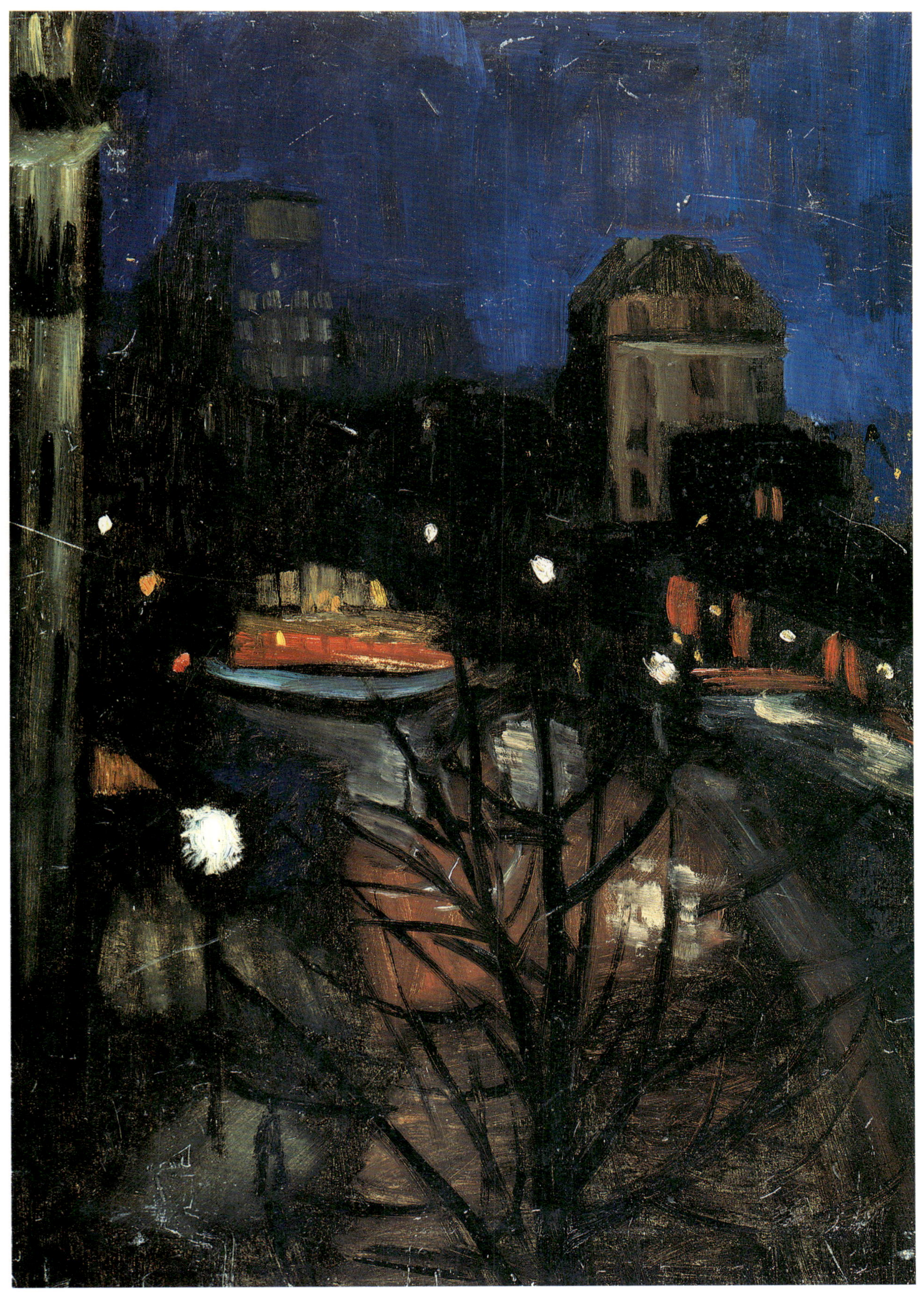

City View by Night, 1910 (Cat. No. 48)

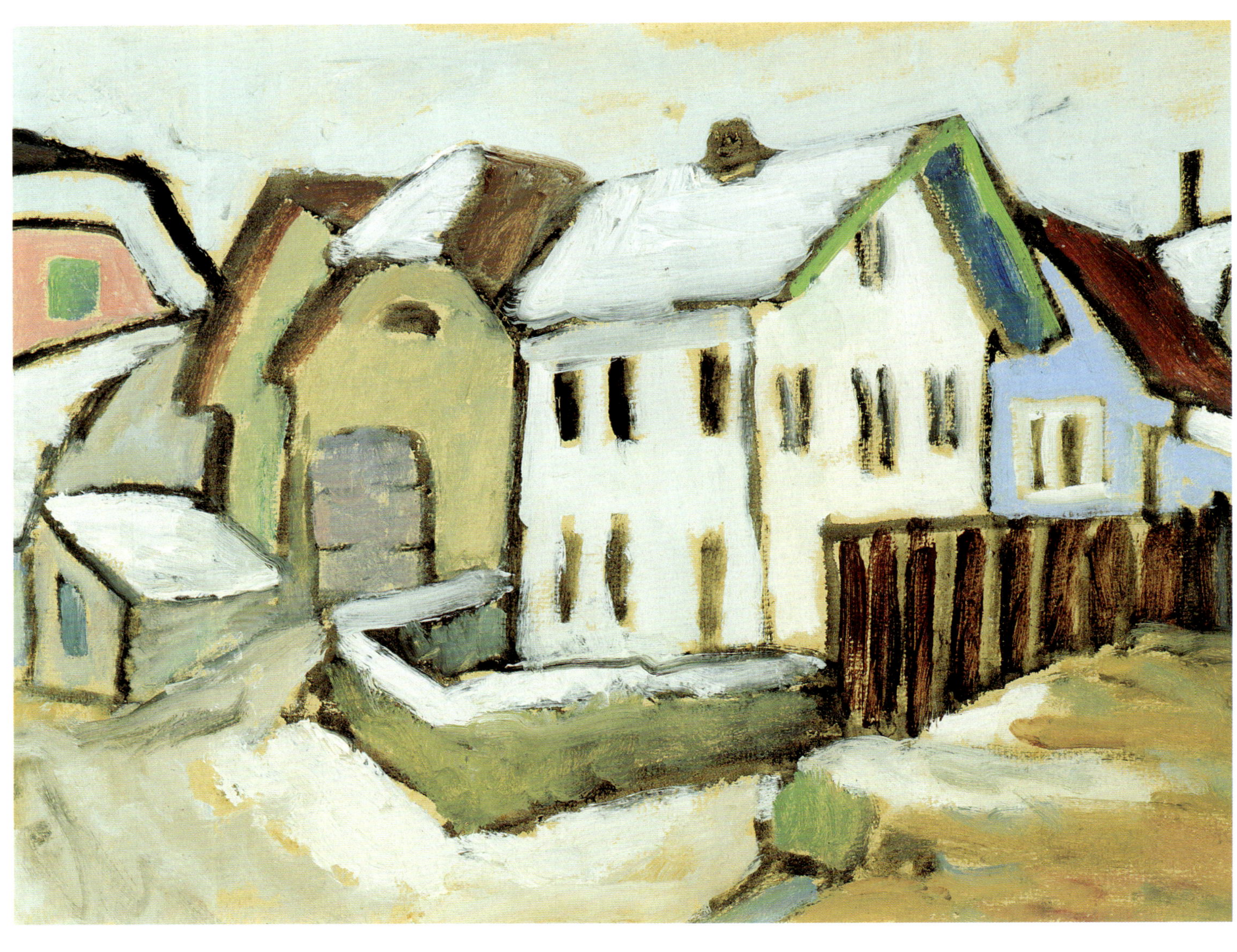

Houses on Wintry Road, 1911 (Cat. No. 51)

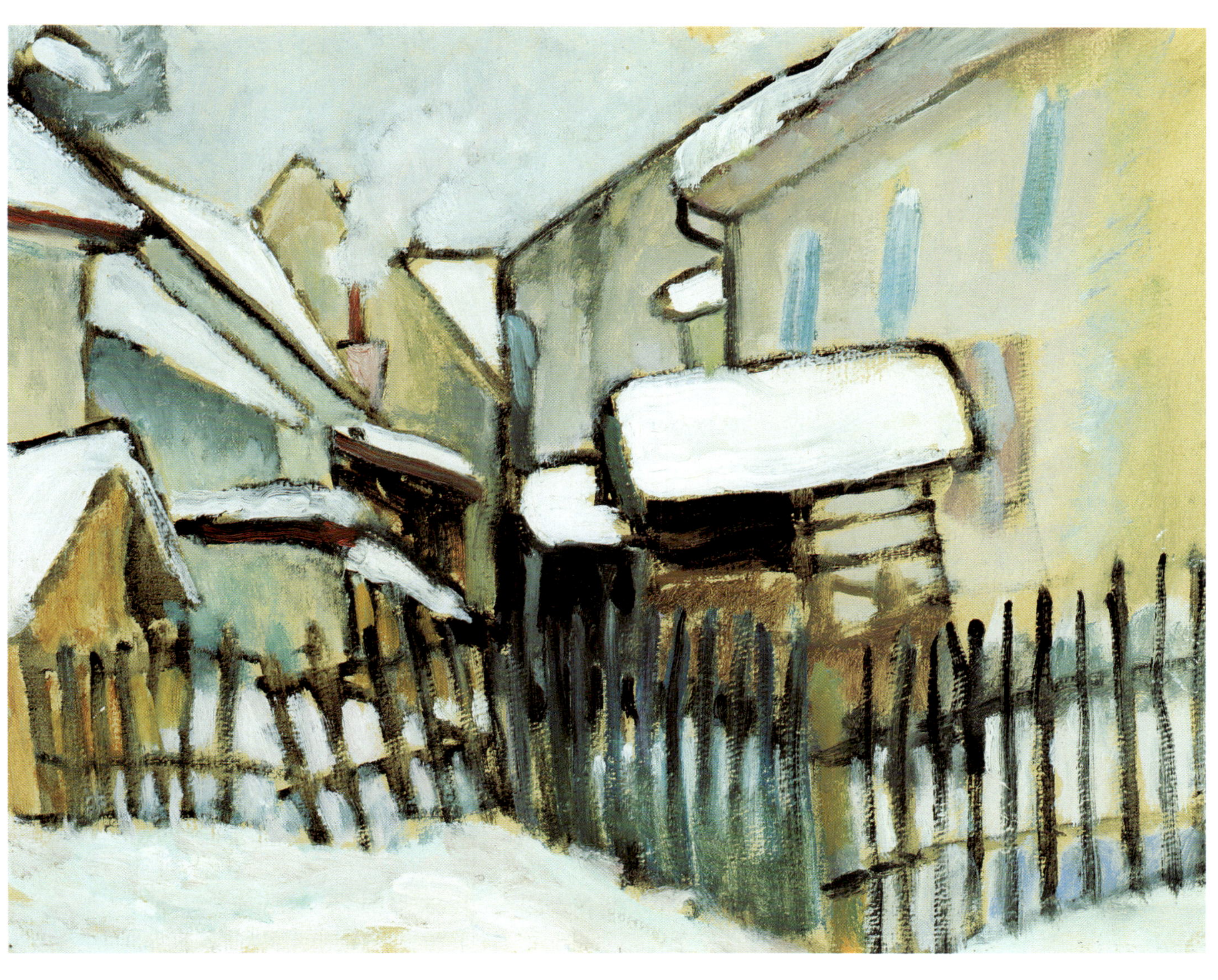

The Brewery, *Murnau*, 1911 (Cat. No. 55)

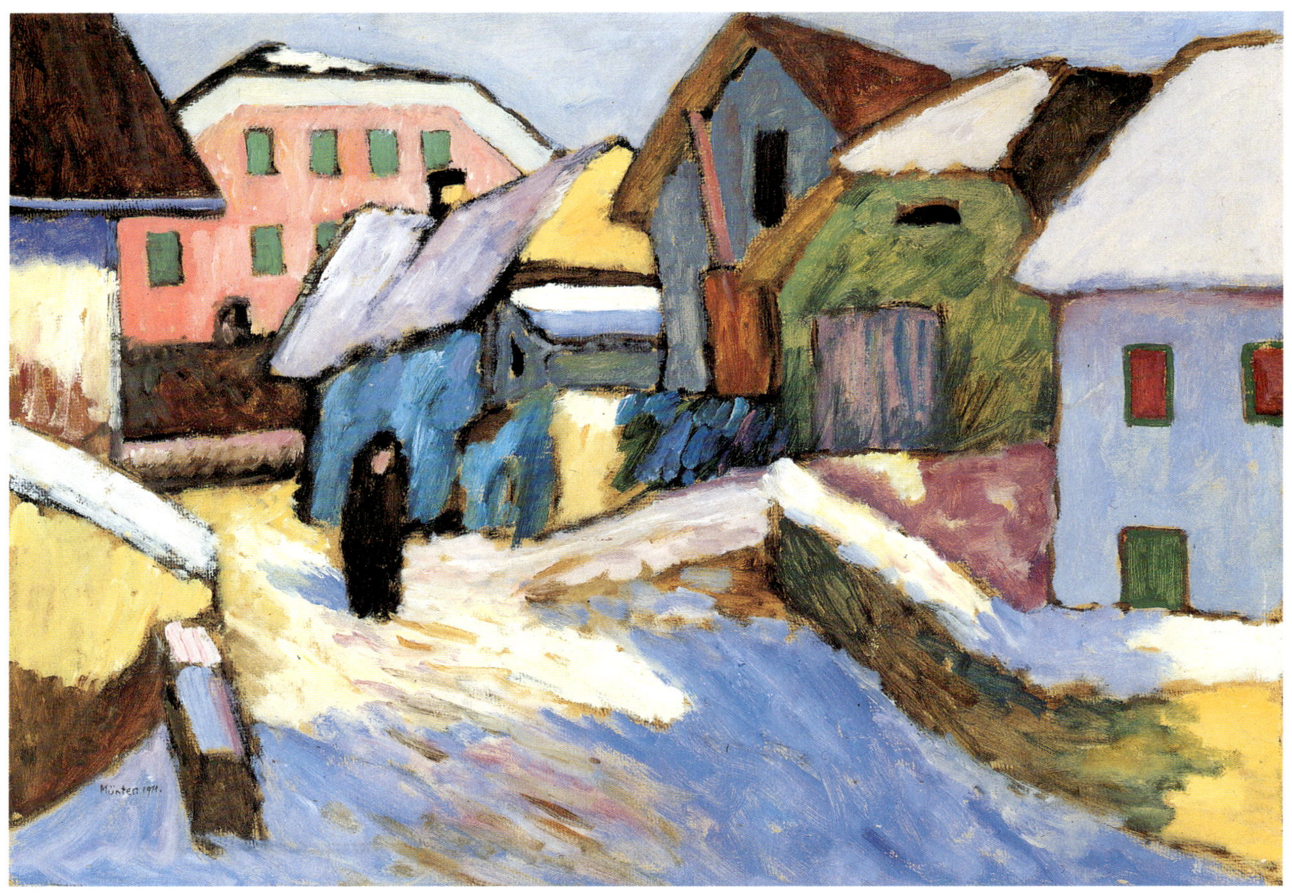

Snow and Sun, 1911 (Cat. No. 56)

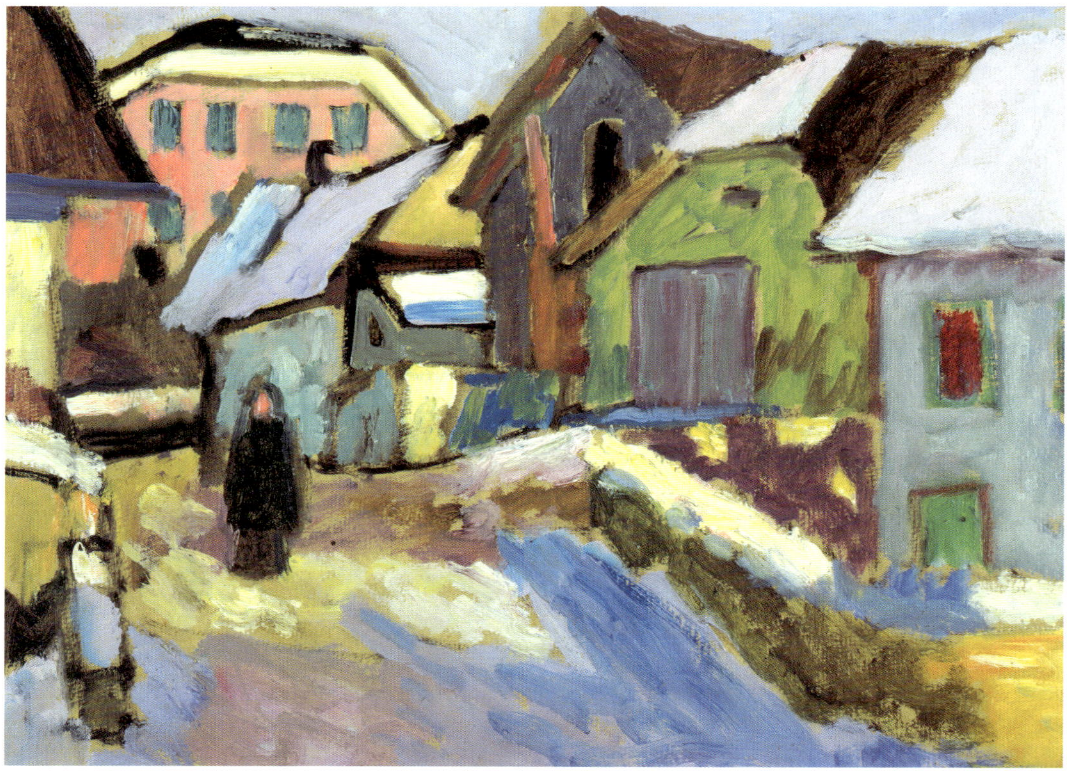

Farmyard in Snow I, 1911 (Cat. No. 57)

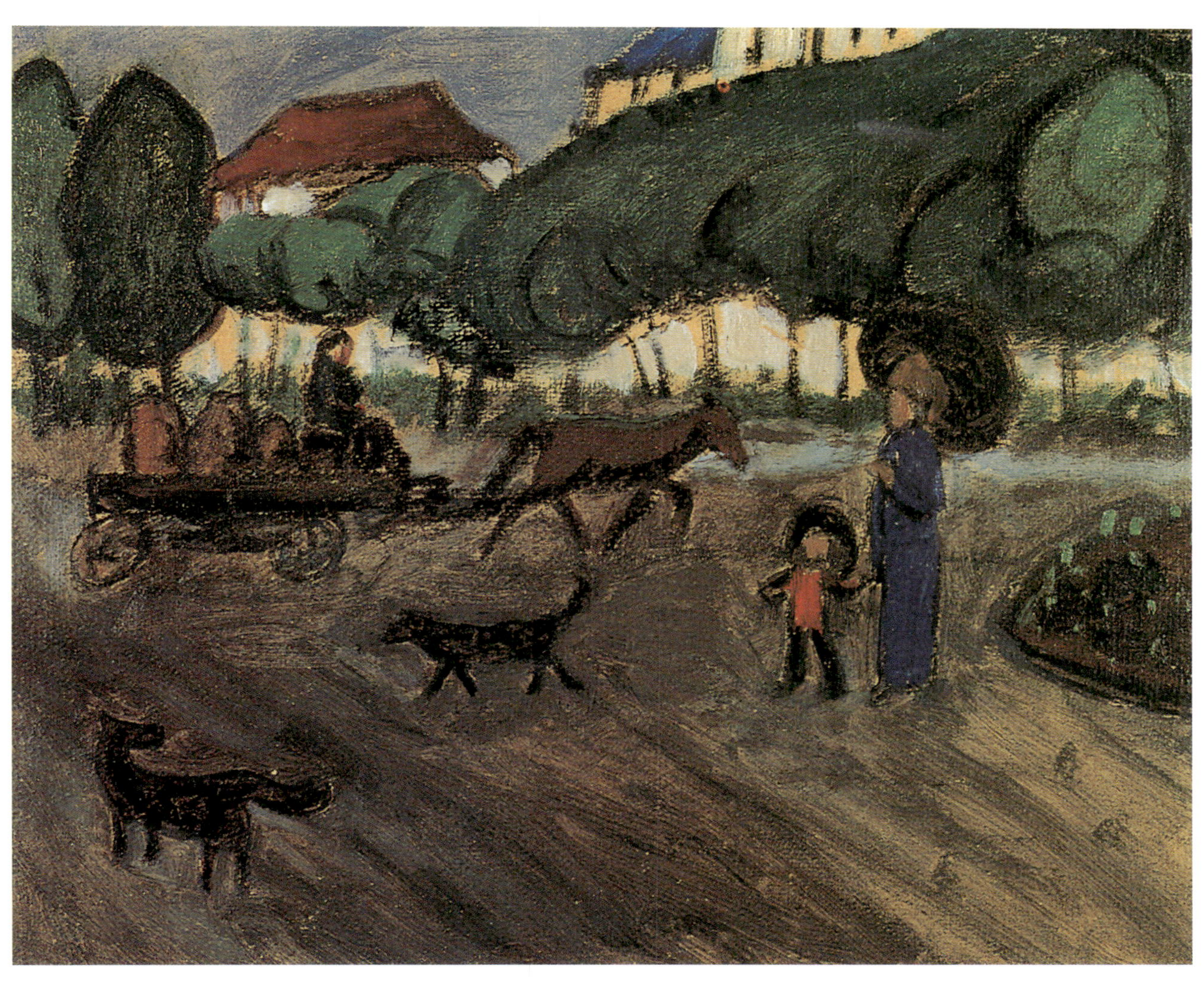

Habsburg Square, Munich, 1911 (Cat. No. 59)

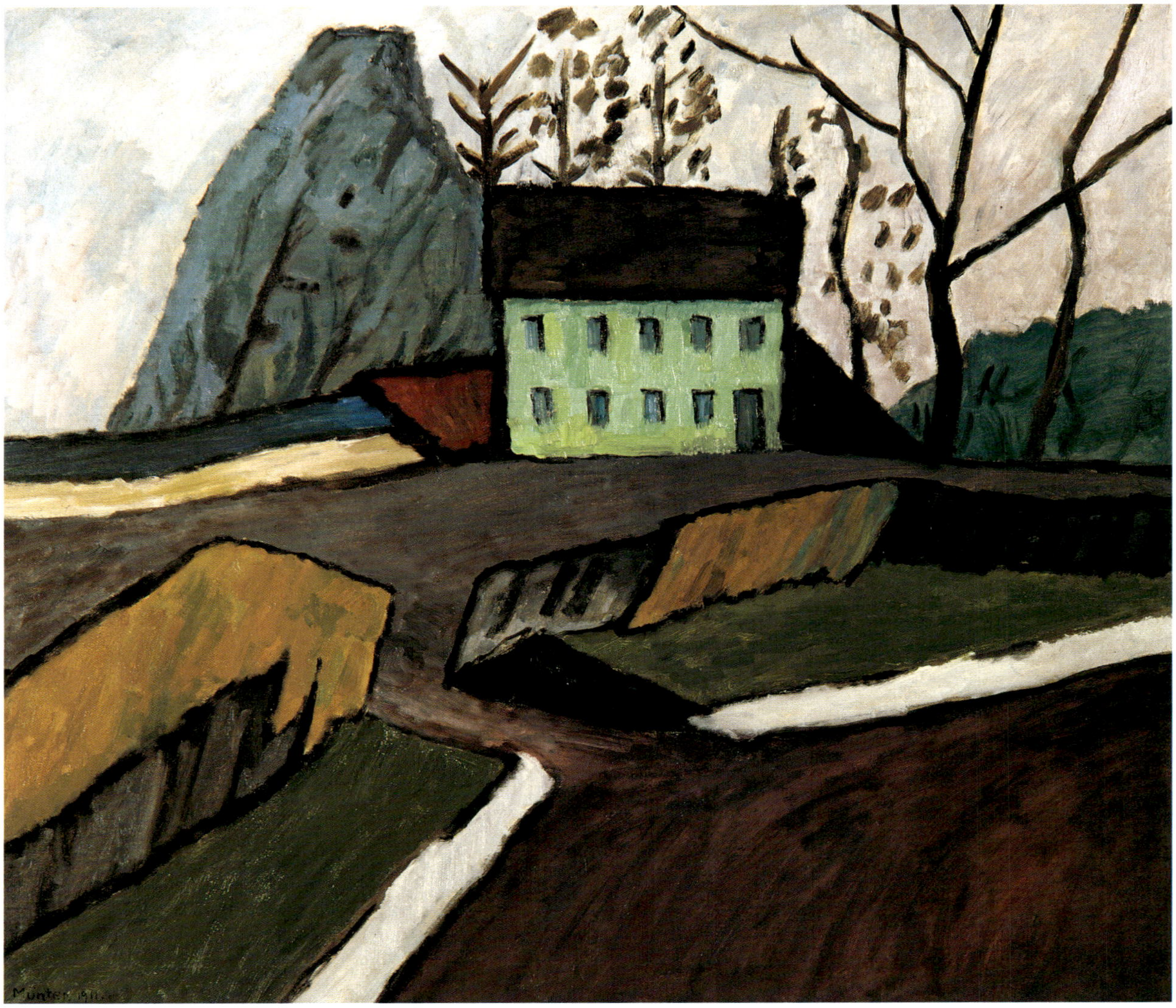

The Green House, Murnau, 1911 (Cat. No. 58)

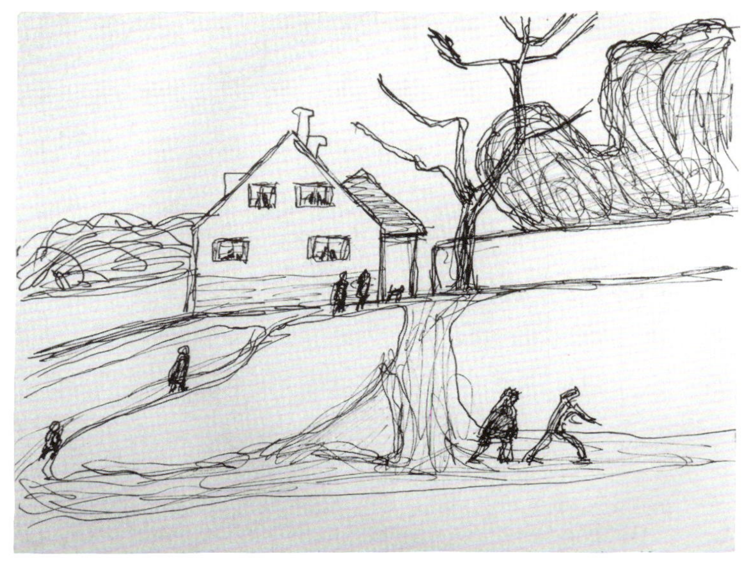

Sketch for: *Green House*, ca. 1911 (Cat. No. 60)

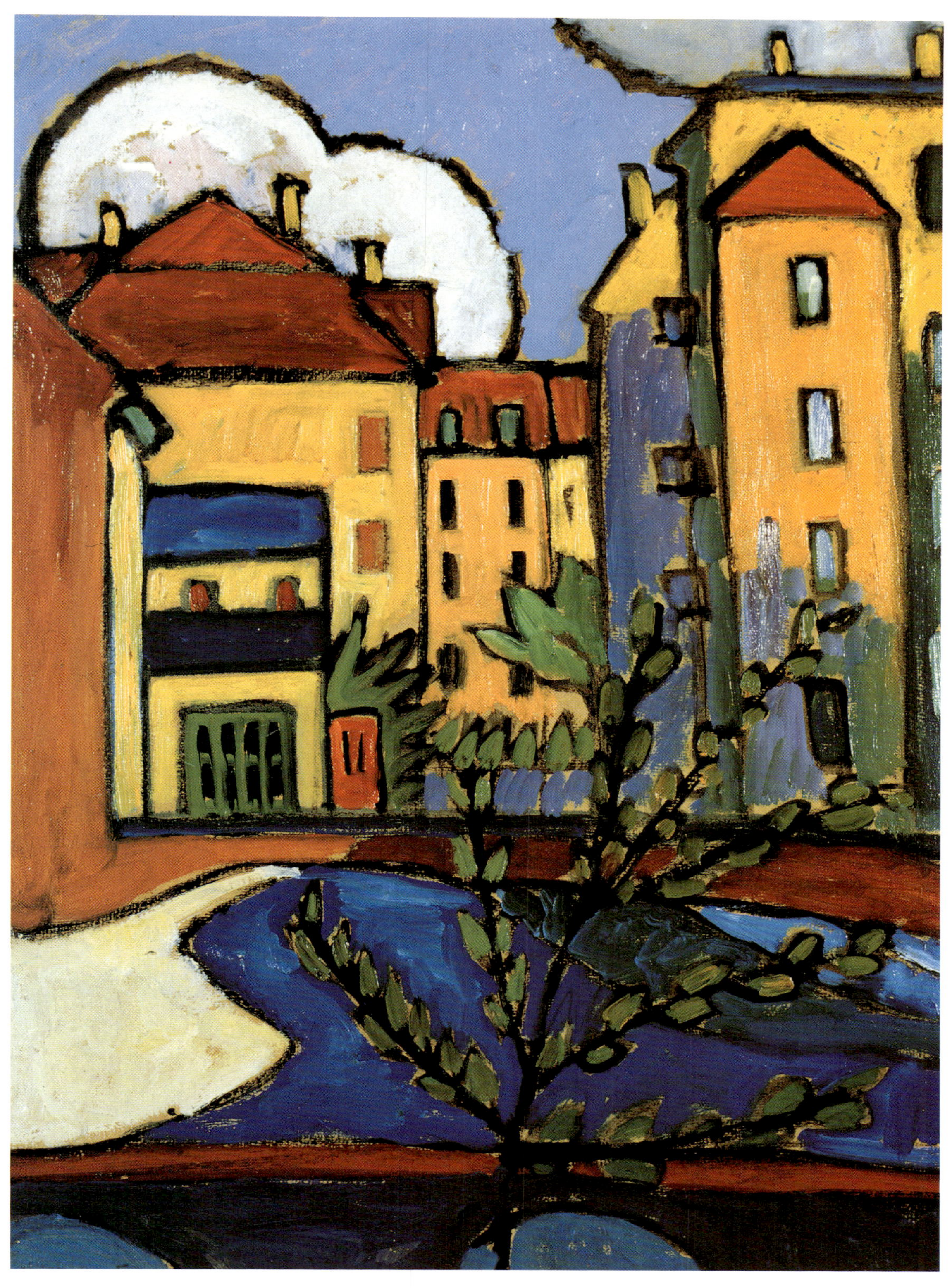

In Schwabing, 1912 (Cat. No. 63)

civilization, its turmoil, its social and political problems, its cities and industry, its materialism and its alienation. Nature purified; it restored feelings of well-being. Characterizing this concept of landscape in 1903, the poet Rainer Maria Rilke, befriended with Paula Modersohn-Becker and the other painters at Worpswede, wrote that modern artists, as they turn towards nature, "...prefer the eternal to the temporal, prefer the essential order of things to passing inventions, and see as their task the embrace of nature in order to accommodate themselves somewhere within her grand interrelationships, since they cannot convince her to be submissive to them. And through these few isolated individuals all of humanity comes closer to nature.... From this point of view it would appear that the theme and intention of all art is contained in the harmony of the individual with the absolute."[5]

The function of landscape painting, according to such a utopian, idealist view, was to restore the unity between humanity and nature, which, it seemed, modern civilization had destroyed. The intent was not to "humanize" nature, but to present an intense, elemental experience of it, to demonstrate a profound involvement with the external world of nature and objects. These become personalized by means of powerful, a-naturalistic and anti-naturalistic presentations of colors and forms in an effort to revitalize the subject/object relationship that was thought to have become cool, neutral and distanced.

In her interactions with Jawlensky, Werefkin and Kandinsky in Murnau, Münter developed the stylistic and technical means to achieve such goals. She did not seek out or construct a primeval pre-Edenic landscape without human presence, however, nor did she imagine an Adamic naturalism with naked individuals in idyllic bucolic surroundings as other Expressionists notoriously did. Instead, she presented the village and its alpine environs as paradigms of human life lived in constant interaction and coexistence with nature, sometimes harmonious, sometimes struggling. A human presence in the landscape, even when figures are absent, was a constant motif employed by Münter.

A row of yellow birch trees, curving boldly from the lower foreground to the painting's center, their golden color and the regular repetition of their lollipop-like shapes unique in the image's inventory of forms, is the dominant feature in *Fall Landscape, Study (Yellow Trees)* (Cat. No. 40), although it takes up little pictorial space.[6] The landscape scene is uninhabited. However, there are indications of human presence in the birch trees. Their regularity and symmetry signify the shaping of the land and its vegetation through acts of cultivation and landscaping. There are further signs of a controlling human presence: the small haystacks known as *Heustanka*, the mowed field and the border of trees that visually and hermeneutically interact with the grand enframing forms of the mountains to produce a scene of human association with nature in propitious, harmonious coexistence. "There are motifs that move you, and, in turn, you want to get hold of them," she jotted in her diary in 1941, "and there are motifs that inspire you to make something out of them, that are not complete as they are. Then I want to...bring order into the chaos. Synthesis. The play of variations."[7] Nature, as viewed by her, gained order by means of human intervention, whether in the agricultural working of the land around Murnau or in the pictorially structured reality of her paintings.

Marks of agricultural activity, plantings and roads appear in Münter's imagery as persistent hieroglyphs of a human presence in Murnau's greater mountainous panorama. The Alps—which in the late eighteenth and nineteenth century were frequently shown to embody the sublime, arousing awe and anxiety simultaneously with their untamed grandeur—were tamed. Human ordering and the submission to pictorial organization extricated the terror, the chaos from the sublimity of the Alps; both offered measure and scale. It is surprising, therefore, that actual figures are rare in Münter's prewar landscapes, and that when they appear they exude the air of an intruding other within the setting where they stand or walk, most commonly alone and isolated (Cat. Nos. 56–58). Even in *Boating* (Cat. No. 47) where the portrayed group plays an atypical, dominant role within the landscape, the figures remain stiffly distinct and—with the significant exceptions of Münter herself and the dog—face away from the green hills and blue mountains to gaze out of the picture at the viewer, not at nature. Their communication is with other, implicitly present human beings, not with nature's forces. With this emphasis, Münter differs dramatically from the German Romantic painters with whom she is otherwise, frequently justifiably, compared. While the figures in paintings by Caspar David Friedrich, for example, commonly face the landscape in order to commune with its majesty, to gain through it access to God's presence, Münter's habitually face away from it. With few exceptions, they are schematic, shadowy representations, depersonalized and out of place. They approach nature less like Friedrich's wanderers and, instead, more like Arnold Böcklin's or Edvard Munch's personages do: tentatively, alone and accompanied by an insurmountable element of apprehension, anxiety and fright . The harmony between nature and humanity that she presents in her landscapes fails to be recognized by the people she places in them.

Although the countryside surrounding Murnau is totally blocked off by a complex of houses and barns in *Snow and Sun*, as well as in the oil sketch that preceded this "synthesis," *Farmyard in Snow I*, it is the snow and sun of nature that intrudes into the settlement. The single, dark form of a woman appears in the snow outdoors, her face featureless, her figure amorphous, a somber shape of blackness quarantined in the gold of reflected sunshine (Cat. Nos. 56, 57).[8] Her place, it might be argued, is not here amid blue shadows and yellow brightness, but within the houses behind her from which she has emerged.

Houses generally figured prominently in Münter's landscape imagery. No other German Expressionist artist imparted signification to them or infused such character into them so consistently, whether seen in isolation or clustered in groups.[9] Emanuel Seidl's multicolored facades in Murnau clearly facilitated this. In both *Snow and Sun* paintings, each structure has a distinct identity in its shape and contours, perhaps because each is painted a different color, with windows and doors in contrasting tones or in a deep brown-black. Color engenders the personality or function of each structure within the jostling assemblage, where they are crowded together as if herded forward by the large pink building with green shutters solidly placed in the background, and where they are gathered together protectively behind the leafless brown hedge separating them from the blues, golds and white of the intruding snow.

The same cluster of houses and barns is seen from a vantage point somewhat higher on the road in *Houses on Wintry Road* (Cat. No. 51), which represents another series of winter scenes in Murnau painted by Münter after she and Kandinsky had spent a week there in January 1911.[10] The coloristic variety of the *Snow and Sun* paintings, here, gives way to a more somber tonality, broken only by the partial view of the domineering pink building. It shares this more monotone approach with *The Brewery, Murnau* (Cat. No. 55)—and both might well be identified as studies in gray—which mixes with virtually all other colors to become the dominant tonality of the scenes. The monotone grayness of houses, snow and sunless sky creates a somber mood, and a certain sense of heaviness, causing one critic aptly to recall the winter scenes by Pieter Brueghel the Elder, not in terms of influence or even prototype but in terms of a shared emotive effect derived from the gray winter setting.[11] Münter enhances the gray mood in both paintings by tightly enclosing the group of houses within the picture space, cutting them off at the sides, having them push upwards to force out most of the sky, allowing no view beyond or around the buildings themselves. Münter fills the very center of the paintings, where we might expect an opening and where their perspectival orientation leads, with houses and sheds tightly locked together, overlapping and dense. She twists and stretches the house facades, making them lean and push one against the other, supporting each other, crowding out the cold. She eschews illusions of depth and space, running her network of wide blue-black outlines, fences and hedges across the painting's surface to further contain, enclose and shut off these huddled signs of human shelter from the encroaching uninhabited cold, in which they glow in pinks and blues to provide a relief in the sober, snowy, sunless winter.

In these winter scenes, Münter chose to depict the outskirts of Murnau, where the village breaks up and opens up into farmyards and fenced enclosures, and where the regularity of its central streets dissipates. Here, at the fraying edges of the village, the dreary drama of winter—with nature shut out, closed off and denied entry, nevertheless, pushing in tenaciously with snow, damp and cold—is played out in irregular but persistent rhythms, alleviated by a hint of playfulness in the facture of Münter's drawing, the unpredictability of her lines and her touches of unexpected color within the all-pervading grayness. The effect Münter chose to create in these winter scenes contrasts strikingly with that of her late summer views of Murnau's market, Main Street and adjoining ones, in 1908 (Cat. Nos. 21, 22). Even if the streets are similarly uninhabited, or show isolated figures, the colored facades in yellow, green and blue glow and breathe beneath pale blue skies, or reflect the light of the setting and rising sun. Here, colors smile. Nature continues to be blocked out or, when incorporated into other paintings of the town streets, appears as an enframing, picturesque accent, blue mountains tamed by their distance from the town, brought into scale with the houses and streets. Murnau seems idyllic, a utopian haven, in such imagery, even as it remains eerily uninhabited, a stage awaiting its actors.

It may be possible to explain Murnau's deserted streets in Münter's paintings by her lack of contact with the town's citizens. Until the 1930s, she seldom spent more than four weeks at a time in her house, more often a few days or a week, with lengthy intervals between visits there. Moreover, that the house should be nicknamed the *Russenhaus*—House of the Russians—by the town's citizens seems less a harmless, charming and naive recognition of the presence of Kandinsky, Jawlensky and other foreign artists than a rejection, an insistence on otherness, alienation, possibly even condemnation—much like the other name given to the house by the conservative Catholic Murnauers, *Hurenhaus* or whorehouse, as a mark of their disapproval of Münter's illicit life together with Kandinsky. That under such circumstances Murnau should take so dominant a role in her landscapes is noteworthy and remarkable. While she was in the town, she stored up an inventory of images that occupied her until she returned to it. Murnau was cast by her to fulfill her dream role of "domesticity as cozy and harmonious as I could make it & [with] someone who wholly & always belongs to me,"[12] but she remained distanced from its inhabitants. One must bear in mind, however, that she deliberately painted her street scenes unpopulated, not as—or not only as—an unconscious psychological reflex against her personal experiences. These views of architectural settings and streets seeming to await their inhabitants or sheltering them unseen behind the windows of their colorful facades are her characterization of the town, an image of potential and expectation, of withdrawal and containment, of nature kept near but at bay.

Unlike other Expressionists, Münter did not construct a counter-image of the small town when she painted views of the city. Indeed, the paintings of Munich's squares and streets seem to share much with the Murnau settings as they, too, show multicolored facades drenched in sunlight. For *In Schwabing* (Cat. No. 63), Münter selected an elevated view, from a window and over a wall that frames the yellow, orange and blue group of recently built four-story apartment buildings, while in the foreground a young tree—or, more likely, a pussy willow branch brought indoors to bud on a window sill—sprouts green against blue shadows, like a screen through which to view the city. Blue-shadowed snow remains in the yard below, but the cold tonality is replaced by incandescent gold, red and orange in the upper half of the painting. The trees among the houses have been rendered in pale green as if to echo the screening pussy willow branch in a visual ode to the arrival of spring in the city, to the greenery amid the ardent glow of facades in the sunshine that overcomes the remaining traces of winter.

For such celebrations of the seasons in the city, Münter did not turn to the historical buildings of Munich, the palaces, churches or parks, but gazed from the window of her apartment onto an anonymous street scene. She offers a colorful arrangement of functional structures, each a variation on the theme of the vertical rectangle, topped by a triangular or a rectangular red roof, the colors not nuanced but presented in broad, bright, flat, juxtaposed planes precisely delineated by thinly stretched black lines. What does distinguish Munich's new apartment houses from the Main Street facades of Murnau is the absolute geometric regularity Münter accentuates in the city view. Unlike Murnau's houses, there is no diversity to counter the relentless geometric symmetry; instead, each Munich building echoes the other. Even the clouds conform to the laws of geometry. Nature seems to intrude in this artificial urban environment in the delicate branches of the pussy willow brought indoors, in the trees and bushes peeking around corners and over walls. Despite its subordinate role, nature's presence is undeniable, as sun and plants transform the view of apartment buildings into a virtual metaphor of spring's arrival within an incongruous urban milieu.

There is nothing truly alienating and anxiety-inducing in Münter's city as in other Expressionist city images. She instead portrays familiarity. The world depicted in her paintings was the fashionably bohemian Schwabing district of Munich, with new apartment houses, buildings testifying to the orderly comfort and sanitary visual appeal of urban modernity, not to Expressionist alienation, crowds or proletarian squalor. If she knew or experienced these, she excluded them from the imagery of her art and from its utopian construct. The city, instead, is a site of colorful variation for her, where the apartments of Schwabing glow in the sunlight or squares are rain-soaked at night, their darkness modulated and nuanced, interrupted by bright street lights and an invitingly illuminated entranceway (Cat. No. 48). Trees as remnants of nature likewise offer cohesion to the view of *Habsburg Square, Munich* (Cat. No. 59), only a block away from Münter's apartment. If nature and a man-made urban setting are seen as the painting's major components, it may be viewed as a record of nature tamed and put into service, with trees planted in even rows, flowers in geometric beds, a harnessed horse pulling a wagon and two dogs roaming the street, either accompanying the mother and child or embodying something between domesticity and wildness. Even the mother and child (or nursemaid and child), in this context, are extensions of this parable of nature in man's service, as they represent a biological process domesticated within the relationships of a family. Certainly, there is the danger of overinterpreting such an engaging painting, but Münter's seriousness of purpose in the motif is indicated by the fact that she repeated the composition several times, worked it up from drawings and published it as a woodcut in the May 1913 issue of *Der Sturm*. She also seems to have been thinking at this time about a major composition devoted to the exploration of work and labor. Several drawn and painted sketches of construction work—men digging and horses pulling wagons (Cat. Nos. 66, 67)—were made, and she returned to the theme in a woodcut as well as later drawings (Cat. No. 72), demonstrating an unusual tenacity with regard to work on a single subject. The work remained unfinished, a concept unrealized, but *Construction Work*, and related depictions of horse-drawn wagons amid the factories of the Rhineland, serve well as antitheses to Franz Marc's monumentalized horses, images of virile, natural strength and militant dynamic energy. Münter's horses work: they pull loads or stand patiently in their harnesses, fulfilling the demands placed on them, most comparable in their function to the women Münter depicted earlier washing laundry (Cat. No. 10), unglamorously, patiently carrying out their menial but essential tasks at the service of men. However these urban images might be understood, they form a major counterpoint to the dominant urban and equine imagery of the male members of Germany's Expressionist avant-garde. They appear as humble and unassuming in comparison to the monumental, ambitious images by the men, but Münter's small paintings and sketches contain within them a radical criticism of the premises underlying precisely those male images. Perhaps for that reason, Münter did not carry out her project on a grander scale and left it incomplete.

Nature in an environment constructed by man is in many ways Münter's primary, if not only, theme manifested in virtually every one of her landscapes and cityscapes. A tree appears in the foreground of the study *City View by Night*, leafless: adapted to the urban world in which it grows, its network of branches plays off the lines and the reflected glow of its darkened surroundings—almost like a diagram of the streets themselves, an extension of, not a contrast to, the city milieu. If *In Schwabing* can be considered an homage to urban spring, this is a similar celebration of late fall or early winter. Even if seen only in climate, weather and intrusive plantings, nature remains a constant presence in Münter's city, while the modern metropolis provides an alternative, man-made environment, appealing and pleasurable in its very artificiality as it illuminates and nuances the natural darkness of night, but also imposing a rigid order, discipline and limit on nature, on life itself within its walls, streets and squares.

The dichotomy and frequently uneasy intersection Münter sees between the products of human existence and nature finds resolution in the surroundings of Murnau. Not in the denseness of the village streets or backyards, but in nearby harvested fields, in the meadows with sheds, and in the single houses and farms that existed outside the village core itself. She often shows these houses standing starkly, isolated, pushed towards the horizon, as simple square blocks of pink, green or white, topped by red roofs and set in the countryside (Cat. Nos. 26, 58). In their plain, geometric simplicity, they represent a dramatic antithesis to the multicolored, irregular natural forms surrounding them. And yet they become harmonized as nature envelops them. They give focus to and punctuate the land, and are themselves surrounded by walled gardens that offer a transition from their own geometric regularity to the erratic growth of nature, avoiding unmediated opposition. In winter, when snow encroaches, it is depicted in majestic patterns of shadow and light, and the small houses emerge almost playfully among them, as miniature counterpoints drawn frontally, roofed rectangles with windows and doors inscribed in them, recalling children's drawings in their naive-like conceptualization (Cat. No. 39).

Münter began collecting children's drawings in 1908, and immediately began to adopt their forms and devices, employing a formal vocabulary also resembling that used in reverse-glass painting. Used most consistently in her landscapes, these child-like practices were to aid in lending her images a sense of the untutored and original, to allow her to share in the apparent innocence, sincerity and immediate expressivity of a child's art. Kandinsky praised "the artist who remains a child in many ways for his entire life [in order to] more readily approach the inner sound of things," and observed that the gifted child possesses the "ability to express the abiding internal [aspect of an object] in terms of a form through which this abiding internal becomes apparent most powerfully and thus works (as one says, 'it speaks'!)."[13] By emulating children's art, like the "folk art" of reverse-glass painting, the most honest form of expression might be achieved.[14]

In *The Green House, Murnau* (Cat. No. 58), Münter again juxtaposes two orders, two varying stylistic and conceptual approaches, within one image: the realm of the child in the upper half, which serves as the background, and a sophisticated variation of perspective in the lower half, the foreground. A curving road, fences and hedges, borders of trapped drifted snow and areas of grass make up the foreground. These elements appear as ambiguous geometric forms, moving into depth, their perspective reversed, flattened into monochrome shapes, so that together they become a disrupted combination of intersecting interpretations of spatial depth and the means of its rendering. In contrast, the house, mountains and trees are rendered flat, without modulation or allusions to volume. Their shapes are simplified, reduced to child-like conceptual renderings: the house is rectangular, the mountain triangular with a curving slope and its peak cut off, trees are vertical lines with very few leaves and branches emerging from them. Centrally placed, enframed by trees and the mountain, the grandly simple shape of the green house gains a powerful presence in this intermixture of artistic orders, while it seems to hug the simplified forms of nature around it. It is distanced from the contrived foreground even as it shares in the geometric order of the forms there. The single house, freestanding, mediates between innocent nature and the harsh, ordered complexity of human constructions.

Solitary dwellings, like the summer villa she herself bought, fascinated Münter and appeared as constant metaphoric presences in her landscape paintings. She demonstrated a similar fascination with the white chapels and their Baroque towers and cupolas common to the alpine valleys and villages near Murnau. They too appear alone, enveloped in nature and emerging grandly from it. During her first visit, she fixed on a small chapel (Cat. No. 17), probably the one in Aidling, a farming community from whose elevation one sees a vast panoramic view of Riegsee lake, of the village Riegsee and of Murnau, with the Alps rising as a magnificent backdrop directly behind the town. Münter, who may have cycled or hiked there, chose not to attempt to portray the overwhelming drama of the scene laid out before her; instead, she painted the chapel, grandly monumental but on a small piece of strawboard. Given the setting, the painting is an ironic commentary on the fundamental impossibility of rendering the grandeur of the alpine landscape as previous artists, who had accented each detail and got lost in minutiae, had done. Münter recognized the need to depict fragments to represent the sense of the whole, and the need to render in simplified forms the magnificent alpine peaks nearby, staged so appropriately for her art in Murnau. During her outing to Aidling, the chapel—standing in the shadow of nearby trees—became an ironic painterly summation of the landscape experience. The plain white building pushes against the limitations of the rectangular field on which it is depicted, as if barely contained, and it blocks off all but small segments of its surroundings. This effect grants the chapel its sense of monumentality, although Münter painted it with humorous incongruity on such a small scale.

Münter refrained from painting interior views of these small Catholic Bavarian chapels and from depicting the religious ceremonies and processions that took place in and near them. Unlike Kandinsky, it was largely the artifacts—the statues, religious figurines and votive paintings—associated with Bavarian Catholicism that intrigued her, not its practices. She was fascinated by the theosophical teachings of Rudolf Steiner and was interested in apparent supernatural phenomena, later participating in séances, for example, but for organized religion she seems to have had little intellectual or emotional concern. The chapels and churches she painted were defined as elements in her landscape experience; their Catholic identity was incidental. Baroque alpine churches rise in her paintings from groves of trees (Cat. Nos. 41, 48), providing focus, much as isolated houses do in other paintings. In color and form they break with their natural surroundings, whose coloristic intensity Münter escalated with the pink and orange of the evening sky so that trees, bushes, fields and rooftops glow almost explosively. She also employed in these paintings a thicker paint application, with more marked brushstrokes, than in her other landscapes of the time, and accented rough, jaggedly irregular, black contours to define the forms. Visual tension results with configurations seeming stolid and on the verge of explosive eruption, as if with these paintings Münter was depicting a landscape analogue to Kandinsky's apocalyptic visions.

Münter altered and adapted her basic stylistic approach—flat, broadly colored forms with dark outlining—to match the meaning she wished to impart through the scene or objects depicted in a painting. Her works, therefore, offer a persistent variety of appearance as she refused to settle on a single stylistic approach. There is an order to the diversity, however. Her town and city views, with clustered houses juxtaposed with streets and squares, she rendered so as to contrast one mass against another, to pictorially explore the intersection of planes, the dematerialization of forms in orchestrations of light and dark, or the staging of a telling scene. The compositions inclined towards relative complexity with a multitude of components, spatial ambiguity, and frequently disparate manners of paint application, brushstrokes and drawing within a single image. Conversely, in views of the alpine countryside around Murnau, she strove for greater simplicity of compositional arrangement and for cohesion in her stylistic approach. Unity, harmony and coherence were stressed, with the human presence emerging in her accented stylizations and vigorous brushwork. The manner of making an image became fused with the subject matter; together, they were interpretive metaphors of her personal response to the motifs depicted.

Questions and Abstraction

Chapter 6

Stockholm and Copenhagen

"[B]ut how am I going to find 'form'—what is 'form' anyway[?] What is appropriate? What not? Should one paint, as I do, in a variety of ways?" Gabriele Münter wrote to Kandinsky in 1910.[1] From Moscow, he warned her to avoid "hard, overly precise form, which 'today' is impossible & anyway leads to a dead end...."[2] The admonition was prompted by her remark that an "undeniable Picasso influence" could be detected in her latest work, painted during Kandinsky's absence. His irritation and jealousy poorly hidden, Kandinsky continued: "What form is, I defined very concisely and well in my brochure. If you really feel what I mean (don't philosophize, just *simply* understand, feel!) you will also find form. One must let the form work on one and forget all the Picassos and Picassoists." In response, she reassured him and assuaged his jealousy: "I am sure you are aware that I never think how does so-and-so do it or how did I see it in this or that picture. I had to try various ways myself, and arrived at the idea of schematization when the thing simply didn't suit me. Don't know if there is much purpose to it—but some surely. [I] believe I really do understand your definition of form."[3]

The exchange reveals much about the artists' personal and artistic relationship. Kandinsky clearly viewed himself as continuing his role as teacher and mentor, while mixing this perception with his role as Münter's lover and companion. If she questioned aspects of his artistic teachings and theories, he would immediately translate this into an accusation and would claim that she was personally disloyal and unfaithful. Münter gave in. She avoided close relationships with other artists, especially men, and seldom overtly questioned Kandinsky's ideas. Sometimes, however, she implied disagreement. Her questions about form and the diversity of her own approach to painting were serious issues for her art, but they also concealed an undertone of criticism. Kandinsky's work in 1909–10 likewise revealed a multiplicity of simultaneous approaches, ranging from stylized but recognizably representational landscapes and interior views emulating Münter's to the virtual abstractions he called "compositions." When Münter spoke of painting "in a variety of ways," she was describing his work as well as her own. Similarly, by asking about the meaning of form, she implied a criticism of his theories in which questions of form prevailed. As was his wont, Kandinsky saw the fault not in himself but in her. The issue of multiple, simultaneous painting modes he simply ignored, then attacked her for being influenced by Picasso, and finally told her that she should not try to understand his ideas of form since she was incapable of doing so. Münter would simply have to feel. He left unsaid that feelings rather than logic were appropriate to a woman. Usually, Münter submitted to such reprimands and characterizations of her nature and women's generally. When she defended herself, it was surreptitiously, more by nuance than forceful argumentative response. Thus, her conclusion that "[I] believe I really do understand your definition of form" emphasized the word "understand" but modified it with "I believe"; it became internalized and subjective in accordance with Kandinsky's admonition. Finally, it was she, not Kandinsky, who resolved the dilemma of multiple, simultaneous modes of painting: "Often my works seem too different from one another to me a[nd] then again I feel that it is, after all, one personality that creates this variety."[4]

Deftly, she turned on its head the common argument that through a given style a personality is revealed, by insisting that singleness of personality can underlie stylistic diversity, and that even within this diversity—indeed through this very diversity—the cohesive unity of the individual is discernible. The personality of the individual, not the manner of painting, guaranteed cohesion and unity. Kandinsky took up the argument in 1912 in *The Blaue Reiter Almanac*:

> *Form is the external expression of the inner content.* Therefore, one should not make an idol out of form. And one should struggle for form no longer than it can serve as the means of expression for inner resonance. Therefore, one should not seek salvation in *one* form....[5]

Although altered, her original formulation remained fundamental to his concepts. Her ideas mixed with his to be incorporated into the Expressionist modernist aesthetic he composed. The frequent characterization of her work as lacking a theoretical component, and of her lack of understanding of others' theories, runs counter to the content of her correspondence with Kandinsky.

For Kandinsky, theory communicated convictions about his art's pioneering historical role. Its function was to proselytize. Theory seconded artistic self-assurance and demanded disciples. For Münter, however, theory was applied to alleviate doubts. "I thought of myself as just a small beginner a[nd] never thought of comparing myself with anyone else," she confessed. "...I see myself readily as 'insignificant'—and the others always seem more important to me."[6] By justifying the variety of her work, she reassured herself of its value. Kandinsky comforted her further:

> ...form is much, but only as a means, and so at the same time it is nothing. A form can be perfect, brilliant and yet not be worth half a penny since it is empty. So, long live form and down with form! You personally need not be afraid, you *must* say something because it is born in you. Just put your ear to your heart and listen! ... And listen carefully to how it resonates.[7]

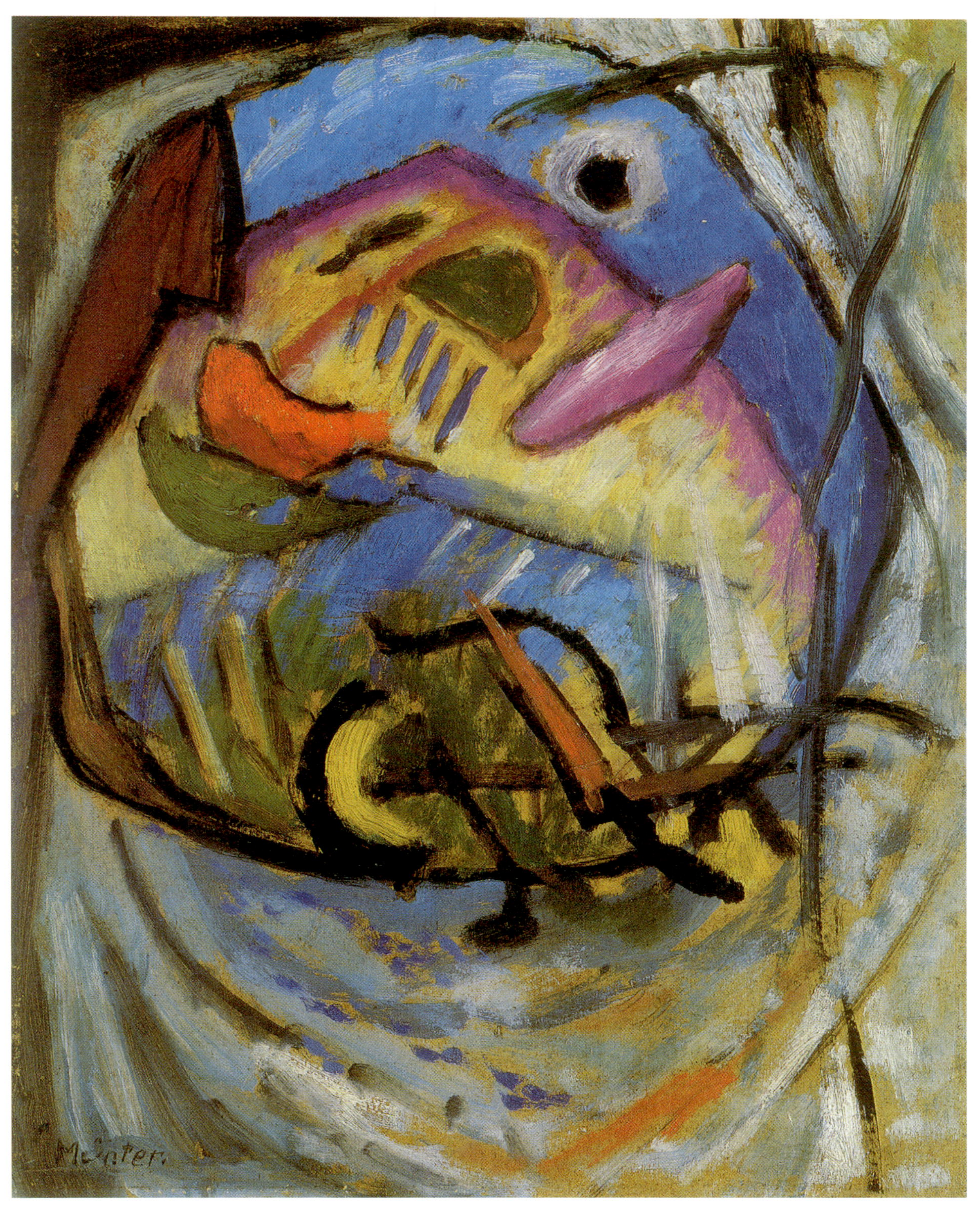

Abstract Study, 1915 (Cat. No. 71)

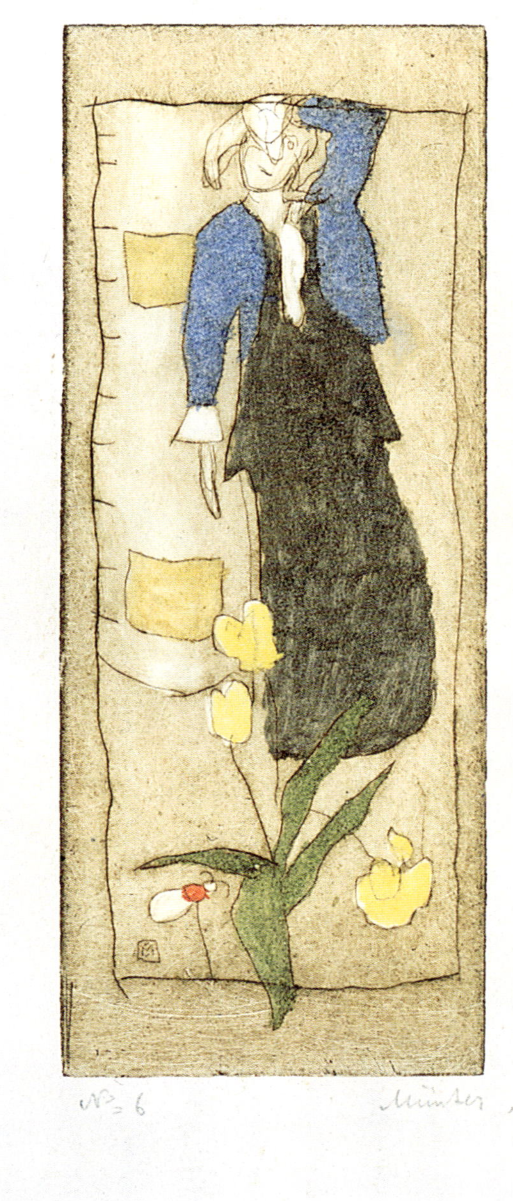

Woman Seeking, 1916 (Cat. No. 76)

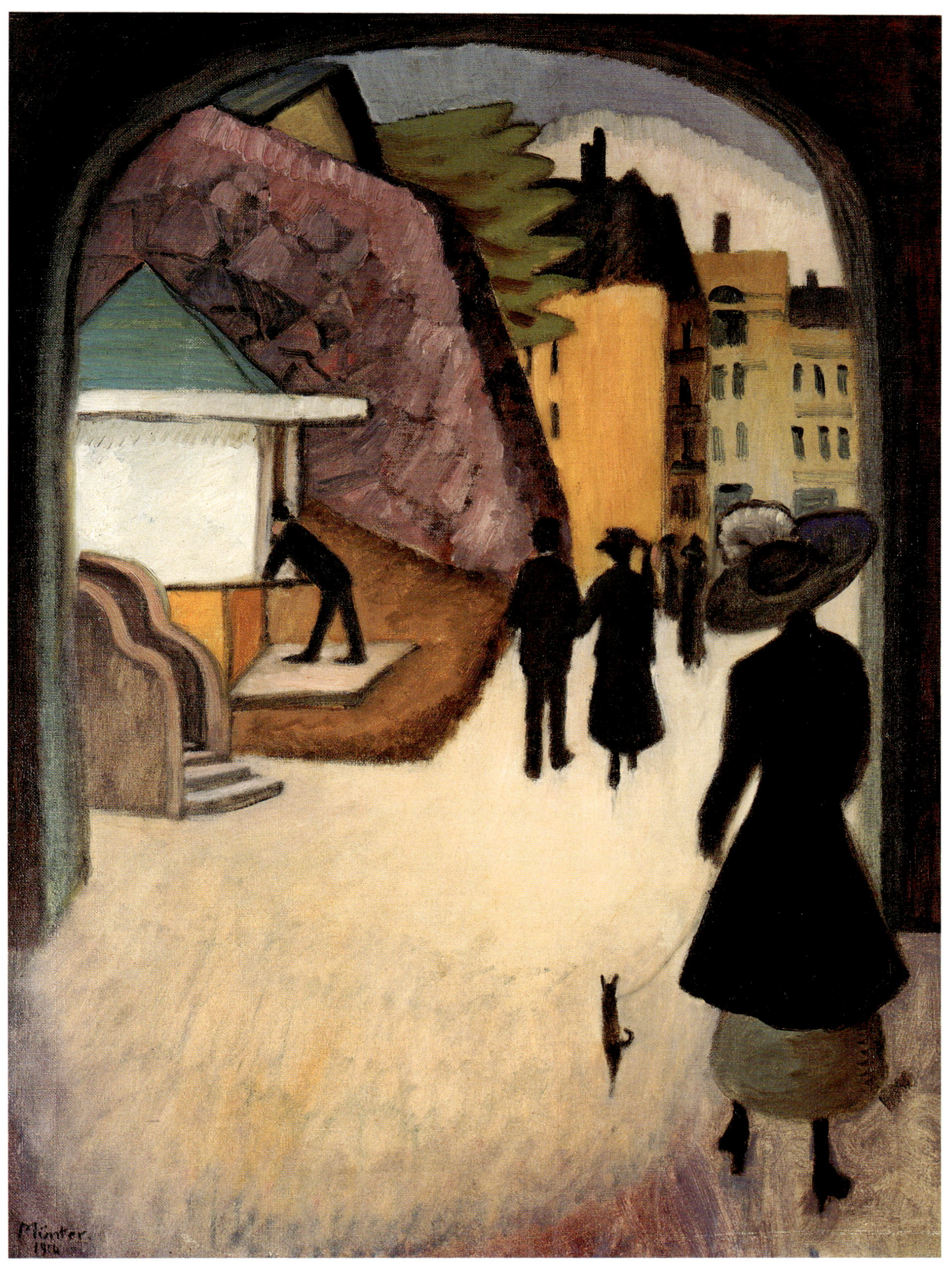

Street in Stockholm (May Evening in Stockholm), 1916 (Cat. No. 77)

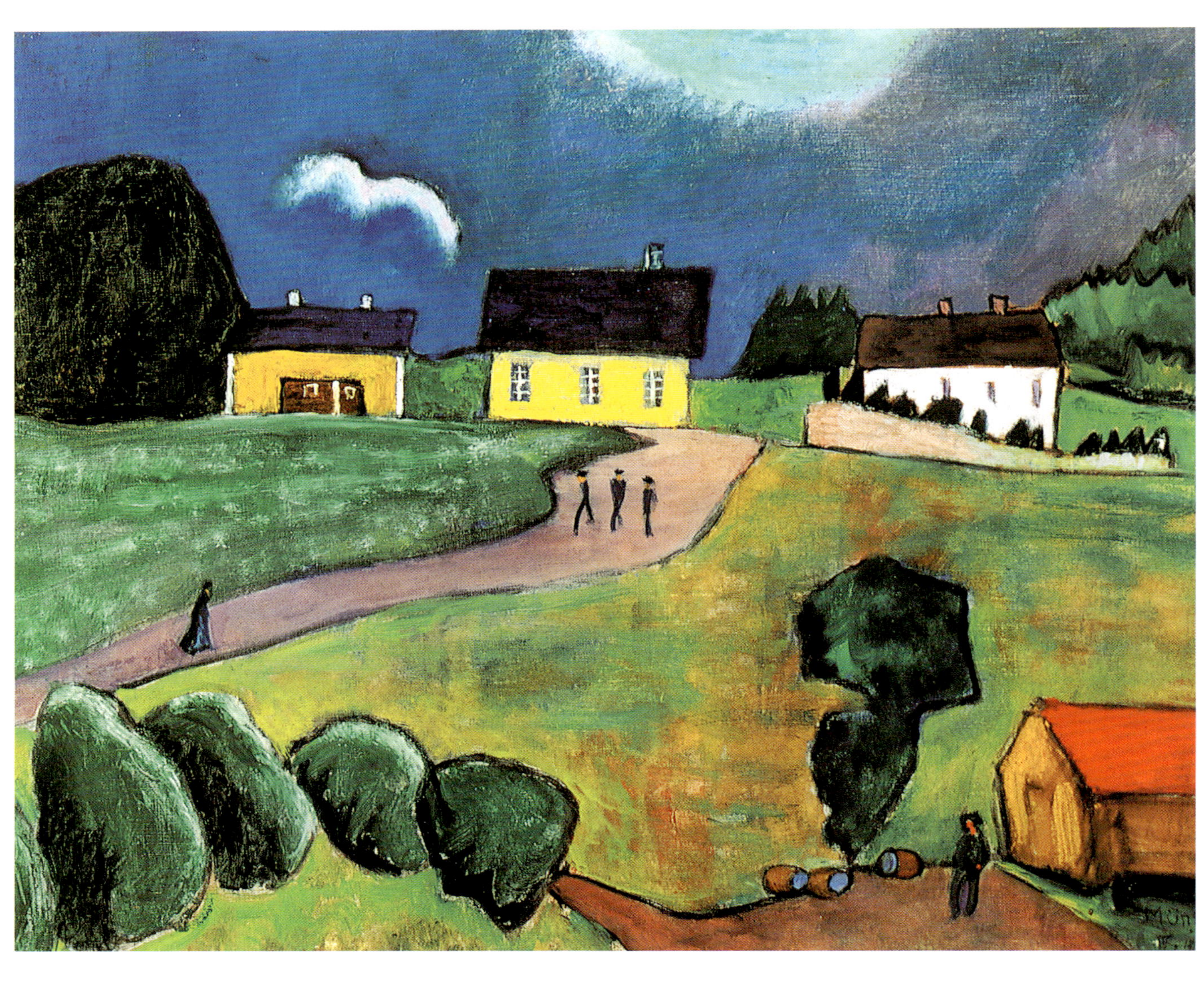

From Norway, Tjellebotten, 1917 (Cat. No. 78)

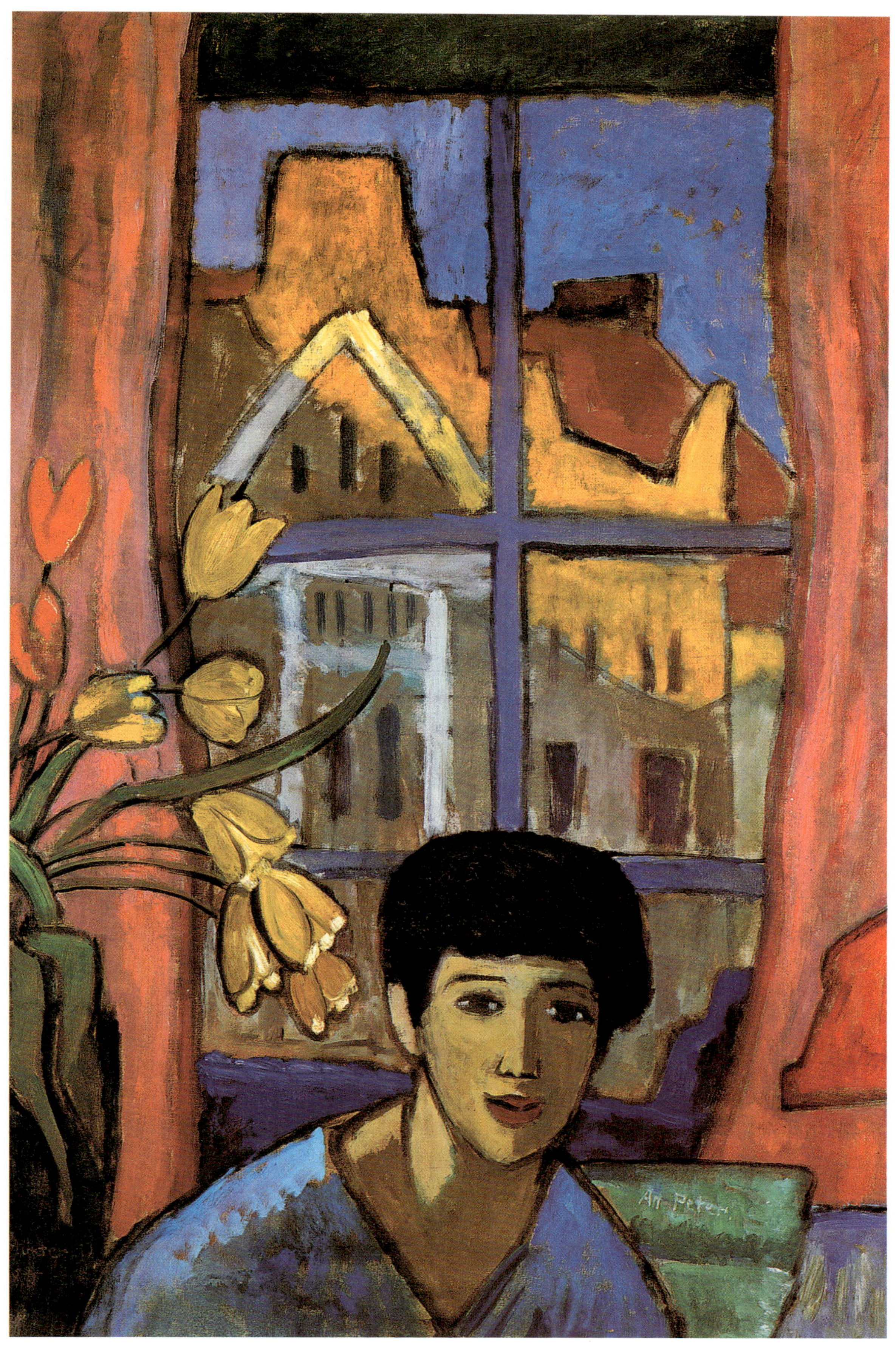

The Future (Woman in Stockholm), 1917 (Cat. No. 79)

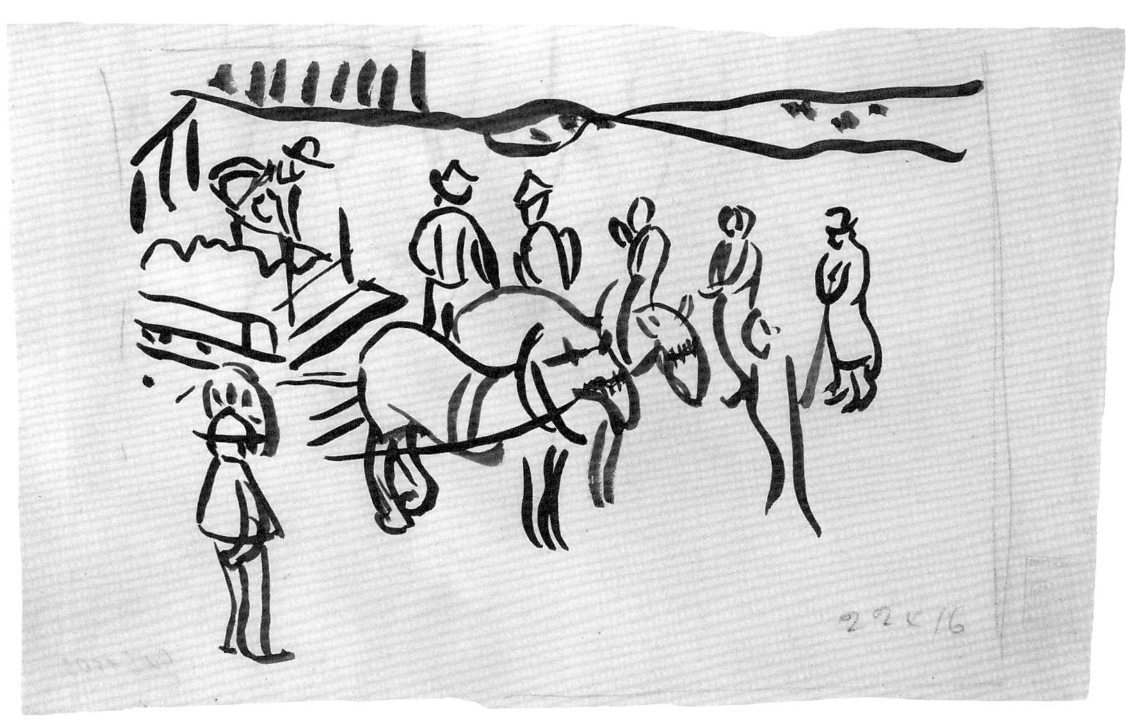

Construction Work, 1916 (Cat. No. 72)

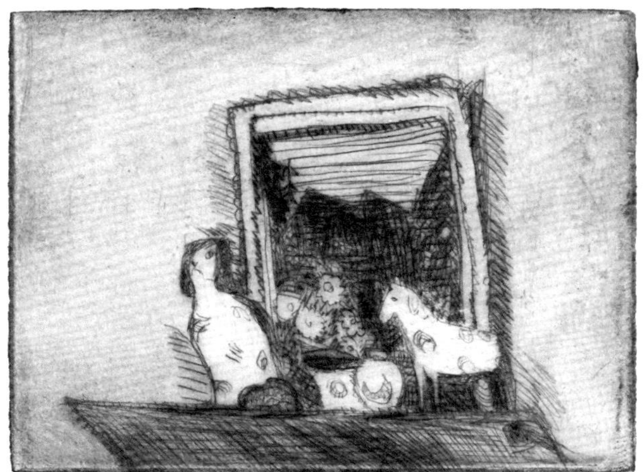

Still Life, 1916 (Cat. No. 73)

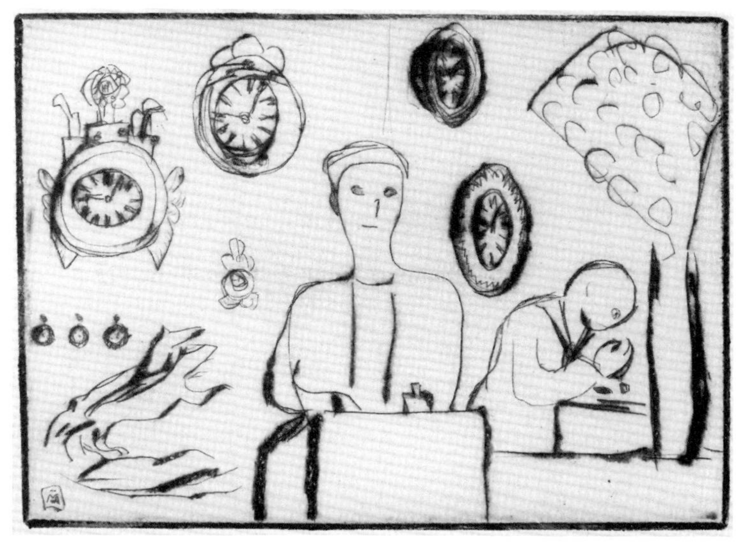

Clockmaker, 1916 (Cat. No. 74)

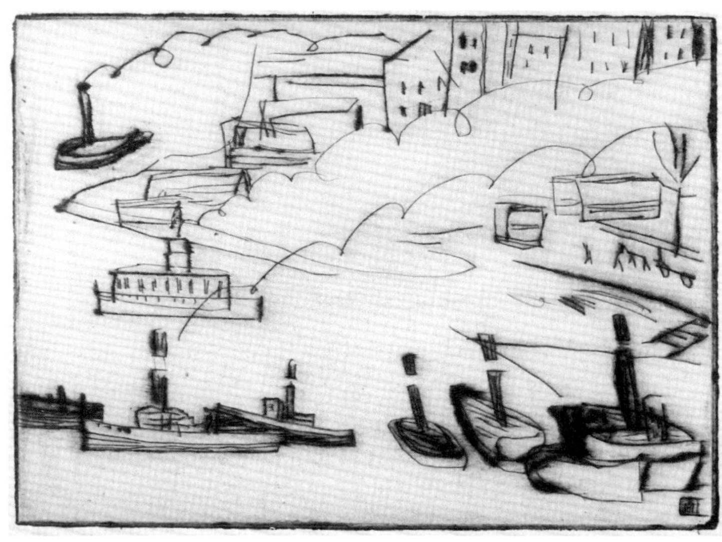

Near the Sluice, Stockholm, 1916 (Cat. No. 75)

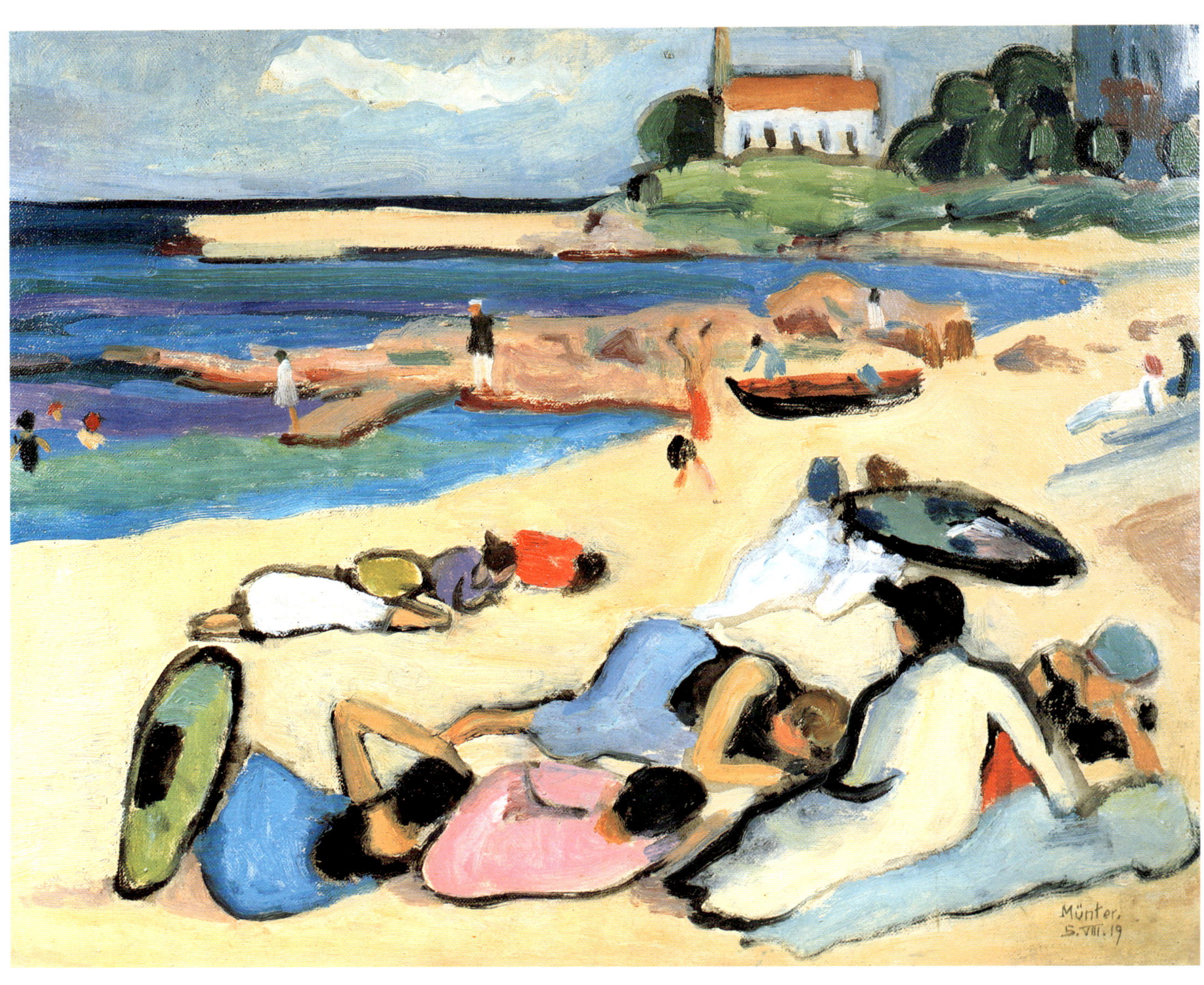

Beach at Bornholm, 1919 (Cat. No. 81)

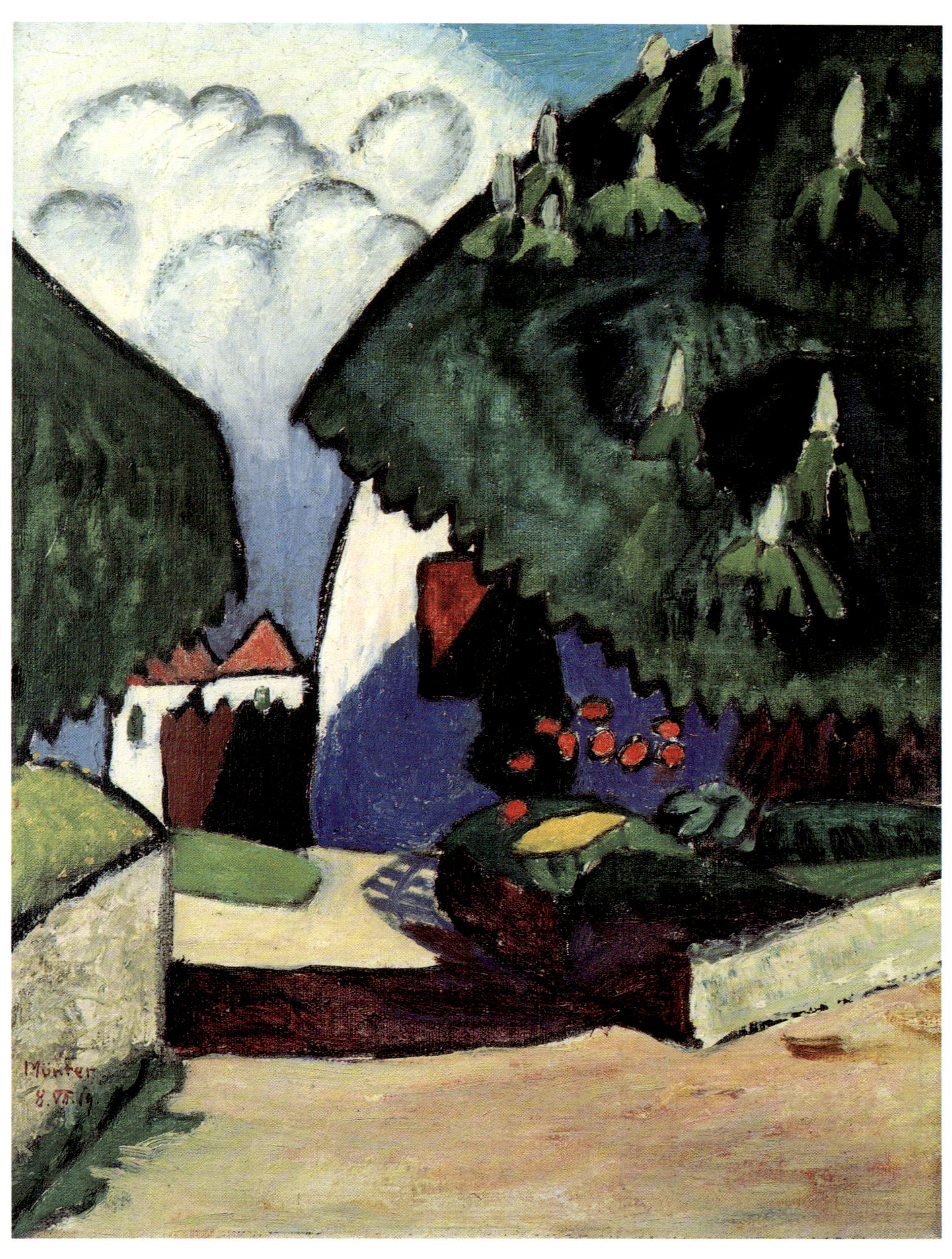

The Chestnut Tree, 1919 (Cat. No. 82)

Such encouragement was constantly needed. "Again I thought about your pictures," he wrote, "and was angry and regretted painfully that you do not work much more energetically. God's divine spark is in you, as is so immensely rare among painters. And your external abilities [i.e. technical skills] are certainly sufficient. Your flowing line and your sense of color!"[8]

In part because of her self-doubt, Münter worked fitfully, alternating between days of extraordinary productivity and days of virtual inactivity, accompanied by moods of listlessness and melancholy. "The last few days I have been restless and incapable of anything," she reported. "Was always intending to work—I couldn't find the time firstly, & secondly when time, no energy. Things are gradually beginning to improve. Now I have been sitting for quite a while & dozing—can't get around to doing anything...."[9] In contrast to such periods of inertia, there were others, such as the first weeks in Murnau in 1908, in which Münter painted between three and five works a day, and made numerous pencil sketches. Her inconsistency, raised additional doubts as to how serious she was as an artist.

Around 1912, she began to feel genuinely dissatisfied with her work and sought solutions for her unease.[10] Projects she initiated failed to find resolution. In painting new versions of earlier works, and taking up motifs from her Sèvres sketchbooks, she was able to distance herself from the present and the milieu which shaped her work during the previous four years.

Her still lifes particularly testify to a process of alienation from the familiar environment of her Munich apartment with its arrangements of figurines and flowers. As early as 1911, she staged her still lifes in such a fashion as to obscure their reality and to construct an artificial milieu around them. *Still Life in Circle* (Cat. No. 52) was an ambiguous scene of figurines that appear as virtual human figures, their reality put into question, however, by the scale of the bird and the vase of flowers. The setting for this shifting reality likewise fails to attain fixity, and encircles the pictorial elements, forming a mysterious ambience of colors seeking form. Identities engage in a mix and shift of referentiality that prevent the painting from being the record of a grouping on Münter's table and towards an abstracted fusion of conceptual, visual and artistic realities.

Kandinsky at this time was engaged in developing a vocabulary of non-referential, or only partially referential, forms for his "absolute painting,"[11] and Münter's practice in part corresponded to his but with significant differences. He employed hermeneutical, figurative signs in which reference to an external world remains, displaced and disguised, but sufficient to be recognized. "[I] did not want to give up the object totally," he explained. "I therefore more or less dissolved the objects ... so that their spiritual resonances could be experienced one after the other by the viewer."[12] In this mixture of recognizability and disguise, Münter shared Kandinsky's goals of seeking a "spiritual resonance" that would "sound" from her pictures, but also offered criticism of, or alternatives to, his grand ambitions. He

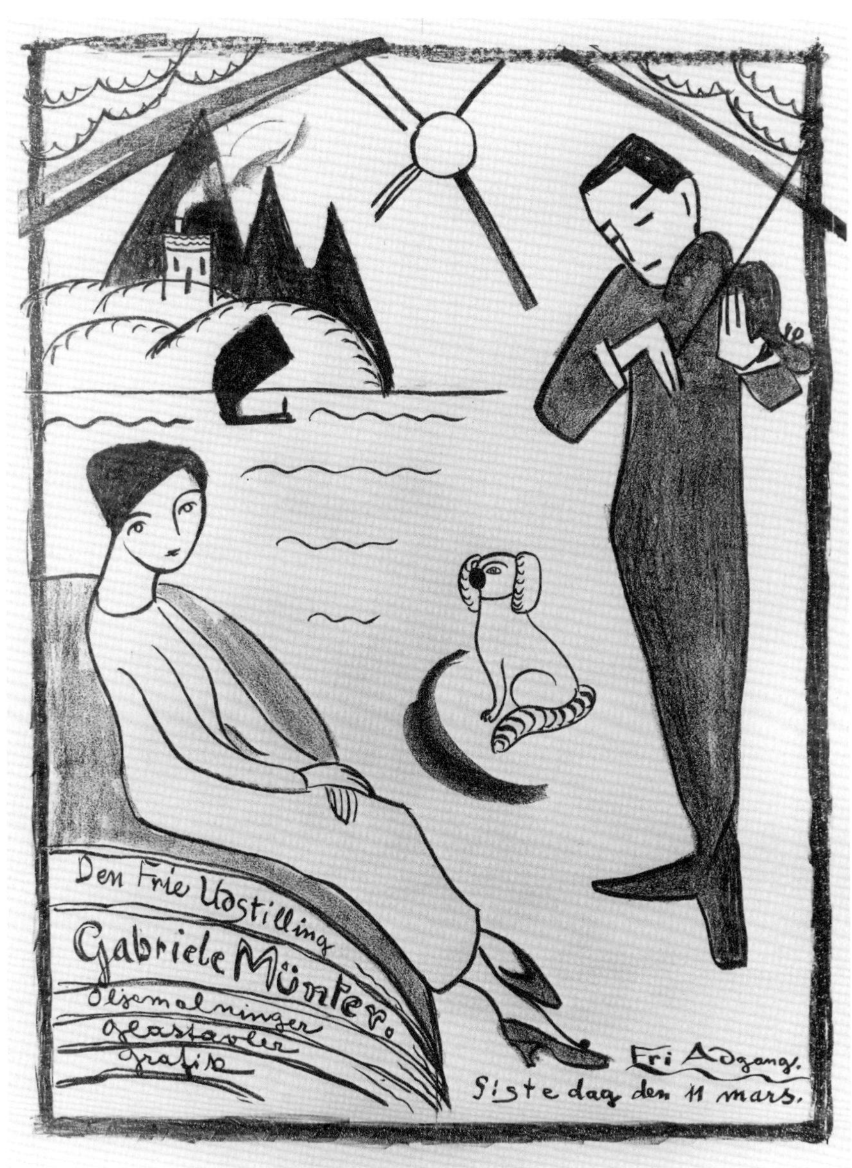

Poster for the Gabriele Münter Exhibition, Copenhagen, 1918 (Cat. No. 80)

spoke of his art as "a thundering collision of different worlds that are destined to produce the new world, called the work [of art], in and from their battle with each other."[13] Münter's worlds, however, do not thunder. The confrontation between art and reality is more playful. In 1913, she used a small Russian folk sculpture of St. George fighting the dragon as the basis for *Dragon Fight*. Two sketchbook drawings, one spreading across two pages, where it jostles against a schematic rendering of a Madonna Dolerosa, and an oil study (Cat. No. 68) preceded the final painting.[14] For Kandinsky the motif of St. George was a personal sign, a disguised self-portrait, a reference to the modern artist's struggle against his opponents and against the "monster" of materialism. As a woodcut print on the cover of *The Blaue Reiter Almanac*, it also became the emblem of the avant-garde artists' group of the same name. Thus, Münter offered a variation on a theme laden with significance for Kandinsky and the Munich artists. However, she employed as a prototype for her image not revered icons or altar paintings, as were Kandinsky's sources, but a small folk figurine included among the *Almanac*'s illustrations. Münter's reference was unmistakable. She stripped Kandinsky's imagery of its burden of connotative symbolism by identifying it with a decorative figurine, a toy. Not an apocalyptic clash, her painting is a lighthearted variation on his theme, injected with irony and humor. As such, it also becomes a gentle criticism of Kandinsky's overblown metaphysical ambitions and of the desire common to the male artists of Munich's avant-garde to view their works as major historical events.

Franz Marc perhaps recognized this humorously critical note in Münter's paintings when he wrote to Kandinsky that "...I am uncertain [about her current works], do not see her goal clearly and have my very personal painter's reservations concerning some of the ways she goes about it."[15] The play of Münter's paintings, their comical and awkward accents, their shifting perspectives and masquerading realities, their overtly inconsequential motifs countered his thoughts about modernism's heroic stance. Münter threatened to transform the men's pioneering Expressionist efforts into "women's work." In a sketchbook, she rendered Kandinsky's painting *Lyrical* (1911, Museum Beumans-van Boynigen, Rotterdam), another St. George image and a decorative bird, to be used as patterns for pearl stitchings, or perhaps for purses.[16] "To create ... *symbols* for their own time ... [for] the altars of a future spiritual religion," was the goal Marc set for the new art.[17] Münter predicted a future in decoration and fashion.

In its compositional arrangement and its use of the St. George motif, *Dragon Fight* also paraphrases Münter's earlier *Still Life with St. George* (Cat. No. 54), the work Kandinsky praised in the *Almanac*. She thereby makes yet another allusion to the *Almanac* and to the theoretical constructs of her male colleagues, but more immediately she offers a variation and a commentary on her own work. In the earlier still life, the figurines and the tabletop setting resemble the actual objects, but simultaneously suggest an ambiguous alternative reality, all the while affirming the painting's own technical and formal independence. The later painting shows a figurine in a seemingly dramatic, religiously significant scene, though, at the same time, reaffirms the stiff naiveté and the monochrome coloration of the figurine. There is a similarity in approach, yet a comical, doubting note enters into Münter's variation on this theme.

Still Life in Circle likewise underwent a significant transformation. A few months before her 1913 exhibition, Münter used its compositional, formal and color arrangements in one of her first abstract "absolute paintings," *Study with White Spots* (Cat. No. 62). In the mid-1950s, she recalled: "From its beginnings I experienced Kandinsky's conversion to non-objective painting, and at the time I told him, I would not join in, because it was appropriate to him a[nd] belonged to him—'I would remain with nature.' And I did, too. But sometimes, when I could not resolve a pictorial problem very well, I allowed myself to 'abstract' or at other times I painted freely without an objective motif. I did not think much of these experiments a[nd] did not show them.... I did not paint abstractly because my eyes constantly provided me with motifs from nature."[18] But Gabriele Münter was equivocating. She not only painted abstract works, but also exhibited them. They provided yet another variation in content and approach in her art, as ironic testimony to her individual personality.

Still Life in Circle left its traces in *Study with White Spots*. The colors are echoed, as is the compositional layout, although the circular surround of the still life was cut. In Münter's terms, the new painting represents a "schematization" that has "crystallized" the major compositional components that now appear in more elemental configurations. The figurative shapes remain as ghosts of themselves, as residues of figurative recollection. The practice parallels Kandinsky's "dissolution" of objects in his striving for abstraction, but where he employed hermeneutical, figurative signs to be decoded by the viewer, she removed the signifying elements, the codes of identifiability, to arrive at a structural substratum of vaguely shaped colors and directionally oriented brushstrokes. Kandinsky abstracted to arrive at meaning, at his "inner resonance"; Münter abstracted precisely to eschew meaning and to engage the play of forms, lines and colors on the cardboard's surface. Rejecting his apocalyptic content, monumental size and mystical intent, she instead affirmed the "objectness" of the painting itself, its very presence as a material object composed of interacting material elements. If Kandinsky's retention of meaning affirmed traditional concepts of art as referencing a world outside itself, then Münter's *Study with White Spots* radically rejects even this remnant of tradition by denying all reality except its own.

When Münter left Germany for Scandinavia, she also left the system of support that ranged from the companionship of Kandinsky to the milieux and landscapes of Munich and Murnau. She could, however, build on the championship of her work by Herwarth Walden and his "Der Sturm" Gallery, which had previously arranged exhibitions in Scandinavia. As she waited anxiously and impatiently for Kandinsky to come, after arriving in Stockholm at the end of July 1917, she renewed her acquaintance with Carl Palme, a fellow Phalanx School student, and sought out Swedish artists who exhibited with Walden—especially Isaac Grünewald and his wife, Sigrid Hjertén.[19] In this way, Münter attempted to recreate her social and professional environment in Munich through artists sharing her modernist convictions, but painted little. She studied Swedish, but failed to become truly integrated into Swedish society. As a woman alone, her contacts remained circumscribed. Much of her energy she devoted to arranging exhibitions of her own and Kandinsky's works.

It is incorrect, however, to consider Münter as inactive, withdrawn, depressed and demoralized after she arrived in Sweden. Her sketchbooks testify to her crisscrossing the city in search of motifs, especially in the historic *Gamla Stan* (old city) with its narrow streets and old houses, along the harbor, in the Djurgård residential and park area, and in the park and museums of Skansen. Aside from Murnau, no other urban space attracted so much of her attention. "I was surprised and fascinated that here in the far North, about which I had only very little knowledge, there is such a wonderfully located and beautiful city," she wrote in a reminiscence to Lilly Rydström-Wickelberg. "Here, I at once felt myself received with friendship and welcomed. Far from the events of the war, I had a time of intense work, promoted by the fine understanding I found among Swedish artists...."[20] The filters of memory and the desire to please play a role in this recollection, from which all unpleasantness is removed, but its emphasis on her activity and friendly reception are readily borne out by the sketchbooks and the daily entries in her pocket calendars. It is also true that from the moment she arrived in Stockholm, the periods of listlessness ended.

After much pleading, Kandinsky finally arrived in Stockholm on 23 December 1915 to help organize his exhibition and to paint new works for it. He stayed until just after Münter's, which closed on 15 March 1916. After he left, Münter resumed sketching and painting views of the city. *Street in Stockholm*, which she also titled *May Evening in Stockholm* and *Summer Evening in Stockholm* (Cat. No. 77), synthesized the altered perceptions she now brought to her work. Compared to her views of Munich, even of Murnau, the painting is remarkable in that it focuses on the broad walkways of the fashionable Kungsgatan and on the people who stroll about on them. Unlike the streets of Munich or Murnau that she depicted, Stockholm's are populated. The figures of women and men dominate the architectural setting, transforming it into a pleasant backdrop—a total reversal of her practice in Germany. Seen from behind, a fashionably dressed woman walks a small dog—Münter humorously accents its tiny, elegant figure and the leash drooping up to its towering owner—as the central motif in the foreground, while a couple walks arm in arm nearby and a man stops to chat at a newspaper stand. The emphasis on quietude and nonchalance, on prosperity and peaceful calm in this painting perhaps implies a contrast to wartime Germany, with its deprivations and regimentation, which Münter had recently left; perhaps it also represents a criticism of neutral Sweden's wartime affluence.[21] If so, however, such didactic content is overpowered by the central elegance of Münter's representation, its very light stylizations and accented, harmonic cohesion that employ the archway as a frame to help define a sense of space and openness virtually unseen in her previous work. With its greater spaciousness and gentle stylization, the painting displays effects found in works by Isaac Grünewald and especially by Sigrid Hjertén, both students of Matisse.[22] Münter was adapting her art to her new surroundings, incorporating the vocabulary of Sweden's progressive artists into it. In effect, she adopted a new Swedish persona. A "Swedish" Münter addressed a Swedish audience.

Considerations of appeal and cost most likely induced her to take up the technique of drypoint engraving on zinc plates for the first time, which were cheaper than the standard copper ones, especially as copper was a material highly valued during the war. Since Kandinsky also produced a series of six drypoints with zinc plates during his stay in Stockholm, he must surely have introduced the technique to her. The two groups of prints, his and hers, are the final products of their lengthy artistic interaction.[23]

Münter's prints offer a variety of motifs, a virtual inventory of her visual interests in Stockholm. The city itself provided the motif in *Near the Sluice, Stockholm* (Cat. No. 75), with tugboats and fishing boats in the foreground, and a view towards Södermalm, partially obscured by the tumbling lines of their smoke. Münter accents the city's activity, the movement and the work being done on the water and on the shore, in accordance with her altered vision of the urban environment. Her exploration of Stockholm's streets and commercial life is similarly reflected in *Clockmaker* (Cat. No. 74), the reversal of a recently completed painting.[24] A motif unlike those in other works by Münter, with its clocks suggesting the passage of time and a sculpture of two horses as an analogous reference to the Blue Rider, it has readily lent itself to psychological and biographical readings, as representative of her waiting for Kandinsky in Stockholm.[25] More directly linked to her life in Sweden is the depiction of the dresser in her room at the guest house (Cat. No. 73), likewise based on a painting.[26] The image represents a continuation of her studies of interiors and interior still lifes, replacing the Bavarian Madonnas and figurines with an English majolica spaniel and a Swedish folk carving of a horse, a *Dalahäst*, frequently used as Christmas decorations in Sweden. If the interior and its dark, empty mirror have biographic associations, even more does the delicately colored drypoint with the suggestive title, *Woman Seeking* (Cat. No. 76). The image may originally have been of a woman sleeping, with one arm covering her eyes, but when given a vertical format, with flowers enigmatically placed in the foreground, the pose of gazing searchingly encapsulates Münter's own quandary. Having left behind the world from which she had drawn the motifs of her art, she sought replacements in a city that, while welcoming, regarded her as foreign and alone.

In her effort to find motifs to replace Murnau and the Alps, but that also might appeal to potential patrons, she undertook a lengthy tour of northern Sweden and the coast of Norway in the summer of 1916. She sketched extensively, returning to Sweden as a guest at the estate Arnäsholm, owned by Leopold Sundbeck; there, she translated sketches into paintings. In its extraordinary simplification *From Norway, Tjellebotten* (Cat. No. 78) recalls the paintings of Murnau, while the coloristic mood reflects Edvard Munch's practices. She appears to have viewed the arctic landscape largely through the eyes of her own art and of the artist she most associated with the Norwegian landscape. However, industry, commercial areas and ports were surprisingly the motifs she sought out most. She painted no views of fjords or mountains, as if refusing to see a dramatic landscape that could vie with her Bavarian memories, nor did she portray the Sami people in their folk dress that she captured in her sketchbooks. "I am truly upset that you are so little satisfied with your voyage," Kandinsky wrote to her. "I hoped that this trip (unique in its type) would give you a boost, ideas for your painting and would renew you and give you peace of soul."[27] However, the trip failed to fulfill such expectations.

She worked diligently in the late summer of 1916, painting over fifteen works during her stay at Arnäsholm. But her doubts about her art and its integrity continued to increase. Between accusations that Kandinsky thought only of himself, that he lied and that he broke all his promises, she wrote to him: "Now I understand that for my art what I lack is culture and discipline. I did not acquire the former and I lack the latter—or I have too little of it. I must work hard."[28]

Münter continued to work despite her intense personal anger and despair caused by Kandinsky's refusal to keep his promise to marry her and despite her insurmountable lack of faith in her own art, and she exhibited her work wherever possible. She maintained a degree of artistic activity that she had never before achieved, and she did it now independently, without the support or preparation Kandinsky had provided earlier. In large, figured compositions, she also asserted a seriousness of purpose unlike in her previous work, inserting allegorical content. Using Gertrude Holz, who accompanied her on her Lapland and Norway tour, as her model in 1917, she painted *The Future*, whose title she later changed to *Woman in Stockholm* (Cat. No. 79). On the large, vertical canvas of *The Future*, bright pinks, yellows and reds dominate areas of blue, green and purple. A woman is seen before a window that offers a view onto the sunlit houses of Stockholm, as she gazes alertly out of the picture at the viewer, her head framed by the window, her face vividly illuminated. The colors, the sunshine and the tulips all combine as signifiers of spring and of hope.

That Münter saw *The Future* as signifying her own entry into a bright new world is doubtful, and points to the danger of interpreting her works as solely reflections of her personal moods and psychological states. Her Scandinavian paintings are not all gloomy, although her state of mind frequently was. Indeed, while living in Copenhagen between 1918 and 1920—the time of her greatest financial need—her paintings became increasingly brighter. On the island of Bornholm, where she wanted to set up an informal art school, on 5 August 1919 Münter depicted the beach in intense colors (Cat. No. 81). Broad, flowing contours define the women that recline on the sand. In theme and mood, this is among Münter's most Impressionist of paintings, particularly recalling the bathing scenes of turn-of-the-century Scandinavian artists, who likewise exaggerated the intensity of the sunlight, employing it as a metaphor of vitality and health. A few months earlier, on 8 June, she painted a similarly bright scene of a chestnut tree in bloom (Cat. No. 82). In her painting manner, it differs significantly, however, as it accents highly stylized forms, flattened and precisely drawn. It demonstrates a sense of control that contrasts with the seeming exhilaration of brushstrokes in the Bornholm painting. Moreover, the poster for her major exhibition in Copenhagen (Cat. No. 80) in 1918 manifests a third simultaneous mode, based on a Swedish painting, with figures simplified into gentle caricatures and set playfully into a fantasized seascape.

The stylistic and thematic multiplicity of the paintings and prints from Münter's last years in Scandinavia is united in one factor. The Expressionist subjectivity that she had developed in Murnau in 1908 and brought with her to Sweden was diminished, transformed or eliminated, to be replaced by more self-conscious stylization, intermittent naturalism and recollections of previous styles. She worked in Copenhagen largely in isolation, her contacts with Swedish artists broken, her links with German artists severed. The Expressionist phase of her art had come to an end.

By the time Münter returned to Germany in 1920, support for her art had ceased to exist. "Because of my absence from Germany," she wrote in a brief autobiographical statement in 1927, "my work has been forgotten and only slowly am I able to regain a foothold."[29] The Germany to which she returned had been transformed. The Empire was gone and a Republic had been declared. The Blue Rider had long since disbanded, Marc and Macke were dead, and Kandinsky was in Moscow, silent, hoping she would believe he, too, was dead. Herwarth Walden and "Der Sturm" championed new artists, and other galleries likewise fostered alternatives to Expressionism, which had now been pronounced dead. In Berlin, when she arrived, Dada artists proclaimed art itself was dead. Münter had to begin again.

Biographic Chronology

This chronology is based freely on the one provided in *Gabriele Münter 1877–1962, Retrospektive,* edited by Annegret Hoberg and Helmut Friedel (Munich, 1992), pp. 10–25, and is supplemented by information from Münter's pocket calendars and other documents at the Gabriele Münter- und Johannes Eichner-Stiftung, Munich. Likewise, Gisela Kleine's *Gabriele Münter und Wassily Kandinsky: Biographie eines Paares* (Frankfurt am Main, 1990) has been consulted.

1 Gabriele Münter, undated recollection written for Johannes Eichner, mid-1950s. Gabriele Münter- und Johannes Eichner-Stiftung, Munich.
2 Gabriele Münter, diary entry of 17 May 1911, author's translation of excerpt in: Annegret Hoberg, *Wassily Kandinsky und Gabriele Münter in Murnau und Kochel: Briefe und Erinnerungen, 1902–1914* (Munich and New York, 1994), pp. 45–46, also published in English as *Wassily Kandinsky and Gabriele Münter: Letters and Reminiscences, 1902–1914* (Munich and New York, 1994).
3 Ibid., pp. 46–47.
4 Ibid., p. 48.
5 Letter from Kandinsky to Münter, dated 31 December 1909. Gabriele Münter- und Johannes Eichner-Stiftung, Munich.
6 Münter (note 1), p. 50.
7 Letter from Münter to Kandinsky, dated 3 August 1911. Gabriele Münter- und Johannes Eichner-Stiftung, Munich. Excerpted in: Gisela Kleine, *Gabriele Münter und Wassily Kandinsky: Biographie eines Paares* (Frankfurt am Main, 1990), pp. 372–73.
8 Letter from Kandinsky to Münter, no. 12, dated 11 March 1915. Gabriele Münter- und Johannes Eichner-Stiftung, Munich.
9 Letter from Kandinsky to Münter, dated 21 September 1915. Gabriele Münter- und Johannes Eichner-Stiftung, Munich. See also, Vivian Endicott Barnett, *Kandinsky and Sweden* (Malmö, 1989), p. 19.
10 Vassily Kandinsky, manuscript for "Über den Künstler." Gabriele Münter- und Johannes Eichner-Stiftung, Munich. Excerpts from the manuscript were first published in Johannes Eichner, *Kandinsky und Gabriele Münter: Von Ursprüngen moderner Kunst* (Munich, 1957), pp. 171–75.
11 Münter's letter of 13 July 1922 and Kandinsky's response of 22 July 1922 are preserved in the archives of the Gabriele Münter- und Johannes Eichner-Stiftung, Munich; they are excerpted in Kleine (note 7), pp. 520–24.
12 Gabriele Münter, "Beichte und Anklage," loose sheet inserted into vol. 3, dated 12 November 1925. Gabriele Münter- und Johannes Eichner-Stiftung, Munich.
13 Münter, entry of 5 May 1928, "Beichte und Anklage," vol. 4, p. 18. Gabriele Münter- und Johannes Eichner-Stiftung, Munich.

Chapter 1: Apprenticeship and Travels in Search of a Style

1 Gabriele Münter, "Gabriele Münter über sich selbst," *Das Kunstwerk* 2:7 (1948), p. 25.
2 Eichner (note 10, Biographic Chronology), p. 26.
3 Ibid., p. 32.
4 Clive Ashwin, *Drawing and Education in German-Speaking Europe, 1800–1900* (Ann Arbor, 1981), p. 44. See also, Renate Berger, *Malerinnen auf dem Weg ins 20. Jahrhundert: Kunstgeschichte als Sozialgeschichte*, vol. 121 (Cologne, 1982), pp. 87ff.
5 Eichner (note 10, Biographic Chronology), p. 28.
6 Gabriele Münter, "Bekenntnisse und Erinnerungen," in: G. F. Hartlaub, *Gabriele Münter: Menschenbilder in Zeichnungen* (Berlin, 1952), n. p.
7 Eichner (note 10, Biographic Chronology), p. 32.
8 See, for example, Eichner (note 10, Biographic Chronology), p. 28, and Kleine, (note 7, Biographic Chronology), p. 40.
9 Eichner (note 10, Biographic Chronology), p. 27.
10 Gabriele Münter in an interview in 1958 with Edouard Roditi in: *Dialogues: Conversations with European Artists at Mid-Century* (San Francisco, 1990), p. 114. The interview was first published as "Interview with Gabriele Münter," *Arts Magazine* 34 (1960), pp. 36–41 and in Roditi's book, *Dialogues on Art* (London, 1960).
11 *Statistisches Jahrbuch für das Deutsche Reich*, vol. 207, part 1 (Berlin, 1909), p. 11.
12 Münter (note 6); Roditi (note 10), p. 114.
13 "St. Louis Art at the Exposition More Valuable than Ever in '98," *St. Louis Post Dispatch*, 11 September 1898, n. p. For bringing this article to my attention and for other information concerning the St. Louis Exposition, I wish to thank Anna Brzyski-Long.
14 Significant, too, is that her subject matter was largely limited to domestic scenes, portraits and renditions of indigenous flowers, all common concerns of *Jugendstil* artists. Quite remarkable, but not easily explained except as an indication of Münter's sophistication in the practices of *Jugendstil*, is the extent to which many of her drawings of domestic life on the American frontier echo contemporary images in the Swedish *art nouveau* artist Carl Larsson's series of watercolors depicting life in his home, *A Home*, known in the United States since 1895. Less frequently, she depicted buildings—the complex of structures constituting Schreiber Mill in Moorefield, Arkansas, for example—but did not group them in landscape contexts, for which she knew no appropriate prototypes on which to model her image. When she did draw landscape scenes from time to time, she selected views that matched European landscape renditions. The emptiness of the Texas prairie, the activities of cowboys and farm laborers and the Mississippi with its paddle-wheel ships were motifs unlike those of European art, which she recorded with her camera rather than making attempts to draw them.
15 Gabriele Münter, entries in pocket calendar for 1 January and 24 February 1901. Gabriele Münter- und

Johannes Eichner-Stiftung, Munich. See also, Kleine (note 7, Biographic Chronology), pp. 87, 680, note 2.

16 Compare the following comments made as late as 1914 in a study of women's art training in Germany: "It is necessary to have gone to such private studios to have any idea of what talentless people dominate, believe they can do art work, [or] achieve artistic results. Especially among women that unbearable horde of dilettantes is fostered that hurls their creations into the world without self-criticism, ruins artistic taste and discredits truly serious women's art as such." Henni Lehmann, *Das Kunststudium der Frauen* (Darmstadt, 1914), pp. 7–8.

17 Karl Scheffler, *Die Frau und die Kunst* (Berlin, 1908), p. 12.

18 Paul de Lagarde, "Program of the Conservative Party of Prussia," 1887, as cited in Berger (note 4), p. 59.

19 Scheffler (note 17), pp. 27–30. See also the discussion of Scheffler's views by Berger (note 4), pp. 66ff.

20 Cited in Kleine (note 7, Biographic Chronology), p. 108. Kleine provides a compilation of antifeminist cartoons in *Simplicissimus*; for similar references from *Die Jugend*, see Berger (note 4), pp. 70–71.

21 Letter from Georg Schroeter to Münter, dated 17 May 1901. Gabriele Münter- und Johannes Eichner-Stiftung, Munich. Cited in Kleine (note 7, Biographic Chronology), p. 91.

22 On Munich's reputation and the challenge posed by Berlin at the turn of the century, see Maria Makela, *The Munich Secession: Art and Artists in Turn-of-the-Century Munich* (Princeton, NJ, 1987).

23 *Kurzer Geschichtsabriß über Gründung und Entwicklung des Künstlerinnen-Vereins München e. V. von 1882–1896* (Munich, 1897), as cited in Kleine (note 7, Biographic Chronology), p. 90.

24 Eichner (note 10, Biographic Chronology), p. 35.

25 Compare the anecdote recalled by Münter of how she went sketching with another student from the Ladies' Academy. Faced with the motif of a woman kneeling and rinsing laundry in the Nymphenburg Canal, "the other dabbed around on the sketchbook page, attempted the outline with numerous small strokes of the pencil, erased most of it, and the result was weak and approximate. I watched her with amazement. Then I drew a few strokes on my paper and the motif was captured precisely and was done." See Münter (note 6).

26 Alexander Koch, "Unser Programm," *Deutsche Kunst und Dekoration* (1897–98), as cited in Eva Huber and Annette Wolde, "Die Darmstädter Künstlerkolonie: Anspruch und Verwirklichung ihrer künstlerischen Zielsetzungen," in: *Ein Dokument deutscher Kunst—Darmstadt, 1901–1976* (Darmstadt, 1977), vol. 5, p. 72. On the significance of the Darmstadt artists' colony for Kandinsky, see Peg Weiss, *Kandinsky in Munich: The Formative Jugendstil Years* (Princeton, NJ, 1979), pp. 61–63.

27 Münter was registered at the Ladies' Academy as student no. 33 for the academic year of 1901–02 and as student no. 265 for the year 1903–04. See Kleine (note 7, Biographic Chronology), p. 681, note 7.

28 On the Phalanx Society, see especially Peg Weiss (note 26), pp. 57ff. and her essay, "Kandinsky und München: Begegnungen und Wandlungen," in: *Kandinsky und München: Begegnungen und Wandlungen, 1896–1914*, ed. Armin Zweite (Munich, 1982), pp. 40ff. See also the recollections of Gustav Freytag and other documentation in Hans Konrad Röthel, *Kandinsky: Das graphische Werk* (Cologne, 1970), pp. 429ff.

29 See Berger (note 4), pp. 140ff. concerning the limitations placed on women artists in life drawing classes. On the Phalanx School, see Röthel (note 28), pp. 435–36.

30 Unpublished letter from Münter to Kenneth Lindsay, dated 7 May 1950. Private Collection.

31 No documentation concerning the opening of the Phalanx School is known, so that it is the recollections of former students, especially Münter and the Swedish artist Carl Palme, that provide an approximate starting date of winter 1901–02. It seems likely that an effort would have been made to coordinate the school's opening with the beginning of the winter semester at other schools and academies, thus January 1902 rather than December 1901. For the second Phalanx exhibition and its contents, see Weiss (note 26), pp. 59–63.

32 See Münter's recollection written for Johannes Eichner, mid–1950s, Gabriele Münter- und Johannes Eichner-Stiftung, Folder 46/7, included in the Biographic Chronology, p. 12. For a fuller citation, see Hoberg (note 2, Biographic Chronology), pp. 31–32.

33 Unpublished letter from Münter to Lindsay, dated 16 July 1956. Private Collection.

34 Münter (note 32); Hoberg (note 2, Biographic Chronology), p. 32.

35 Postcard from Kandinsky to Münter, dated 9 September 1902. Gabriele Münter- und Johannes Eichner-Stiftung. See also, Hoberg (note 2, Biographic Chronology), pp. 35–36.

36 Gabriele Münter, note dated 12 October 1902. Gabriele Münter- und Johannes Eichner-Stiftung. The unsent letter to Kandinsky in the envelope is published by Hoberg (note 2, Biographic Chronology), pp. 37ff.

37 Letter from Kandinsky to Münter, dated 7 November 1902. Gabriele Münter- und Johannes Eichner-Stiftung.

38 Roditi (note 10), p. 120.

39 Eichner (note 10, Biographic Chronology), p. 193.

40 Vassily Kandinsky, unpublished introduction to an exhibition of works by Gabriele Münter, 1913, in: *Sammlungskatalog 1: Der Blaue Reiter*, Städtische Galerie im Lenbachhaus (Munich, 1966), p. 119.

41 Eichner (note 10, Biographic Chronology), p. 38. Eichner cites a note written by Münter for him in the mid-1950s as he researched his book, Gabriele Münter- und Johannes Eichner-Stiftung, Folder 14. Münter originally placed the recollection in a significantly less positive context in

1925, see Biographic Chronology, pp. 27–28.

42 The trope of the Münter-nature-woman parallelism is discussed further by Sabine Windecker, *Gabriele Münter: Eine Künstlerin aus dem Kreis des "Blauen Reiter"* (dissertation, Universität Kiel, 1990; Berlin, 1991); Johanna Werckmeister, "'Blauer Reiter' im Damensattel: Rezeptionsraster für eine Künstlerin," *kritische berichte* no. 1, 1989, pp. 70–77; Christiane Keim, "'Ich komme mir leicht "wenig" vor—und die anderen scheinen mir immer mehr' (Gabriele Münter)," *kritische berichte* no. 2, 1994, pp. 18–25; and Barbara U. Schmidt, "Gabriele Münter (k)eine Künstlerin aus der Gruppe 'Blauer Reiter,'" *kritische berichte* no. 2, 1994, pp. 26–39.

43 Gabriele Münter, note dated 5 February 1933. Gabriele Münter- und Johannes Eichner-Stiftung. Cited in: *Gabriele Münter, 1877–1962*, exh. cat., Städtische Galerie im Lenbachhaus (Munich, 1962), n. p.

44 The dichotomy is noted by Annegret Hoberg, "Gabriele Münter in München und Murnau, 1901–1914," in *Gabriele Münter, 1877–1962, Retrospektive*, ed. Annegret Hoberg and Helmut Friedl (Munich, 1992), p. 33.

45 According to Eichner (note 10, Biographic Chronology), p. 37, during 1902 she produced a woodcut, larger than life size, of a woman's head at the graphics school of Heinrich Wolff and Ernst Neumann in Munich. This print seems to have been lost.

46 On the woodcut revival in Germany, see Robin Reisenfeld, *The Revival of the Woodcut in Germany, 1890–1920* (Ph. D. dissertation, The University of Chicago, 1993).

47 Letter from Kandinsky to Münter, dated 16 April 1903. Gabriele Münter- und Johannes Eichner-Stiftung.

48 Letter from Münter to Kandinsky, dated 19 December 1903. Gabriele Münter- und Johannes Eichner-Stiftung.

49 Letter from Münter to Kandinsky, dated 31 December 1903. Gabriele Münter- und Johannes Eichner-Stiftung.

50 Münter (note 1).

51 Letter from Kandinsky to Münter, dated 6 November 1904. Gabriele Münter- und Johannes Eichner-Stiftung.

52 The temptation to compare Münter's Holland studies to similar views of canals with reflected trees painted at the same time by Piet Mondrian is great. That either artist knew of the other is extremely unlikely. Instead, both worked from analogous artistic premises and stylistic principles to arrive at related conclusions.

53 In a footnote in his "Reminiscences" (1913), Kandinsky observes: "The 'light and air' problem of the Impressionists interested me very little. I always found that erudite conversations about this problem had very little to do with painting. Later, the theories of the Neo-Impressionists seemed to me more important, since they were talking ultimately about the *effects of colors* and left the atmosphere alone." Vassily Kandinsky, "Reminiscences/Three Pictures," in: *Kandinsky: Complete Writings on Art*, ed. Kenneth C. Lindsay and Peter Vergo (New York, 1994), pp. 363–64.

54 Röthel (note 28), No. 35.

55 "...this evening I—traced!—your study, and will begin painting it tomorrow morning." Letter from Münter to Kandinsky, undated (ca. early 1904). Gabriele Münter- und Johannes Eichner-Stiftung.

56 Letter from Münter to Kandinsky, dated 1 July 1904. Gabriele Münter- und Johannes Eichner-Stiftung.

57 Letter from Münter to Kandinsky, dated 3 March 1904. Gabriele Münter- und Johannes Eichner-Stiftung.

58 Eichner (note 10, Biographic Chronology), p. 43. See also, *Gabriele Münter, 1877–1962, Retrospektive* (note 44), pp. 32–33.

59 Münter (note 6).

60 See Reisenfeld (note 46) for a discussion on the spread of these influences in Germany.

61 Eichner (note 10, Biographic Chronology), pp. 53–54.

Chapter 2: Modernity, Munich and Murnau

1 *Statistisches Jahrbuch für das Deutsche Reich*, vol. 207, part 1 (Berlin, 1909), pp. 11, 255 and 273.

2 Significant debate exists about the term "Expressionism," its historical usage and its applicability. At its simplest, it is identified with the two artists' groups *Brücke* (Bridge), founded in Dresden in 1905, and *Der Blaue Reiter*, founded in Munich in 1911 by Kandinsky, Franz Marc and Gabriele Münter after they seceded from the New Artists' Association Munich (*Neue Künstlervereinigung München*)—a progressive exhibition society founded two years earlier in 1909—as well as by artists active in Germany and Austria (including but not limited to the members of these groups) represented by the Berlin periodical and gallery "Der Sturm," founded by Herwarth Walden in 1910. For a recent discussion of the problematic nature of the term, see especially Marit Werenskiold, *The Concept of Expressionism: Origin and Metamorphosis* (Oslo, 1984); Ron Manheim, "'Expressionismus': Zur Entstehung eines kunsthistorischen Stil- und Periodenbegriffs," *Zeitschrift für Kunstgeschichte* 49:1 (1986), pp. 73–91; Charles Haxthausen, "A Critical Illusion: 'Expressionism' in the Writings of Wilhelm Hausenstein," in: *The Ideological Crisis of Expressionism: The Literary and Artistic German War Colony in Belgium, 1914–1918*, ed. Rainer Rumold and O.K. Werckmeister (Columbia, SC, 1990), pp. 169–91; and Reinhold Heller, "Expressionism," in: *Encyclopedia of Aesthetics*, ed. Michael Kelly (Oxford, forthcoming).

3 An alternative reading, in part suggested by Anne Mochon in *Gabriele Münter: Between Munich and Murnau*, exh. cat., Busch-Reisinger Museum (Cambrigde, MA, 1980), p. 16, would be the contrast between the United States as she experienced it with its informality, diversity and friendliness, all perhaps personified by Uncle Sam and the teddy bear named after the then president, Theodore Roosevelt, and Prussia with its social rigidity and militaristic ethos. The suggestion offered by Peter Lahnstein, *Gabriele Münter* (Ettal, 1971), p. 18, that Uncle Sam, the bear and the soldier are a "playful reference to her theme of America-Germany-Russia," while it may have a certain basis in Münter's interest in, or identification with, the three countries (which never became a "theme" of her work), seems to be largely a product of mid-twentieth-century Cold War ideology.

4 For an itemization of collections and exhibitions Münter and Kandinsky may have seen in Paris, as well as contacts they made, see Jonathan David Fineberg, *Kandinsky in Paris 1906–1907* (Ann Arbor, MI, 1984), p. 44

5 Mochon (note 3), pp. 17–18.

6 See Biographic Chronology, p. 16, for a more extensive citation of Münter's diary entry of 17 May 1911.

7 The most extensive documentation of this phenomenon can be found in Gerhard Wieteck, *Deutsche Künstlerkolonien und Künstlerorte* (Munich, 1976).
8 Franz Zell, "Hausmalereien in Murnau," *Velhagen und Klasings Monatshefte* 22:11 (1907–08), pp. 842–48.
9 On Seidl's renovations, see also Brigitte Salmen, *Gabriele Münter malt Murnau: Gemälde 1908–1960 der Künstlerin des "Blauen Reiters,"* exh. cat., Schloßmuseum Murnau (Murnau, 1996), pp. 118–19, notes 17, 18 and 24.
10 Lydia L. Dewiel, *Oberbayern: Kunst und Landschaft zwischen dem Altmühltal und den Alpen* (Cologne, 1996), p. 260.
11 Peg Weiss, "Kandinsky und München: Begegnungen und Wandlungen," in: *Kandinsky und München: Begegnungen und Wandlungen, 1896–1914*, ed. Armin Zweite (Munich, 1982).
12 Letter from Kandinsky to Alexei Jawlensky, dated 24 April 1934. As cited in Jelena Hahl-Koch, "Der frühe Jawlensky," in: *Alexej Jawlensky: 1864–1941,* ed. Armin Zweite, exh. cat., Städtische Galerie im Lenbachhaus (Munich, 1983), p. 43.
13 Eichner (note 10, Biographic Chronology), p. 89. But also compare Münter's undated note to him: "The emphasis on Jawlensky is wrong. He had no significance for me." Folder 14/77, Gabriele Münter- und Johannes Eichner-Stiftung.
14 For Jawlensky's artistic development, see especially *Alexej Jawlensky, 1864–1941* (note 12) and *Alexei Jawlensky*, ed. Rudy Chiappini, exh. cat., Kunsthalle Emden (Emden, 1989–90).
15 Van Gogh's significance is also confirmed by Münter's statement, "If I had a formal prototype ... then it is surely Van Gogh through Jawlensky and his theories." Undated note, ca. mid-1950s. Gabriele Münter- und Johannes Eichner-Stiftung.
16 See Biographic Chronology, pp. 15–17.
17 See Biographic Chronology, p. 16.
18 Paula Modersohn-Becker, frequently counted among Expressionism's pioneers, preceded Münter, but worked in isolation and did not become widely known until considerably later. Marianne Werefkin, while also in Murnau in 1908, retained a greater link to Symbolist aesthetics, and with few exceptions did not paint in an Expressionist manner.
19 Gabriele Münter, undated note, ca. mid-1950s. Gabriele Münter- und Johannes Eichner-Stiftung.
20 Siegmar Gerndt, *Unsere bayrische Landschaft: Ein Naturführer*, 4th edn. (Munich, 1978), as cited in Dewiel (note 10), p. 264.
21 Münter (note 1, chap. 1), p. 25.
22 Münter's "Lourdes Woods" reference is to a small emulation of the Marian grotto at Lourdes situated in the woods overlooking the Murnau Moors.
23 Cited by Wladislawa Jaworska, *Paul Gauguin and the School of Pont-Aven* (London, 1972), p. 129.
24 Neue Künstlervereinigung München, Gründungzirkular, 1909, as reprinted in Rosel Gollek, *Der Blaue Reiter im Lenbachhaus München: Katalog der Sammlung in der Städtischen Galerie*, 4th edn. (Munich, 1988), p. 10.
25 Eichner (note 10, Biographic Chronology), p. 89.

Chapter 3: Still Lifes and Interiors

1 Münter and Eichner, while cataloguing her collection, inscribed titles and dates on the reverse of her works. This painting was dated simply "prewar," rather than being given a more precise date.
2 See, for example, the design for a purse in Münter's sketchbook, Folder 43/23 (Gabriele Münter- und Johannes Eichner-Stiftung), p. 101, among sketches dated to June 1908.
3 Gabriele Münter, undated note, ca. mid-1950s. Folder 14, Gabriele Münter- und Johannes Eichner-Stiftung. See also, Roditi (note 10, chap. 1), p. 120.
4 Roditi (note 10, chap. 1), p. 120.
5 Gabriele Münter, undated note, ca. mid-1950s. Folder 14, Gabriele Münter- und Johannes Eichner-Stiftung.
6 Norman Bryson, *Looking at the Overlooked: Four Essays on Still Life Painting* (Cambridge, MA, 1990), p. 61. The term was first applied to still-life painting by Charles Sterling, *Still Life Painting from Antiquity to the Twentieth Century*, 2nd edn. (New York, 1981).
7 Paula Modersohn-Becker, who also painted numerous still lifes during her brief career, and who often is identified as a forerunner of Expressionism, should likewise be mentioned. She worked in isolation in Worpswede and remained little known until after World War I, unlike Münter who participated actively in the formation and exhibition of prewar Expressionist art. Similarly, a separate issue—the decorum of subject matter in differing stylistic ideologies—is raised by the significance of still-life painting among German Impressionist painters.
8 *Tendances Nouvelles* 4:42 (May 1909), pp. 924 and 939.
9 See note 24, chap. 2.
10 Brochure printed on the occasion of the second exhibition of the New Artists' Association Munich, reproduced in Gollek (note 24, chap. 2), p. 394. I have used the translation, with slight modification, found in *Kandinsky: Complete Writings on Art* (note 53, chap. 1), p. 82.
11 Letter from Münter to Kandinsky, dated 12 November 1910. Gabriele Münter- und Johannes Eichner-Stiftung. In: Annegret Hoberg, *Wassily Kandinsky and Gabriele Münter: Letters and Reminiscences, 1902–1914* (Munich and New York, 1994), p. 84.
12 Letter from Münter to Kandinsky, dated 30 October 1910. Gabriele Münter- und Johannes Eichner-Stiftung.
13 Letter from Münter to Kandinsky, dated 3 November 1910. Gabriele Münter- und Johannes Eichner-Stiftung.
14 Walter Benjamin, *Das Passagen-Werk*, vol. I (Frankfurt am Main, 1982), p. 281.
15 For Münter's terminology and her use of it, see Reinhold Heller, "Innenräume: Erlebnis, Erinnerung und Synthese in der Kunst Gabriele Münters," in: *Gabriele Münter, 1877–1962, Retrospektive* (note 44, chap. 1), pp. 52–53.
16 Based on photographs taken by Münter of the exhibition, a reconstruction of the content and hanging of the first Blue Rider exhibition is provided by Maria Andreas von Lüttichau, "Der Blaue Reiter," in: *Stationen der Moderne—Die bedeutenden Kunstausstellungen des 20. Jahrhunderts in Deutschland*, exh. cat., Berlinische Galerie (Berlin, 1989), pp. 109ff.
17 Letter from Münter to Kandinsky, December 1910. Gabriele Münter- und Johannes Eichner-Stiftung. Cited in: *Gabriele Münter, 1877–1962, Retrospektive* (note 44, chap. 1), p. 39.
18 Kandinsky, "Content and Form" (1910) in: *Kandinsky: Complete Writings on Art* (note 53, chap. 1), p. 87.
19 It is useful to compare Münter's and

Kandinsky's Murnau home and life to that of the Swedish artist Carl Larsson at Dallarna, which was conceptually and ideologically significantly related. See Michelle Facos, "The Ideal Swedish Home: Carl Larsson's Lylla Hyttnäs," in: *Not at Home: The Suppression of Domesticity in Modern Art and Architecture*, ed. Christopher Reed (London, 1996), pp. 81–91. Also comparable is Heinrich Vogeler's *Barkenhoff* home in the artists' colony of Worpswede; see Wieteck (note 7, chap. 2).

20 Benjamin (note 14), p. 286.

21 Letter from Münter to Kandinsky, dated 12 November 1910. Gabriele Münter- und Johannes Eichner-Stiftung. In: Hoberg (note 11), p. 84.

22 Letter from Münter to Kandinsky, dated 3 November 1910. Gabriele Münter- und Johannes Eichner-Stiftung. See also the discussion of this below, chap. 6, p. 155.

23 Kandinsky, "On the Question of Form," *The Blaue Reiter Almanac*. The author has modified the translation cited in: *Kandinsky: Complete Writings on Art* (note 53, chap. 1), pp. 255–56. Kandinsky was writing specifically about Cat. No. 54, *Still Life with Saint George*.

Chapter 4: Portraits

1 Münter (note 6, chap. 1).

2 This and the following quotation, ibid.

3 G.F. Hartlaub and Münter collaborated on the publication of a selection of her portrait drawings, most of which were from the 1920s; see note 6, chap. 1. Several of her Scandinavian portrait sketchbooks, which she called "Criminals' Albums," are in the collection of the Gabriele Münter- und Johannes Eichner-Stiftung, Folders 46/50 and 46/51.

4 Münter (note 6, chap. 1).

5 In a photo-album catalogue of Münter's portraits of women, Johannes Eichner identifies the painting as *Young Polish Woman*, and provides the dates "1908 or 9." The Polish model, whose further identity is not currently known, appears in at least one other portrait by Münter from early 1909.

6 See entries to Cat. Nos. 49 and 50 in: *Gabriele Münter, 1877–1962* (note 44, chap. 1), p. 262.

7 On the history and technique of *Hinterglasmalerei*, see particularly Gislind Ritz, *Hinterglasmalerei: Geschichte, Erscheinung, Technik* (Munich, 1972); Leopold Schmidt, *Hinterglas: Zeugnisse einer alten Hauskunst* (Munich, 1979); and Eckhardt Feuchtmayr, "Zur Entwicklung der Hinterglasmalerei im Staffelseeraum," *Schriften des Historischen Vereins Murnau am Staffelsee e. V.*, 6:10 (1985). The influence and reception of reverse-glass painting among Munich avant-garde artists has been extensively researched by Ursula Glatzel, *Zur Bedeutung der Volkskunst beim Blauen Reiter* (dissertation, Ludwig-Maximilians-Universität, Munich, 1975), and summarized by Windecker (note 42, chap. 1), pp. 103ff.

8 Münter, personal reminiscence, dated 10 February 1933. Folder 10/2, Gabriele Münter- und Johannes Eichner-Stiftung. The note was most likely written for Eichner, whose writings during the 1930s particularly emphasized Münter's links to Bavarian folk art.

9 Most of her early reverse-glass paintings Münter did not date; later, she inscribed on the back of several paintings: "about 1909/10" or "about 1910." However, the copies after Rambold are generally dated to 1908/09 in the literature on her, without offering further justification. See Rosel Golleck, *Gabriele Münter: Hinterglasbilder* (Munich, 1981), p. 57, and the extensive listing of her reverse-glass paintings in: *Gabriele Münter, 1877–1962: Gemälde, Zeichnungen, Hinterglasbilder und Volkskunst aus ihrem Besitz*, exh. cat., Städtische Galerie im Lenbachhaus (Munich, 1977), pp. 115ff. An interesting side note to the issue of Münter's discovery of reverse-glass painting is provided by Alesandra Comini, "Gender or Genius? The Women Artists of German Expressionism," in: *Feminism and Art History: Questioning the Litany*, ed. Norma Broude and Mary D. Garrard (New York, 1982), pp. 283–84, who discovered that the Ginocchio Hotel and Restaurant in Marshall, Texas, decorated its rooms with American reverse-glass paintings at the time of Münter's visit there.

10 Münter (note 6, chap. 1).

11 "11. Ausstellung Der Sturm: Gabriele Münter Kollektiv-Ausstellung," Der Sturm, Berlin, Jan.–Feb. 1913, No. 7: *Kind mit Puppe*.

12 During 1909–10, Jawlensky seems to have used the same or a similar model for several portraits using compositions and stylistic devices similar to Münter's but, significantly, achieving effects of coquetry or anxiety quite unlike her work. See *Alexei Jawlensky* (note 14, chap. 2), Cat. Nos. 26 and 32. Similarly telling are comparisons with Edvard Munch's painting *Puberty* (1893) and the numerous depictions of the models Franzi and Marzella by the *Brücke* artists in Dresden. Among Expressionist-related artists, only Paula Modersohn-Becker's portrayals of young girls achieve a content akin to Münter's.

13 See note 11, No. 5, and "Kollektiv-Ausstellung G. Münter (1904–1913)," Der Neue Kunstsalon, Munich, March–April 1913, No. 6.

14 Remaining in the collection of the Gabriele Münter- und Johannes Eichner-Stiftung are: *Girl's Head (with Pigtails)*, 1909 (Estate No. P58), and *Girl's Head (Blue Blouse)*, 1909 (Estate No. P38). The location of the fourth portrait in the Sturm exhibition, *Girl's Head (Black Dress)*, is unknown.

15 See her recollections of 1911 above, Biographic Chronology, p. 16. The portraits might also be compared to Jawlensky's later series of heads and—especially *Child in White*—to Paul Gauguin's portrait of his mother (1890; Staatsgalerie Stuttgart), exhibited in 1910 in Dresden, where Ernst Ludwig Kirchner employed its motif in a woodcut poster.

16 It is of interest that Münter did not exhibit the various portraits of young boys she painted during 1908–10, while she presented the girl's portraits as a conscious serial entity.

17 Roditi (note 10, chap. 1), p. 117.

18 An additional portrait of Olga von Hartmann is in the Gabriele Münter- und Johannes Eichner-Stiftung, Estate No. P162. For an alternative reading of Olga von Hartmann's face as a mask, see David Morgan, "Varieties of 'Expression' in German Art, 1890–1922," in: *A Breadth of Vision: The Ritz Collection*, compiled by Sue Taylor (Milwaukee, WI, 1992), p. 23.

19 Shulamith Behr, "Die Arbeit am eigenen Bild: Das Selbstporträt bei Gabriele Münter," in: *Gabriele Münter, 1877–1962* (note 44, chap. 1), p. 86, views the painting as "an uncertain compromise between the serious effort of the artist to capture her image and the accentuation of her proud dressage that underlines her femininity." Anne Mochon (note 3, chap. 2), p. 35, accents the linkage to

eighteenth-century women artists.

20 The various versions of the painting, and sketches for it, are discussed in Heller, "Innenräume: Erlebnis, Erinnerung und Synthese in der Kunst Gabriele Münters" (note 44, chap. 1), pp. 57–59.

21 Kandinsky employs Münter's works as representatives of "great realism," coequal to but contrasting with his own "great abstraction" in his essay "On the Question of Form," in *The Blaue Reiter Almanac* in 1912.

22 Given Münter's connections to the United States, the similarity of situation between Kandinsky in her painting and George Washington in Emanuel Leutze's famous depiction of his historic crossing of the Delaware River is too intriguing to ignore.

23 The dichotomy of Münter's physical labor and Kandinsky's visionary attitude in this painting has been remarked upon by Shulamith Behr, *Women Expressionists* (Oxford and New York, 1988), p. 38.

Chapter 5: Landscapes

1 Roditi (note 10, chap. 1), p. 120.

2 Münter, diary entry dated 26 December 1941. Gabriele Münter- und Johannes Eichner-Stiftung.

3 Münter, diary entry dated 9 January 1940. Gabriele Münter- und Johannes Eichner-Stiftung.

4 Münter, diary entry dated 6 April 1941. Gabriele Münter- und Johannes Eichner-Stiftung.

5 Rainer Maria Rilke, Worpswede, in: *Sämtliche Werke*, vol. 5 (Frankfurt am Main, 1965), p. 11.

6 A variant of the painting, incorrectly dated to 1912, is in a private collection. See Lahnstein (note 3, chap. 2), Plate 29.

7 Münter, diary entry dated 20 September 1941. Gabriele Münter- und Johannes Eichner-Stiftung.

8 At the very least, *Snow and Sun* is thematically identical to the painting purchased by Franz Marc for 55 Marks at an auction held by the New Artists' Association Munich in March 1911, for which *Farmyard in Snow I* was identified by Münter as a study. See *Gabriele Münter, 1877–1962* (note 44, chap. 1), entry to Cat. No. 94, *Hof im Schnee I*, 1911, p. 270. In an inventory of her paintings in private collections, compiled in 1917, Münter more appropriately entitled the painting *Hinterhäuser in Schnee und Sonne* (Rear Buildings in Snow and Sun), since what is depicted is not a farmyard, but a street in the northern section of Murnau (Pechmannstrasse) faced not by houses as such, but by ancillary structures, such as sheds and barns, and by commercial buildings. Compare the view from a different angle in *Village with Yellow Church (Murnau)*, ca. 1910, and the accompanying photograph of the street in Salmen (note 9, chap. 2), pp. 36–37. Both paintings also serve as fine examples of the distinction between "sketch" and "synthesis" in Münter's practice. Not only is *Farmyard in Snow I* "sketchier" with its thinned paint, rapid brushwork and moderate use of black outlining, which gives the impression that it was painted *in situ* or was a rough preliminary study, but it also is less systematically composed than *Snow and Sun*, with its forms less sharply delineated and coloristic interactions less developed or exploited.

9 The houses of Van Gogh's village scenes painted in St. Rémy and Auvers-sur-Oise in 1890 are at least conceptual precursors of, and probable influences on, Münter's depictions of Murnau's houses and streets, as are Edvard Munch's paintings of houses and villages from the 1890s and early 1900s. Among German Expressionists, Ludwig Meidner's somewhat later Berlin scenes, although using a dramatically different formal vocabulary, perhaps most nearly approach Münter's house imagery as they, too, impart an overwhelming sense of vitality and veritable movement in the houses and facades. In his dependence on Italian Futurism, however, and in his restricted focus on the city, Meidner is dramatically far removed from Münter's example.

10 Several sketches related to these paintings are contained in a small notebook, Folder 46/37, Gabriele Münter- und Johannes Eichner-Stiftung. With colors often indicated, they served as a means to recall the scenes as well as to initiate the process of distancing them from nature. It is significant that Münter seldom alters the resulting painting compositions in major ways from those of the initial sketches.

11 Unidentified critic, 1921, cited in: *Gabriele Münter, 1877–1962* (note 44, chap. 1), entry to Cat. No. 87, *Landschaft im Winter*, 1911, p. 268.

12 Münter, unsent letter addressed to Kandinsky, 12 October 1902, cited in: Hoberg (note 11, chap. 3), p. 37 (incorrectly dated 10 October 1902).

13 See *Kandinsky: Complete Writings on Art* (note 53, chap. 1), pp. 251–52.

14 For further consideration of the emulation of children's art by Münter and other Expressionists, see Reinhold Heller, "Expressionism's Ancients," in: *Parallel Visions: Modern Artists and Outsider Art*, ed. Maurice Tuchman and Carol S. Eliel (Princeton, NJ, 1992), pp. 78ff.

Chapter 6: Questions and Abstraction

1 Letter from Münter to Kandinsky, dated 3 November 1910. Gabriele Münter- und Johannes Eichner-Stiftung. See note 22, chap. 3.

2 Letter from Kandinsky to Münter, dated 26 October/8 November 1910. Gabriele Münter- und Johannes Eichner-Stiftung. Excerpt in: Hoberg (note 11, chap. 3), p. 83. The brochure to which Kandinsky refers is his essay "Content and Form," published in Russian in 1910 in: *Kandinsky: Complete Writings on Art* (note 53, chap. 1), pp. 84ff. The German manuscript is in the Gabriele Münter- und Johannes Eichner-Stiftung.

3 See note 11, chap. 3, p. 83. I have slightly altered the translation.

4 Letter from Münter to Kandinsky, 5 November 1910. Gabriele Münter- und Johannes Eichner-Stiftung.

5 Kandinsky, "On the Question of Form" (1912), in: *Kandinsky: Complete Writings on Art* (note 53, chap. 1), p. 237. I have altered the translation. Emphasis in the original text.

6 Münter, personal reminiscence, mid-1950s. Gabriele Münter- und Johannes Eichner-Stiftung. For a fuller citation, see *Gabriele Münter, 1877–1962, Retrospektive* (note 44, chap. 1), p. 43.

7 Letter from Kandinsky to Münter, dated 3 December 1912. Gabriele Münter- und Johannes Eichner-Stiftung. Excerpted in: Hoberg (note 2, Biographic Chronology), pp. 93–94.

8 Letter from Kandinsky to Münter, dated 6 January 1915 (24 December 1914). Gabriele Münter- und Johannes Eichner-Stiftung.

9 Letter from Münter to Kandinsky, no date (ca. 8 October 1912). Gabriele Münter- und Johannes Eichner-Stiftung. Hoberg (note 2, Biographic Chronology), pp. 129-30.

10 Compare *Gabriele Münter, 1877–1962, Retrospektive* (note 44, chap. 1), p. 41.

11 Kandinsky employed the term in his "Cologne Lecture" in 1913. See *Kandinsky: Complete Writings on Art* (note 53, chap.1), p. 396.
12 Ibid. I have altered the translation.
13 Kandinsky, "Reminiscences," in: *Kandinsky: Complete Writings on Art* (note 53, chap.1), p. 373.
14 The final painting is illustrated in *Gabriele Münter, 1877–1962, Retrospektive* (note 44, chap. 1), entry for No. 135, p. 276. The drawings are contained in the Folder 46/42, pp. 6–9, Gabriele Münter- und Johannes Eichner-Stiftung.
15 Letter from Franz Marc to Kandinsky, dated 23 March 1912, in: *Wassily Kandinsky/Franz Marc: Briefwechsel*, ed. Klaus Lankheit (Munich and Zurich, 1983), p. 151.
16 Folder 36/11, p. 7. Gabriele Münter- und Johannes Eichner-Stiftung.
17 Marc, "The 'Savages' of Germany," in: *The Blaue Reiter Almanac*, ed. Vassily Kandinsky and Franz Marc. *New Documentary Edition*, ed. Klaus Lankheit (New York, 1974), p. 64.
18 Letter from Münter to Prof. Kenneth Lindsay, dated 19 January 1956. Private Collection.
19 Münter's stay in Sweden is presented by Annika Öhrner, "'Ich lebte im Prophetenland—jetzt bin ich Weltkind geworden'—Gabriele Münter in Skandinavien, 1915–1920," in: *Gabriele Münter, 1877–1962, Retrospektive* (note 44, chap. 1), pp. 67ff. See also Sara H. Gregg, "Gabriele Münter in Sweden: Interlude and Separation," *Arts Magazine* 55 (1981), pp. 116–19, and Chapter VI of her master's thesis, *The Art of Gabriele Münter: An Evaluation of Content* (State University of New York at Binghamton, 1980), pp. 80ff.
20 Lilly Rydström-Wickelberg, "Gabriele Münter," *Konstrevy* 28:4/5 (1952), p. 217.
21 Compare Windecker's rather overstated reading of the large interior portraits of 1916 as a criticism of bourgeois values and society in Sweden (note 42, chap. 1), pp. 159–61 and 176.
22 The stylistic affinities between Münter and Hjertén were quickly recognized by Swedish critics, especially at the exhibition "Swedish Women Artists" that featured Münter and Hjertén at Liljevalchs Konsthall in January 1917. August Brunius, after comparing the artists, intriguingly found Münter the most "Nordic." See Elisabeth Lidén, *Expressionismen och Sverige* (Stockholm, 1974), pp. 51 and 243, note 32.
23 On Kandinsky's Swedish drypoints, see especially Barnett (note 9, Biographic Chronology), pp. 43–44.
24 *Gabriele Münter, 1877–1962*, Galerie Orangerie/Reinz, Cologne, 1981, illustrates *Clockmaker*, Estate No. V80, p. 19.
25 See Gregg, "Gabriele Münter in Sweden" (note 24), and Windecker (note 42, chap. 1), pp. 161–62.
26 Katalog 4, Galerie Gunzenhauser, Munich, 1980, p. 42 illustrates the painting.
27 Letter from Kandinsky to Münter, dated 22 July/4 August 1916. Gabriele Münter- und Johannes Eichner-Stiftung.
28 Unsent letter from Münter to Kandinsky, dated 8–9 May 1916. Gabriele Münter- und Johannes Eichner-Stiftung.
29 Letter from Münter to Hans Hildebrand, dated 6 July 1927. Getty Center for the History of Art and the Humanities, Santa Monica, CA.

Exhibition Checklist

Prints are accompanied by the numbers given to them by Sabine Helms, *Sammlungskatalog II: Gabriele Münter: Das druckgraphische Werk*, Städtische Galerie im Lenbachhaus (Munich, 1967). * = not exhibited at the Milwaukee Art Museum, Milwaukee, WI; † = not exhibited at the Columbus Museum of Art, Columbus, OH; ‡ = not exhibited at the Virginia Museum of Fine Arts, Richmond, VA; § = not exhibited at the Marion Koogler McNay Art Museum, San Antonio, TX.

1. *Kallmünz*, 1903
Oil on canvas-covered cardboard
9 7/8 x 6 1/2 in. (25 x 16.5 cm)
Munich, Städtische Galerie im Lenbachhaus, Gabriele Münter Bequest
(GMS 650)
Page 41

2. *Study from Holland*, 1904/05
Oil on canvas-covered cardboard
10 5/8 x 8 5/8 in. (27 x 22 cm)
Munich, Gabriele Münter- und Johannes Eichner-Stiftung (L440)
Page 45

3. *Kandinsky*, 1906
Color linocut (Helms 5)
9 5/8 x 6 7/8 in. (24.4 x 17.7 cm)
New York, The Solomon R. Guggenheim Museum of Art
Page 47, left

4. *M. Vernot*, 1906
Color linocut (Helms 7)
7 3/4 x 6 7/8 in. (19.7 x 17.7 cm)
Munich, Städtische Galerie im Lenbachhaus, Gabriele Münter Bequest
Page 47, top right

5. *Mme Vernot with Aurelie*, 1906
Color linocut (Helms 8)
6 7/8 x 4 3/4 in. (17.8 x 12.2 cm)
Munich, Städtische Galerie im Lenbachhaus, Gabriele Münter Bequest
Page 47, bottom right

6. *Washerwomen*, 1906/07
Pencil on gray paper
7 7/8 x 13 1/16 in. (20 x 33.2 cm)
Munich, Städtische Galerie im Lenbachhaus, Gabriele Münter Bequest
(GMS 1066)
(Not illustrated)

7. *Woman with Petroleum Lamp*, 1906/07
Charcoal
13 3/8 x 10 3/8 in. (34 x 26.5 cm)
Munich, Gabriele Münter- und Johannes Eichner-Stiftung (Folder 30/17)
(Not illustrated)

8. *Fall Evening — Sèvres*, 1907
Color linocut (Helms 14)
4 5/8 x 6 7/8 in. (11.9 x 17.7 cm)
Munich, Städtische Galerie im Lenbachhaus, Gabriele Münter Bequest
Page 48

9. *Path*, 1907
Color linocut (Helms 18)
4 5/8 x 6 3/16 in. (11.8 x 15.8 cm)
Munich, Städtische Galerie im Lenbachhaus, Gabriele Münter Bequest
Page 49, top

10. *Washing at the Shore*, ca. 1907/08
Color linocut (Helms 27)
5 1/4 x 9 5/16 in. (13.4 x 23.7 cm)
Munich, Städtische Galerie im Lenbachhaus, Gabriele Münter Bequest
Page 69, top

11. *Rose Garden*, ca. 1907/08
Color linocut (Helms 28)
6 1/2 x 7 7/8 in. (16.5 x 20 cm)
Munich, Städtische Galerie im Lenbachhaus, Gabriele Münter Bequest
Page 49, bottom

12. *Child with Bottle*, ca. 1907/08
Color linocut (Helms 29)
6 11/16 x 9 3/8 in. (17 x 23.9 cm)
Munich, Städtische Galerie im Lenbachhaus, Gabriele Münter Bequest
Page 69, bottom

13. *Sleeping Child*, ca. 1907/08
Color linocut (Helms 30)
6 9/16 x 9 3/8 in. (16.7 x 23.9 cm)
Munich, Städtische Galerie im Lenbachhaus, Gabriele Münter Bequest
Page 60

14. *Uncle Sam and Company (Toys, No. 2)*, 1908
Color linocut (Helms 33)
5 1/4 x 8 9/16 in. (13.2 x 21.8 cm)
Munich, Städtische Galerie im Lenbachhaus, Gabriele Münter Bequest
Page 61

15. *In Conversation (Toys, No. 4)*, 1908
Color linocut (Helms 34)
6 3/8 x 7 3/8 in. (16.7 x 18.8 cm)
Munich, Städtische Galerie im Lenbachhaus, Gabriele Münter Bequest
(Not illustrated)

16. *Interior (Still Life)*, 1908
Oil on cardboard
20 1/8 x 26 1/4 in. (51 x 66.4 cm)
New York, The Museum of Modern Art, Gift of the Glickstein Foundation (§)
Page 85

17. *The Village Church*, 1908
Oil on canvas-covered cardboard
13 x 16 1/2 in. (33 x 41.9 cm)
Milwaukee Art Museum, Gift of Mrs. Harry Lynde Bradley (M1975.155)
Page 128

18. *The Murnau Moors*, 1908
Oil on cardboard
13 x 17 1/2 in. (33 x 44.5 cm)
Collection of Mr. Norbert Adler
Page 72

19. *View of the Murnau Moors*, 1908
Oil on cardboard
12 7/8 x 15 7/8 in. (32.7 x 40.5 cm)
Munich, Städtische Galerie im Lenbachhaus, Gabriele Münter Bequest
(GMS 654)
Page 73

20. *Village Street in Murnau (Manure Pile)*, 1908
Oil on canvas-covered cardboard
13 x 16 in. (33 x 40.6 cm)
Collection of Mr. Norbert Adler
Page 76

21. *Small Street in Murnau*, 1908
Oil on cardboard
14 1/2 x 17 5/8 in. (36.8 x 44.8 cm)
Collection of Muriel Goldstone, Munster, IN
Page 81

22. *Main Street, Murnau*, 1908
Oil on cardboard
13 x 17 in. (33 x 43.2 cm)
Collection of Ruth and Bruce Dayton
Page 77

23. *Fisherman's House*, 1908
Oil on cardboard
12 1/4 x 15 1/2 in. (31.1 x 39.4 cm)
Collection of Mr. and Mrs. Frank E. Taplin, Jr.
Page 129

24. *Oberau*, 1908
Oil on cardboard
32 3/8 x 44 5/8 in. (82.3 x 113.3 cm)
Collection of Esther Leah Ritz
Page 130

25. *Factory*, 1908
Oil on cardboard
33 x 44 5/8 in. (83.8 x 113.3 cm)
Storrs, The William Benton Museum of Art, University of Connecticut
Page 131

26. *The Pink House (Country Home near Murnau)*, 1908
Oil on cardboard
13 x 16 1/4 in. (33 x 41.3 cm)
Private Collection
Page 133

27. *Return from Shopping (In the Streetcar)*, 1908/09
Oil on cardboard
18 7/8 x 12 3/8 in. (48 x 31.5 cm)
Munich, Gabriele Münter- und Johannes Eichner-Stiftung (S44)
Page 86

28. *Girl with Doll*, 1908/09
Oil on cardboard
27 1/2 x 19 in. (69.9 x 49.3 cm)
Milwaukee Art Museum, Gift of Mrs. Harry Lynde Bradley (M1966.165)
Page 113

29. *Grave Crosses in Kochel*, 1909
Oil on cardboard
15 7/8 x 12 7/8 in. (40.5 x 32.8 cm)
Munich, Städtische Galerie im Lenbachhaus, Gabriele Münter Bequest (GMS 658)
Page 134

30. *Still Life, Yellow*, 1909
Oil on cardboard
16 1/2 x 13 in. (41.9 x 33 cm)
Milwaukee Art Museum, Gift of Mrs. Harry Lynde Bradley (M1975.156)
Page 87

31. *Still Life, Red*, 1909
Oil on cardboard
20 7/8 x 15 3/8 in. (53 x 39 cm)
Private Collection
Page 88

32. *Still Life with Armchair*, 1909
Oil on cardboard
28 9/16 x 19 5/16 in. (72.5 x 49 cm)
Munich, Gabriele Münter- und Johannes Eichner-Stiftung (S119)
Page 89

33. *Interior (Still Life, Bedroom)*, 1909
Oil on cardboard
20 7/8 x 27 15/16 in. (53 x 71 cm)
Munich, Gabriele Münter- und Johannes Eichner-Stiftung (V107)
Page 90

34. *Portrait of a Young Woman (Young Polish Woman)*, 1909
Oil on canvas
27 3/4 x 20 5/8 in. (70.5 x 52.4 cm)
Milwaukee Art Museum, Gift of Mrs. Harry Lynde Bradley (M1966.164)
Page 116

35. *Listening (Portrait of Jawlensky)*, 1909
Oil on cardboard
19 5/8 x 26 1/8 in. (49.7 x 66.2 cm)
Munich, Städtische Galerie im Lenbachhaus, Gabriele Münter Bequest (GMS 657)
Page 117

36. *Self-Portrait in Front of an Easel*, ca. 1909
Oil on canvas
29 1/2 x 22 5/8 in. (75 x 57.5 cm)
Princeton, The Art Museum, Princeton University, Gift of Mr. and Mrs. Frank E. Taplin, Jr. (y 1992–21)
Page 120

37. *The Yellow House*, 1909
Oil on cardboard
13 x 15 3/4 in. (33 x 40 cm)
Bonn, Kunstmuseum (‡, §)
(Not illustrated)

38. *Country Road in Winter*, 1909
Oil on cardboard
10 x 13 3/4 in. (25.4 x 34.9 cm)
Private Collection
Page 132

39. *House in Winter*, 1909
Oil on cardboard
19 3/4 x 23 1/2 in. (50 x 59.5 cm)
Collection of Mr. and Mrs. Dan Garson
Page 135

40. *Fall Landscape, Study (Yellow Trees)*, 1909
Oil on cardboard
13 x 17 5/8 in. (33.1 x 44.8 cm)
Collection of Lester and Betty Guttman
Page 136

41. *Landscape with Church*, 1909
Oil on cardboard
12 7/8 x 17 1/2 in. (32.8 x 44.6 cm)
Saarbrücken, Saarland Museum (inv. no. 1896) (*, †)
Page 137

42. *Still Life with Russian Tablecloth*, 1910
Oil on cardboard
27 3/16 x 19 7/8 in. (69 x 50.5 cm)
Munich, Gabriele Münter- und Johannes Eichner-Stiftung (S96)
Page 92

43. *Still Life with Elf*, 1910
Oil on canvas-covered cardboard
25 x 22 7/16 in. (63.5 x 57 cm)
Collection of Muriel Goldstone, Munster, IN
Page 91

44. *Still Life with Figure II (Mrs. Simonovich)*, 1910
Oil on canvas
29 7/8 x 31 1/4 in. (76 x 79 cm)
Munich, Gabriele Münter- und Johannes Eichner-Stiftung (S105)
Page 93

45. *Portrait of Olga Hartmann*, 1910
Oil on cardboard
20 1/8 x 15 5/8 in. (51.1 x 39.7 cm)
Collection of Esther Leah Ritz
Page 121

46. *Child in White*, 1910
Oil on cardboard
17 1/2 x 12 15/16 in. (44.7 x 33 cm)
Munich, Städtische Galerie im Lenbachhaus, Gabriele Münter Bequest (GMS 663)
Page 124, left

47. *Boating*, 1910
Oil on canvas
49 1/4 x 28 7/8 in. (125.1 x 73.3 cm)
Milwaukee Art Museum, Gift of Mrs. Harry Lynde Bradley (M1977.128)
Page 125

48. *City View by Night*, 1910
Oil on cardboard
21 7/16 x 14 15/16 in. (54.5 x 38 cm)
Munich, Gabriele Münter- und Johannes Eichner-Stiftung (L103)
Page 139

49. *Landscape with Church*, 1910
Oil on cardboard
13 x 17 5/8 in. (33 x 44.8 cm)
Collection of Sylvia and Ulrich Ströher
Page 138

50. *Landscape*, ca. 1910
Oil on cardboard
34 15/16 x 39 5/8 in. (88.8 x 100.7 cm)
Champaign, Krannert Art Museum, University of Illinois
(Not illustrated)

51. *Houses on Wintry Road*, 1911
Oil on canvas-covered cardboard
13 x 16 in. (33 x 40.6 cm)
Milwaukee Art Museum, Gift of Mrs. Harry Lynde Bradley (M1975.153)
Page 140

52. *Still Life in Circle*, 1911
Oil on cardboard
33 1/4 x 17 9/16 in. (84.5 x 70 cm)
Collection of Mr. Harlan J. Berk
Page 96

53. *Still Life, Pink*, 1911
Oil on canvas
43 5/8 x 39 1/3 in. (88 x 100 cm)
Saarbrücken, Saarland Museum (inv. no. 3082) (*, †)
Page 94

54. *Still Life with Saint George*, 1911
Oil on cardboard
20 1/16 x 26 3/4 in. (51.1 x 68 cm)
Munich, Städtische Galerie im Lehnbachhaus, Gabriele Münter Bequest (GMS 666)
Page 95

55. *The Brewery, Murnau*, 1911
Oil on cardboard
13 x 16 in. (33 x 40.6 cm)
Milwaukee Art Museum, Gift of Mrs. Harry Lynde Bradley (M1975.150)
Page 141

56. *Snow and Sun*, 1911
Oil on cardboard
20 x 27 1/2 in. (50.8 x 69.9 cm)
Iowa City, The University of Iowa Museum of Art, Gift of Owen and Leone Elliott (1968.63)
Page 142, top

57. *Farmyard in Snow I*, 1911
Oil on cardboard
13 x 17 5/8 in. (33 x 45 cm)
Collection of Mr. and Mrs. Frank E. Taplin, Jr.
Page 142, bottom

58. *The Green House, Murnau*, 1911
Oil on canvas
34 3/4 x 39 1/2 in. (88.3 x 100.3 cm)
Milwaukee Art Museum, Gift of Mrs. Harry Lynde Bradley (M1977.127)
Page 144, top

59. *Habsburg Square, Munich*, 1911
Oil on cardboard
13 1/4 x 16 in. (33.7 x 40.7 cm)
Milwaukee Art Museum, Gift of Mrs. Harry Lynde Bradley (M1975.151)
Page 143

60. Sketch for: *Green House*, ca. 1911
Pen and ink
16 3/8 x 8 1/4 in. (16.5 x 21.1 cm)
Munich, Gabriele Münter- und Johannes Eichner-Stiftung
Page 144, bottom

61. *Habsburg Square, Munich*, 1911
Tusche over pencil
8 9/16 x 10 in. (21.8 x 25.4 cm)
Munich, Gabriele Münter- und Johannes Eichner-Stiftung (Folder 40/6)
(Not illustrated)

62. *Study with White Spots*, 1912
Oil on cardboard
15 1/4 x 10 in. (38.5 x 25.5 cm)
Munich, Städtische Galerie im Lenbachhaus, Gabriele Münter Bequest (GMS 667)
Page 97

63. *In Schwabing*, 1912
Oil on canvas
27 x 20 in. (68.6 x 50.8 cm)
Milwaukee Art Museum, Gift of Mrs. Harry Lynde Bradley (M1975.152)
Page 145

64. *Country Homes (Kandinsky in the Garden)*, 1912
Oil on cardboard
13 x 16 in. (33 x 40.7 cm)
Private Collection (Courtesy Salis & Vertes, Salzburg)
Page 100

65. *Still Life with Queen*, 1912
Oil on canvas
31 5/16 x 22 1/4 in. (79.5 x 56.5 cm)
The Art Institute of Chicago, Arthur Jerome Eddy Memorial Collection
Page 101

66. Sketch for: *Construction Work*, 1912
Tusche
6 x 8 1/4 in. (15.5 x 21 cm)
Munich, Städtische Galerie im Lenbachhaus, Gabriele Münter Bequest (GMS 933,1)
(Not illustrated)

67. Sketch for: *Construction Work*, 1912
Tusche
6 x 8 1/4 in. (15.5 x 21 cm)
Munich, Städtische Galerie im Lenbachhaus, Gabriele Münter Bequest (GMS 933,2)
(Not illustrated)

68. *Dragon Fight*, 1913
Oil on cardboard
14 3/16 x 17 in. (36 x 43.2 cm)
Munich, Gabriele Münter- und Johannes Eichner-Stiftung (V117)
Page 104

69. *Portrait of Kandinsky's Mother*, 1913
Oil on cardboard
27 3/4 x 19 3/4 in. (70.5 x 50.2 cm)
Collection of Mr. and Mrs. Frank E. Taplin, Jr.
Page 124, right

70. *Still Life Abstract (Abstraction)*, 1914
Oil on cardboard
12 15/16 x 16 1/8 in. (33 x 41 cm)
Munich, Gabriele Münter- und Johannes Eichner-Stiftung (V13)
Page 105

71. *Abstract Study*, 1915
Oil on cardboard
16 x 12 5/8 in. (40.8 x 32.2 cm)
Munich, Gabriele Münter- und Johannes Eichner-Stiftung (V113)
Page 157

72. *Construction Work*, 1916
Tusche and pencil
6 5/8 x 8 5/8 in. (17 x 22 cm)
Munich, Städtische Galerie im Lenbachhaus, Gabriele Münter Bequest (GMS 1103)
Page 162, top

73. *Still Life*, 1916
Drypoint engraving, zinc plate (Helms 50)
2 1/2 x 3 1/4 in. (6.2 x 8.1 cm)
Munich, Städtische Galerie im Lenbachhaus, Gabriele Münter Bequest
Page 162, bottom

74. *Clockmaker*, 1916
Drypoint engraving, zinc plate (Helms 53)
2 7/8 x 3 7/8 in. (7.4 x 9.9 cm)
Munich, Städtische Galerie im Lenbachhaus, Gabriele Münter Bequest
Page 163, top

75. *Near the Sluice, Stockholm*, 1916
Drypoint engraving, zinc plate (Helms 54)
2 7/8 x 3 7/8 in. (7.4 x 9.9. cm)
Munich, Städtische Galerie im Lenbachhaus, Gabriele Münter Bequest
Page 163, bottom

76. *Woman Seeking*, 1916
Color drypoint engraving, zinc plate (Helms 55)
6 1/4 x 3 1/4 in. (16 x 6.3 cm)
Munich, Städtische Galerie im Lenbachhaus, Gabriele Münter Bequest
Page 158

77. *Street in Stockholm (May Evening in Stockholm)*, 1916
Oil on canvas
23 3/4 x 17 3/4 in. (60 x 45 cm)
Collection of Judy and Harold Prince
Page 159

78. *From Norway, Tjellebotten*, 1917
Oil an canvas
21 1/2 x 25 3/4 in. (54.5 x 65.5 cm)
Collection of Mr. and Mrs. Frank E. Taplin, Jr.
Page 160

79. *The Future (Woman in Stockholm)*, 1917
Oil on canvas
39 3/4 x 26 3/16 in. (100.5 x 66.5 cm)
Cleveland Museum of Art, Gift of Mr. and Mrs. Frank E. Taplin, Jr.
Page 161

80. Poster for the Gabriele Münter Exhibition, Copenhagen, 1918
Color lithograph (Helms 57)
34 1/4 x 24 3/8 in. (87 x 62 cm)
Munich, Städtische Galerie im Lenbachhaus, Gabriele Münter Bequest
Page 167

81. *Beach at Bornholm*, 1919
Oil on canvas-covered cardboard
13 1/4 x 17 3/4 in. (33.3 x 46.2 cm)
Collection of Mr. and Mrs. Richard D. Smith
Page 164

82. *The Chestnut Tree*, 1919
Oil on cardboard
16 1/4 x 12 1/2 in. (41.3 x 31.8. cm)
Collection of Beatrice Riese
Page 165

Photographic Acknowledgments

Photographs of works by Gabriele Münter were provided by the individuals and institutions credited in the Exhibition Checklist. Photographs for the Biographic Chronology were provided by the Gabriele Münter- und Johannes Eichner-Stiftung, Munich. Individual credits are as follows:

AB Nordiska Kompaniet, Stockholm: p. 23
Sigrid Bührig: p. 30
Henry Goodwin, Stockholm: frontispiece, p. 25
Hennon & Dodson, St. Louis: p. 9
Hänse Herrmann, Berlin: p. 27
Leonard Hutton Galleries, New York: Cat. No. 38
Milwaukee Art Museum: Cat. Nos. 17 (Photo: Larry Sanders), 18, 20, 22, 23, 24 (Photo: Larry Sanders), 26, 28 (Photo: Efraim Lev-er), 30 (Photo: Larry Sanders), 34 (Photo: P. Richard Eells), 39, 45, 48, 51 (Photo: Larry Sanders), 52, 55 (Photo: Larry Sanders), 57, 69, 71, 77–79, 81, 82
Photostudio Alfons Coreth, Salzburg: Cat. No. 64 (Courtesy Salis & Vertes, Salzburg)
The David and Alfred Smart Museum of Art, The University of Chicago: Cat. No. 40
Städtische Galerie im Lenbachhaus, Munich: Cat. No. 60
The William Benton Museum of Art, The University of Connecticut, Storrs, CT: Cat. No. 25 (Photo: E. Irving Blomstrann)